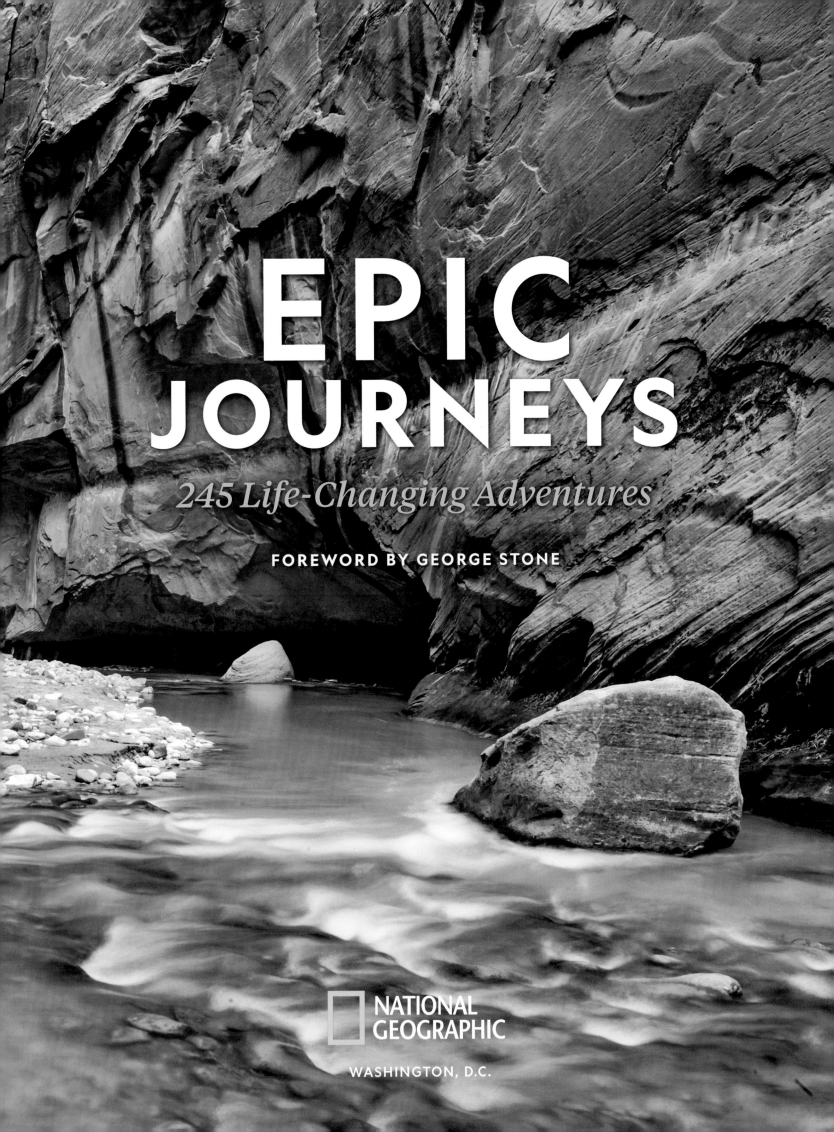

EPIC
JOURNEYS

245 Life-Changing Adventures

FOREWORD BY GEORGE STONE

NATIONAL
GEOGRAPHIC

WASHINGTON, D.C.

ABOVE: Hot-air balloons float over
ancient temples in Bagan, Myanmar.
PREVIOUS PAGES: A hiker walks through
The Narrows in Zion National Park, Utah.

CONTENTS

FOLLOW YOUR DREAMS

Our journeys are as epic as our ambitions. Our ambitions are as soaring as our imaginations. This book is for dreamers with adventurous inclinations—people who think about what's possible and then set about discovering what's achievable. People, in short, who are propelled by the National Geographic spirit of exploration. • One of the best things about working at National Geographic is that many of the world's foremost explorers pass through our doors (and our yellow borders) every week. It's not uncommon to see legendary oceanographer Sylvia Earle darting through the cafeteria like an angelfish swimming through sea anemone. Or famed underwater archaeologist Bob Ballard, who located the wreck of the *Titanic*, searching in vain for a hidden conference room. Everyone is a fish out of water from time to time, but that hardly dampens the spirits of our greatest adventurers. On the contrary, National Geographic explorers and grantees—funded, in part, by readers like you—passionately push the boundaries of what is known about our world. And they always come home with an unforgettable tale.

So can you. The idea of pursuing an ambition of exploration—no matter how crazy it may seem at the time—is one way to honor our dreams and our unique potential in life. It's not a competition; it's about embracing the world on our own terms. One of National Geographic's most inspiring recent adventure stories is about climber Alex Honnold's free solo ascent of Yosemite's 3,000-foot (914.4 m) El Capitan, a 2017 scaling that was accomplished without rope or safety equipment and is now considered the greatest feat in rock-climbing history. Famously modest, Honnold characterizes rock climbing as a low-adrenaline sport because it's slow and methodical. And hardly anything—including global renown—can shift his focus from realizing the ambitions that bring him joy. "The whole pursuit of this dream has allowed me to live my best life," Honnold said immediately following his landmark climb. "That makes me hopefully the best version of me."

What's the best version of you? Perhaps the 245 life-changing adventures—and countless woodlands, rivers, reefs, slopes, summits, trails, vales, whales, and cultural treasures—in this book will awaken and enrich your ambitions to explore the world and honor your hopes of being the best version of yourself. To those who worry that the world is getting small, fear not. From Aconcagua to Everest, Banff to Borneo, Namibia to Norway, the Zambezi to the Zanskar River (and hundreds of places beyond), this book reminds us that our exterior and interior geographies are perfectly matched.

All that's left is a story to be told—your story about how you turned a dream into a journey and your life into a pursuit of meaningful adventure. Let the epic begin.

—GEORGE W. STONE
Editor in Chief, National Geographic Travel

A pack of Alaskan huskies—part of Hey Moose! Kennel in Healy, Alaska—pull mushers through Denali National Park.

CKWISE FROM TOP LEFT: A toucan
   nal, Costa Rica; the Temple of the
  t the Ingapirca ruins in Ecuador;
  oreline of Isla del Sol in Lake Titi-
  a sunrise horseback tour of Easter
 d, Chile

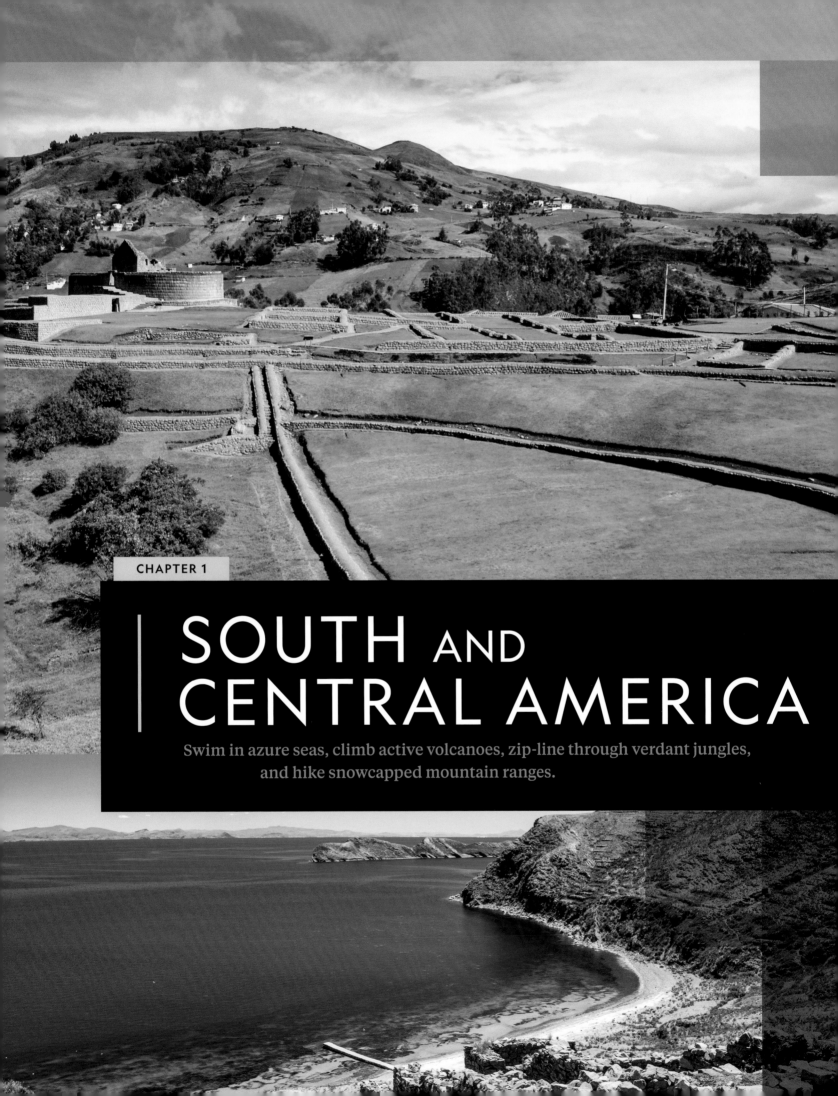

CHAPTER 1

SOUTH AND CENTRAL AMERICA

Swim in azure seas, climb active volcanoes, zip-line through verdant jungles,
and hike snowcapped mountain ranges.

VOLCANO BOARDING AND CLOUD SOARING

Whether you are hiking, boarding, or swimming, Nicaragua has an experience for everyone.

When Cerro Negro, Nicaragua's youngest volcano, last erupted, in 1999, boulders tumbled down the western slope, creating a rocky, ascendable path. On the opposite side, the wind deposited dark, smooth ash that is perfect for sliding. In 2004, this unique pairing of terrains sparked an outlandish idea: volcano boarding.

"This is the only place in the world where you can sit upright on plywood, feet-first, and coast down a cindery flank of a still-active volcano," says Nick Porter, an affable tour guide who left his job at a bank in Manchester, England, in 2013, went traveling, and never returned.

Figuring out how to slide the volcano's ashy slopes took some time. Volcano boarding's inventor, Daryn Webb, made early attempts to slide down Cerro Negro on a table, a mattress, and a mini-refrigerator before landing on plywood.

Should a thrilling ride down one of the world's most active volcanoes (it has erupted at least 23 times in its 159-year history) prove not enough for your adrenaline fix, Nicaragua is the land of opportunity. Beyond the verdant hills surrounding Cerro Negro, you can find sunny coastlines, rich historic cities, exotic wildlife, and enchanting cloud forests.

Travel Tips

WHEN TO GO: Visit in Nicaragua's dry season, which runs from November through April, when temperatures are mild and the days are sunny.

PLANNING: A number of outfitters offer volcano boarding, the country's most extreme sport; Bigfoot Hostel was the world's first. A high-end version offers helicopter transport from Mukul resort and a snowboard-style ride. Nonprofit Quetzaltrekkers provides a less hardcore version of the excursion.

WEBSITES: bigfoothostels.com; mukulresort.com; quetzaltrekkers.com/xela; vianica.com

Hammocks hang on Little Corn Island.

WHAT TO DO

Go With the Flow

The adventure begins with a bumpy drive past small villages and farms and into the Cerro Negro national park. The barren volcano, whose name means "black hill," has loomed over the countryside as a constant specter since it first erupted in 1850 and is the perfect playground for adrenaline junkies.

Visitors pay a five-dollar (U.S.) entrance fee and can opt to pay another five dollars for a local to tow the boards uphill. Boards are provided by operators but can also be rented at the park. Riders then endure an hour-long hike up a wind-beaten path that curves past four craters that belch sulfur and dry heat, an impolite reminder that the next eruption could happen anytime. (Don't worry: The volcano is closely monitored by the Nicaraguan Seismic Network.)

At the 2,388-foot (728 m) summit, riders slip into orange jumpsuits and safety goggles and take a quick lesson on maneuvering the board, which is basically a sled with a rope handle. Using their feet, riders create friction with the ground to steer and control speed.

One by one, the participants launch themselves over the edge, accelerating as the incline steepens. The entire ride takes three to five minutes, depending on whether you stop or roll off your board. Small rocks fly from under the board, and riders who spill end up with blistered appendages and soot in the suit. Most come out unscathed, though, and as they approach the bottom, guides snap photographs and clock top

speeds—the record is 60 miles an hour (96.6 kph)—with a radar gun.

Ride the Roads

Horseback riding in the lush Nicaraguan countryside beyond Cerro Negro is something not to miss. Tours take you on an exploration of the back roads right outside the city of Grenada. The best part of this experience is a visit to the Apoyo Lagoon, a nature reserve that originated about 23,000 years ago. It is a welcome respite after riding in the hot sun and worth the swim, so be sure to pack a bathing suit.

Hike in the Clouds

The Mombacho Volcano sits 6.2 miles (10 km) from Granada and is known for a cloud forest at the summit that is home to pumas, howler monkeys, and many other species. The two-hour hike isn't an easy

one, but it is a rewarding experience and will get your heart racing. You can look forward to beautiful views of several of the four craters, spotting wildlife, and enjoying the cooler temperature. It is recommended that you book a tour guide at the welcome center to the reserve to get the most of your adventure.

Zip Through the Forest

If you want to get your adrenaline pumping, zip-lining opportunities are vast in the Nicaraguan cloud forest. The reserve is situated at the foot of the Mombacho Volcano, which you'll ascend by truck to get to your first platform. Covering 1.25 miles (2 km) of the forest with 17 platforms and three hanging bridges, Miravalle Canopy Tour offers a unique chance to glide past howler monkeys and exotic flora and fauna.

Catch Some Rays

Not all activities have to be adrenaline inducing. Take a break and enjoy the sunshine on the Corn Islands, located about 43 miles (69 km) off the coast of Nicaragua. Sunny, with warm weather year-round, these islands make for the perfect escape. Visitors can enjoy scuba diving excursions, kayaking, snorkeling, and lazy beach days by the crystal clear blue waters of the Caribbean Sea.

OPPOSITE: Riders zip down the ashy slopes of Cerro Negro at speeds up to 60 miles an hour (96.6 kph). ABOVE: A zip-liner soars through Mombacho and makes it through a keyhole in the trees.

Trail horses await riders overlooking
Lake Laguna de Apoyo.

ECUADOR

CRUISING THE GALÁPAGOS

Explore Darwin's living laboratory of evolution.

Close animal encounters of the Galápagos kind are unlike any other on Earth. Isolation from the mainland (the archipelago is 620 miles/ 997.7 km west of Ecuador in the Pacific Ocean) means no large animal predators ever reached the 19 active volcanic large islands and hundred-plus islets. The rugged terrain gave rise to a trove of bizarre endemic creatures, such as flightless cormorants, giant Galápagos tortoises, and lava lizards. In addition, the four main ocean currents of varying temperatures swirling around the islands produced the Galápagos's wondrous array of native marine species, such as marine iguanas (the planet's only seafaring reptile) and the tiny Galápagos penguin, the only species of its kind found north of the Equator.

As a result, the creatures residing in Charles Darwin's living laboratory have no fear of humans and are present in large numbers. In many cases, the species you'll see exist only here: about 97 percent of the land mammals and reptiles, 80 percent of the land birds, and more than 20 percent of the marine species are endemic.

The only way to experience the Galápagos is to cruise among the islands much as Darwin did during his voyage on the H.M.S. *Beagle* in the 1830s. The Galápagos National Park Service strictly regulates ship routes, expedition itineraries, and land excursions to protect the archipelago from one of its greatest threats—us.

Travel Tips

WHEN TO GO: June to November for cool, dry conditions; December to May (the warm and slightly rainy season) for fewer visitors and good underwater visibility.

PLANNING: You cannot cruise the Galápagos islands on your own. You must be with a licensed tour operator like National Geographic Expeditions. The best way to protect these delicate islands is to closely heed park rules, including staying at least six feet (2 m) away from all wildlife.

WEBSITES: nationalgeographic.com/ expeditions; galapagos.org

A Pacific green turtle swims among baitfish.

7-DAY ITINERARY

Day 1

From Isla Santa Cruz, the Galápagos's most populous island, set sail for Isla San Cristóbal, one of the geologically oldest (more than 2.4 million years) places in the archipelago and home to its oldest surviving permanent settlement, El Progresso, established in 1869. Starting off here is symbolic, because it is the first island Darwin visited in 1835. Follow in his footsteps by going ashore to see roaming tortoises, nesting blue- and red-footed boobies, San Cristóbal mockingbirds, and lava lizards. Watch for the endemic San Cristóbal mockingbird and *Calandrinia* plant, and see—and hear the raucous barking of—the largest colony of sea lions in the Galápagos.

Day 2

Cruise south to Isla Española, a birder's paradise with 95 recorded species. Scan the skies for Española mockingbirds, blue-footed and Nazca boobies, and swallow-tailed gulls. The island is also the main breeding grounds of the waved albatross—the Galápagos's largest bird, with a wingspan of up to eight feet (2.4 m). You can see the colossal birds on land April to December and in the skies January to March. Breeding season is April to June, when eggs are produced. Hatchlings flee the nest by the next January and head out to sea for six years before coming back to choose a lifelong mate.

Walk the trail out to Punta Suarez on the westernmost point of the island to see nesting albatross, vivid green and red marine iguanas, and sea lions. Along the way, keep a running tally of the Galápagos lava lizards you spot—the ubiquitous reptiles have a penchant for sunbathing atop lava rocks.

Day 3

Today's destination, Isla Floreana, has the longest Galápagos human history: first resident (1807–1809), first island to be colonized by Ecuador (1832), and first post office (1793). The post office was a barrel used by 18th-century whalers who stopped at Floreana when traversing the oceans. Homesick seamen left mail in the barrel, and sailors on passing ships hand-delivered those addressed to locations near their final destinations. The stampless system still operates out of Post Office Bay. Write a postcard to drop in the current barrel, and then sift through the collected mail to find any you can send, or, in keeping with tradition, hand-deliver when you return home. Next, snorkel among sea lions at Champion Islet, an extinct shield volcano, and hike to a turtle nesting beach.

Day 4

Watch for whales, dolphins, and the occasional mola—a gigantic sunfish that can weigh as much as 5,000 pounds (2,268 kg)—in the cool waters surrounding Isla Isabela. The seahorse-shaped island is the largest in the Galápagos, stretching 74 miles long (119 km) and covering more land than all the other islands combined. Go ashore to hike against a backdrop of giant shield volcanoes and to see marine iguanas, sea turtles, the only species of flightless cormorant in the world, and the only wild penguins found north of the Equator.

Day 5

Sail to Isla Santiago, the second island Darwin visited, and disembark on the northwest coast at James Bay. Follow the trail north to the sea turtle nesting site on Espumilla Beach (remember to keep an appropriate distance from the nests as determined by your guide) and then inland past a lagoon where you might see flamingos and white-cheeked pintail ducks. The trail loops through an arid zone teeming with land birds. At the southern end of the bay, hike the coastal path among tide pools and caverns in search of Galápagos fur

seals, marine iguanas, sea lions, shore-birds, and Sally Lightfoot crabs. If time permits, walk the southern inland trail, ending atop an abandoned salt mine crater.

Cruise to the eastern side of Santiago to see the volcanic landscape and walk across black pahoehoe lava at Sullivan Bay. Directly off the coast lie the red-sand beaches of Ràbida Island. The rocky islet is a good spot to snorkel among playful sea lions and graceful manta rays with wingspans reaching 12 to 23 feet (3.6 to 7 m).

Day 6

Resume your sail along Santiago's south-eastern coast en route to Isla Bartolomé, a lava rock island covering an area less than half the size of New York City's Central Park. The barren islet is a breeding and nesting ground for green turtles, but the two main attractions are the volcanic-cone summit views (after you make the 376-step climb to the top) of famous Pinnacle Rock and snorkeling with Galápagos penguins, sharks, rays, and sea turtles in the waters surrounding it.

Day 7

Spend your final day living the giant tortoise life on Isla Santa Cruz. Visit the Charles Darwin Research Station, home to several species of giant tortoise, and tour the Galápagos National Park Service's captive breeding program for endangered Galápagos giant tortoises. After lunch in Puerto Ayora, venture into the highlands to observe and photograph giant tortoises in the wild.

HIGHLIGHTS

• Cruise to Isla Española, a bird-watcher's paradise with mockingbirds, blue-footed and Nazca boobies, and waved albatrosses.

• Meet endangered giant tortoises at a captive breeding program.

• Snorkel and kayak among sea lions, sea turtles, and the Northern Hemisphere's only wild penguins.

About half of all breeding pairs of blue-footed boobies live on the Galápagos Islands.

Hiking Peru's Iconic Inca Trail to Machu Picchu

By Boyd Matson

THE SECURITY LINE at my home airport in Washington, D.C., isn't where I expected to get my first reminder that I should have trained a little more for 19 days of trekking in the mountains of Peru.

Before I even board the plane, the security agent tells me, "Sir, you need to remove those items from your shirt pockets"—forcing me to explain that those "items" can be removed only through diet and exercise.

Admittedly, one of the bonuses I'm anticipating from this trip is the excess body baggage I hope to leave in the Andes, as there's no escaping the physical effort required to hike over mountain passes, some higher than 15,000 feet (4,572 m).

The Inca built many of these trails 500 years ago, and they're still the only way to reach all of our destinations— Machu Picchu and a few lesser visited yet equally impres-

sive Inca sites, such as Choquequirao; the water shrine Picha Unuyoc; and Vilcabamba, also called Espíritu Pampa, the last city of the Inca.

Our guide has arranged for tents, food, supplies, mules to transport our gear, mule handlers, cooks, and—as insurance—a couple of horses should anyone need the assistance of an equine taxi. In spite of these amenities, we will for the most part be sleeping on the ground and surviving without internet and electricity. We'll also be facing a high probability of occasional rain—maybe even snow—at altitudes where we sea-level dwellers have difficulty breathing. Inexplicably, my son Taylor agrees to join me. He thinks it sounds like fun.

BELOW: Visitors climb the ancient steps of Machu Picchu. OPPOSITE: Choquequirao, three times the size of Machu Picchu, sits on the far end of the Apurímac Valley.

My wife, Betty, reacts differently: "That sounds like the worst trip ever." Near the end of our first full day on the trail, I have a gnawing fear I will be forced to confess the three most difficult words in any relationship: "You were right."

I had expected the beginning to be an easy warm-up—all downhill, from the village of Cachora to the Apurímac River, and then a short climb to camp. But after eight hours and some 5,000 feet (1,524 m) of steep descent, I remember that downhill is worse than uphill on old knees with no cartilage.

The reality of where I am—both on the mountain and on the scale of high-altitude cardio fitness—hits with an unexpected thud. My legs announce that they've put in their eight hours and are through for the day. Unfortunately, we are less than a hundred feet (30.5 m) into a 2,000-foot (609.6 m) climb to the next campsite. No pumping adrenal glands speed to the rescue, so I have to concentrate on each step, willing my body forward like a toddler learning to walk, as the air hangs hot and heavy without even a whisper of a breeze.

I'm sweating so profusely I have to dry my ears with a bandanna to hear, though the only sounds are my own noisy gasps for air. Taylor has also hit the wall, and neither of us can afford the energy to offer encouragement. When we finally collapse into our tent after 11½ hours on the trail, he summons the strength to ask, "Are you as embarrassed as I am?" "No," I reply. "I'm just relieved—the day's over and we made it."

I assure him that the days will get a bit easier as we acclimatize. And they do, at least cardio-wise, with Taylor practically running the trails by day three. But there are unexpected setbacks—any one of which, when later described to friends, elicits that familiar response: "That sounds like the worst trip ever."

We endure 10 straight days of rain. On day five, we stop for lunch on a beautiful pass, but my knee locks up and I'm forced to descend the next 2,200 feet (671 m) using trekking poles like canes. On day seven, the rain becomes a heavy snowstorm as we make our way up and over a 15,000-foot (4,572 m) pass. The snow further complicates the process of going down 3,500 steep Inca stone steps.

Still, wherever we go, the scenery is breathtakingly beautiful, and when heavy rains trap Taylor and me in our tent for hours at a time, we have no choice but to talk—father and adult son, discussing everything that's ever happened in our lives. For us, the accomplishment of not only surviving but also being able to laugh about our struggles at the end of each day leaves us both saying this is "the best trip ever."

Oh yeah—and I've also lost 15 pounds (7 kg).

• *Adventurer and journalist Boyd Matson has hosted radio shows and documentaries for National Geographic.*

OPPOSITE: Stone steps up Huayna Picchu lead to a view overlooking all of Machu Picchu. ABOVE: Queshuachaca is the last remaining Inca rope bridge above the Apurímac River.

COSTA RICA

PADDLE, SWIM, AND FLY IN COSTA RICA

Take a canopy-to-coast road trip in the land of Pura Vida.

Costa Rica is a treasure trove of biodiversity and big-thrill outdoor adventure. The compact country—which, at its narrowest point, extends only about 75 miles (120.7 km) between the Pacific Ocean and the Caribbean Sea—is home to more than 2,000 species of trees and 9,000 different kinds of flowering plants. Rainforests and cloud forests cover one-fifth of a landscape dominated by mountain ranges and rivers.

A world leader in conservation and environmental protection, Costa Rica established its national park system in the 1970s. In addition to sparing wild spaces from development, the parks inspired sustainable tourism activities, such as zip-lining through the rainforest and rappelling down waterfalls. Among the country's natural wonders chockablock with wild adventure opportunities are the Monteverde Cloud Forest Reserve, the largest of its kind in Central America, and the Guanacaste coast, boasting white-sand beaches and azure Pacific waters.

Experience the best of Costa Rica's wild side by taking a canopy-to-coast excursion from the capital city, San José, westward to the Pacific. The nonstop adventure route will take you deep into dense jungles buzzing with chattering monkeys and birds, through remote river gorges filled with dancing white water, and onto secluded beaches fringed by rainforests.

Travel Tips

WHEN TO GO: Since Costa Rica has several different climatic regions, visit January to March or during July for relatively dry weather throughout the trip. Rafting trips run year-round on the Pacuare River.

PLANNING: National Geographic Expeditions regularly offers small group tours. To make the trip solo, rent a four-wheel-drive vehicle, and prepare for Costa Rica's notoriously poor road conditions, including ubiquitous potholes and washed-out roads.

WEBSITES: nationalgeographic.com/expeditions; riostropicales.com; desafiocostarica.com; arenal.net

Rafters paddle the Pacuare River's rapids.

7-DAY ITINERARY

Day 1

From San José, Costa Rica's capital, make the short drive to Finca Rosa Blanca Coffee Plantation and Inn, a National Geographic Unique Lodge of the World. Spending your first day and night at the inn—a coffee-scented retreat perched in the highlands above the cloud forest–ringed Valle Central—offers a preview of the adventures that lie ahead. From its terraces, tropical gardens, and guest rooms you can see volcanoes, such as dormant Barva, which sits directly above the resort, and nearby Poás, an active volcano with three craters.

Day 2

Start the day by walking among thousands of shade-grown banana and coffee trees on a guided tour of the lodge's organic coffee farm. The bean-to-cup tour includes a chance to see how red coffee cherries are de-pulped to harvest the beans, which are then fermented, dried, sorted, and roasted. Soak up the intoxicating aromas and flavors in a "cupping" session, the fresh roasted coffee equivalent of a wine tasting. An infusion of caffeine will help get you in gear for an afternoon white-water trip on the Pacuare River, which begins in the high Talamanca mountains, then runs east down the slopes of the inactive Irazu volcano and on to the Caribbean Sea.

Considered one of the world's premier rafting rivers, the Pacuare boasts Class II to IV rapids as it winds through the towering green walls of the gorge. For a white-knuckle, expert run, tackle the Upper Pacuare, particularly during the rainy season (typically May to November) when the water is high, fast, and fierce. The more common put-in for rafting groups is on the Lower Pacuare, which offers tamer—yet still challenging—Class II and III rapids. Either way you'll be tumbling through a tropical rainforest teeming with wildlife including capuchin monkeys, sloths, parrots, and toucans. Overnight at the remote Rios Tropicales Lodge, a 2,409-acre (974.8 hectare) private reserve located at the mouth of the Pacuare River Gorge and accessible only by raft or hiking through the rainforest.

Day 3

Spend the day exploring the surrounding jungle on Rios Tropicales Lodge's guided hikes, bird-watching expeditions, rainforest restoration tours, and adventure activities, such as horseback riding to a local village. Experience the adrenaline rush of a ground-to-treetops climb on the combination canyoning and canopy tour. The adventure includes rappelling down the face of a nearly 200-foot-high (60.9 m) waterfall and soaring high across the river on a series of three zip lines.

Day 4

Return to the Pacuare River for a half-day rafting trip on Class II, III, and IV rapids.

Then drive northwest (about three hours) to Arenal Volcano National Park. The park is named for Costa Rica's most famous volcano; it's currently in a passive phase (the last eruption was in 2010), but it regularly billowed smoke and spewed sizzling lava from a vent on its western flank for 42 years. Stay close to the entrance of the park at the Hotel Arenal Manoa or Arenal Springs Resort. The first is on a dairy farm and the latter has thermal pools filled with mineral-rich water naturally heated (93 to 104°F/33.8-40°C) by the volcano.

Day 5

Arenal Volcano National Park is an adrenaline junkie's dream destination. Plan a play-day in the park by combining a couple of the activities offered by experienced outfitter Desafio Adventure Company. Its Gravity Falls Waterfall Jumping tour begins with rappelling down a 14-foot-high (4.3 m) waterfall and manages to top that big-thrill descent with a series of free-fall jumps off waterfalls and cliffs into the deep emerald waters of canyon pools. The slightly tamer Lost Canyon Adventures Canyoneering tour

OPPOSITE: In La Fortuna, a woman relaxes in hot springs warmed by the Arenal Volcano. RIGHT: A plethora of wildlife, including the red-eyed tree frog, live in the rainforest of Costa Rica.

combines rappelling, bouldering, jumping, hiking, river tracing, and a guided canyon free fall.

_____

Day 6

Drive northwest about two hours through rolling farmland to Tenorio Volcano National Park. Dominated by its eponymous dormant volcano and surrounding wildlife-rich rainforest, the park may be best known for its otherworldly, azure blue Rio Celeste waterfall. Hike through the lush green canopy to the roaring cascade, which you will hear well before you can see the rushing waters. Swimming isn't permitted in the cold, mist-covered pool beneath the falls, but you can descend the 250 steps for an up close view.

Following the waterfall hike, drive west another two hours to Costa Rica's Pacific Guanacaste coast. Spend the night at an oceanfront Hermosa Beach property such as the beach-level Hotel Bosque del Mar or the cliffside Villas Sol Hotel and Beach Resort.

_____

Day 7

Spend your last full day exploring the Guanacaste coast on a guided kayaking or stand-up paddleboarding tour. Some operators offer snorkeling as an option on kayaking trips. Whether as part of another tour or as a dedicated snorkeling excursion, don't miss the opportunity to discover the rich marine life—including sea turtles, moray eels, octopus, and tropical fish in a kaleidoscope of dazzling colors—swimming just under the surface of the water. Close the day, and the adventure, with a sunset cruise.

HIGHLIGHTS

• Watch for monkeys and sloths on a white-water rafting adventure down the Pacuare River.

• Hike in the jungles of Arenal Volcano National Park, and cross hanging bridges through the lush forest canopy.

• Explore the Pacific coast on kayaking and snorkeling excursions.

Standing 5,437 feet (1,657 m) tall, Arenal Volcano looms over Costa Rica's verdant landscape.

CHILE

ENIGMATIC EASTER ISLAND

Face time with one of the planet's greatest mysteries

Known as Rapa Nui by its native Polynesian inhabitants, Easter Island has a common Western name that borders on the incredible. European explorers bumped into the remote island on Easter Day, 1722, and thus bestowed on it the Dutch name Paaseiland (Easter Island), a moniker that had nothing to do with the people or land they encountered and everything to do with the pride of a few floundering seafarers.

Regardless of what it's called, there is no denying that this island is a treasure chest of cultural and natural riches. It's the planet's most remote inhabited island, a volcanic castaway more than 2,000 miles (3,219 km) west of the Chilean coast. Most famous, some 900 enormous stone figures, called *moai*, guard its shores. Carved from lava tuff between the 11th and 17th centuries, the towering busts served as ceremonial embodiments of ancestral spirits. Since the arrival of European explorers, scientists have pondered and debated how these multiton monoliths were moved into position miles from the quarry where they originated. Local legend holds that the statues walked themselves to their resting places.

It's a far-fetched theory but a compelling invitation to explore this enigmatic land on foot. Venture from volcano peaks to subterranean caves to moai-lined platforms, cultivating your own ideas about this unusual place along the way.

Travel Tips

WHEN TO GO: Pleasant weather prevails year-round, with the island attracting the largest crowds from January to March.

PLANNING: Rent a car or bike in the main town of Hanga Roa to explore the island's scattered archaeological sites. Hire local guides for cultural insight. Access to many sites requires national park admission, and Orongo and the quarry of Rano Raraku can be visited only once per ticket.

WEBSITES: imaginaisladepascua.com/en; islandheritage.org

Ruins of a stone village and ceremonial site

4-DAY ITINERARY

Day 1

Kick off your Easter Island cultural immersion on a dramatic note: Witness the sun rise over the 15 stunning moai statues at the legendary platform of Ahu Tongariki, standing sentinel along the Pacific coast. Then head to Rano Raraku, the quarry where most of the moai stone originated. Walk in the footsteps of the Rapa Nui along trails the ancient people took as they transported the statues to their ceremonial platforms.

In the afternoon, ride horseback or cycle around the Poike Peninsula and trace the north coast to the stone petroglyphs of Papa Vaka. Carved several centuries ago, the engravings feature marine creatures and other symbols of sea life. Then continue on to Ovahe beach, a remote pink-sand paradise teeming with colorful fish, sea turtles, and purple corals just beyond the shore. Finish your cycling tour under the swaying palm trees of nearby Anakena beach, known for golden sand, gentle waves, and an impressive lineup of moai statues.

Day 2

Set out on a hike to the top of the extinct Rano Kau volcano, which formed 2.5 million years ago. A historic footpath leads up the side of the 3,000-foot-wide (914 m) crater and around the rim. Enjoy views of the crater lake below before continuing on to the ancient ceremonial village of Orongo, nestled into the volcano slopes. Here the ancient tribal leaders once convened in an annual spring competition called Tangata Manu to gather the first egg of the manu-

tara (luck) bird. The winner ruled the island for the coming year.

Later, charter a boat off the coast of Orongo for a tour of Moto Nui islet. Take in a fresh perspective of the towering cliffs, and snorkel in the crystal-clear waters off the most westerly point of South America.

Day 3

Spend the morning riding the gently rolling waves of Pea Beach in Hanga Roa, the island's main town. Beginners can stay in this shallow bay and take a surfing lesson, while more seasoned surfers head to bays on the island's south side and chase crashing swells (up to 20 feet/6 m) on the west side.

In the afternoon, don snorkeling gear and swim with green sea turtles in the Hanga Roa harbor. For a deeper dive in these crystalline waters, hire a scuba outfitter in town who can point out endemic creatures, tropi-

cal fish, and the volcanic seabed punctuated by cliffs and arches. Don't miss your chance to marvel at an underwater moai (not an authentic statue, but rather a prop from a 1990s movie set).

End the day with an unforgettable sunset at the ceremonial platform of Tahai, which dates to A.D. 700. Stay here to gaze up at the clear night sky and twinkling stars that Polynesian voyagers once followed.

Day 4

Volcanic landscape and archaeological sites await on the island's northwest coast. On a spelunking trip in Ana Kakenga cave, peer through its natural window that overlooks the cobalt Pacific Ocean. Discover the impressively intact ruins of an ancient village at Ahu Te Peu and descend into its sprawling lava tubes, the island's largest lava channel, where banana trees grow inside. The circuit culminates at the impressive inland platform of Ahu Akivi, situated on the lower slopes of Terevaka volcano, where seven moai gaze out at the sea—the island's only statues to face the water. From here, set off on a moderately challenging afternoon trek to the 1,676-foot (511 m) summit of Terevaka, the island's tallest and youngest volcano. Wind along rugged trails to reach the peak, where 360-degree panoramas of the island await. Or opt to cycle to the Puna Pau crater, a sacred quarry for red scoria.

OPPOSITE: Tourists walk by 15 behemoth *moai* statues at Tongariki on Easter Island. ABOVE: Some 900 moai statues, carved from volcanic rock centuries ago, dot the island.

1 CHOQUEQUIRAO TO MACHU PICCHU, PERU

National Geographic's strenuous 10-day "Machu Picchu Inn to Inn Trek" travels between coffee plantations and mountain lodges across the Cordillera de Vilcabamba. Hike Machu Picchu Mountain through orchid- and butterfly-filled cloud forests and stop at quieter Inca ruins. Spend a full day exploring Machu Picchu's 150-plus temples, ancient dwellings, and ceremonial centers.

2 RAO RARAKU TRAIL, EASTER ISLAND

Ancient Easter Island's athletes competed in "the Birdman," when contestants clambered down a cliff, paddled to Motu Nui, and stole an egg from a red-breasted Mahoke's nest. The Rapa Nui's February Tapati Festival honors the tradition with the Tau'a trail race: a paddle across a volcanic lake in bulrush kayaks, run carrying 44 pounds (20 kg) of bananas, and ascent of the crater past rows of ancient moai.

3 INGAPIRCA TRAIL, ECUADOR

Ecuador's Ingapirca Inca Trail was constructed 1,000 years ago to connect Cusco to the Tomebamba and Quito. The three-day trek crosses the Espíndola River valley and Andean grasslands of Sangay National Park to the curved and terraced temple ruins of Ingapirca. Ecuador's best preserved archaeological complex, the site features both Inca and Cañari constructions.

4 CAMINO REAL, COLOMBIA

Long-used by indigenous Guane people as a local trade route, Colombia's Camino Real connects Baricharas to the charming village of Guane via six miles (9.6 km) of canyon rims, cactus fields, and cobbled trails. Stone walls, mature trees, and tiny villages border the path as you hike between goat farms and expansive valleys.

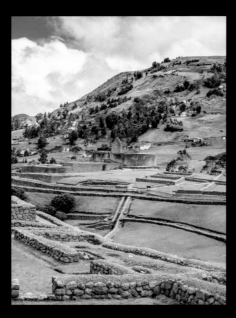

OPPOSITE: The road from Baricharas to Guane on the Camino Real in Colombia ABOVE: The Inca ruins of Ingapirca, one of Ecuador's most important archaeological sites

5 TRILHA DO OURO, BRAZIL

First laid out by Guaianazes Indians, then painstakingly paved by African slaves in the 18th century, the Portuguese used the Trilha do Ouro to transport gold. Today, the trail is a 1,200-mile (1,931 km) living example of Brazil's diverse culture, nature, and history. Hire a local guide to learn more as you trek through the Mata Atlântica rainforest past waterfalls and natural rock waterslides.

6 ANCIENT QUERCUS TREE HIKE, PANAMA

This hike traces pre-Columbian Indian paths into the remote cloud forest of Baru Volcano National Park. The trail parallels Quebrada La Mina creek, arriving at five enormous old-growth millenary quercus trees. Watch for howler monkeys, white-faced capuchins, two-toed sloths, and elusive quetzal birds as you hike beneath Baru Volcano, the highest point in Panama.

7 RUTA 40, ARGENTINA

The nomadic Tehuelche people carved trails through Patagonia that are still in use. Argentina's 3,227-mile (5,193 km) Ruta 40 traces many of their paths. Road trippers can kayak the milky Marble Caves over neon blue General Carrera Lake, hike to the Cave of Hands rock paintings left by Tehuelche ancestors more than 10,000 years ago, and visit the pre-Inca Quilmes ruins in the Calchaquí Valley.

8 ANCIENT INCA TRAILS, LAKE TITICACA, BOLIVIA

Every year kayakers, parasailers, and mountain bikers travel to Lake Titicaca to explore its true-blue shores. Hike an ancient trail from the lakeshore to Inca Anatawi ruins, where polished stone seats look toward the Andes. Similar trails lead to Inca temple ruins on the lake's Moon Island, Sun Island, and Los Uros. For the complete experience, advanced scuba tours of Lake Titicaca descend to an ancient underwater road and submerged pre-Inca temple, discovered in 2000.

9 TAKESI TRAIL, BOLIVIA

The advanced aqueducts and retaining walls along Bolivia's Takesi Trail reveal the engineering prowess of Inca builders. Once frequented by ancient couriers, this route takes two to three days to complete and is best hiked from May to October (dry season). Although the path is not strenuous, hikers will want to make sure to acclimatize to the high altitude before starting off.

10 MAYA HIGHLANDS TRAIL, GUATEMALA

Guatemala's three-day Maya Highlands Trail follows ancient trade routes between beautiful Lake Atitlan and Quetzaltenango, once a royal capital of the Xelajú kingdom. Fifteen volcanoes (two active) peek into view as hikers approach Zunil's Siete Cruces ridge. Guided excursions often end with a volcano-heated thermal soak in the Fuentes Georginas hot springs, set in a serene rainforest.

WONDERS BEYOND THE SACRED VALLEY

From stunning hikes to archaeological mysteries, Peru's wonders extend far and wide.

For many visitors to Peru, Machu Picchu is the number one draw. But the country is such an ecologically, topographically, and historically rich place that it'd be a waste to travel all that way without tacking on an extra day or three to appreciate some of Peru's other wonders.

Peru boasts more than 10,000 years of rich cultural history. Home to imposing archaeological complexes, 12 UNESCO World Heritage sites, and numerous natural reserves, it's an adventure lover's dream. The Amazon covers nearly half of Peru, providing a home to animals and plants that live nowhere else on earth—the Andean condor, spectacled bear, Amazonian pink dolphin, and yellow-tailed woolly monkey, to name a few. Plus, some scientists believe there are even indigenous tribes that have never seen the outside world. The Amazon also affords tourists opportunities for thrilling adventures and unique sights. Another third of the country is dominated by the Andes mountain range, and its west coast includes a narrow strip of desert 1,555 miles (2,500 km) long.

With its unique terrain and rich cultural history, there is loads on offer beyond the ancient walls of Machu Picchu. Step outside the traditional itinerary and instead paddle a sacred river, hike a stunning canyon, soar high above ancient geoglyphs, go mountain biking in the Andes, and explore the wonders of a national park.

Travel Tips

WHEN TO GO: Peru's winter (May to September) is the driest season and best time to visit Cusco or make the trek to Machu Picchu. December through March, Peru's summer offers warmer weather but frequent heavy showers.

PLANNING: Cusco sits at 11,152 feet (3,399 m) above sea level, so give yourself time to acclimate to the higher altitude. It's also a great starting point for higher hikes and levels in the Sacred Valley.

WEBSITES: peru.travel/en-us

The sacred valley is dotted with Inca ruins.

WHAT TO DO

Raft a Sacred River

The Andes are veined with white water, the inevitable product of steep slopes funneling glacial meltwater into tight canyons. As a result, Peru is a fantastic place for river rafting. A popular spot for paddling, the Urubamba River, which the Inca revered as a deity, runs through the Sacred Valley near Cusco and eventually winds in an omega shape around Machu Picchu. A typical trip on the Chuquicahuana stretch, a lovely part of the Upper Urubamba, features Class III rapids and can be done as a day trip from Cusco. (Avoid downriver Urubamba trips, which pass through a polluted section of the river.) More adventurous paddlers can tackle the Class IV and V white water of the Apurimac River. The translation of its name, "Great Speaker," offers a hint of the roaring rapids that await.

Hike the Colca Canyon

No one's entirely sure how deep the Colca Canyon is, but scientists have determined that the distance from its rim to its bottom measures more than 10,000 feet (3,048 m)— twice the depth of the Grand Canyon. The Colca is also generally agreed to be one of the most beautiful places on Earth. The immense space within those towering walls is filled with some of South America's most spectacular scenery: untouched valleys, pre-Columbian agricultural terraces still in use, dormant volcanoes, and green oases. The vicuña, a smaller cousin of the llama, runs wild here. The Colca's calling card, though, is the majestic Andean condor, a bird whose populations are dwindling elsewhere but which is regularly spotted here at the Cruz del Condor mountain pass. It's possible to reach the Colca overland from Cusco, but the easiest way is to take a 45-minute flight to Arequipa, which also happens to be Peru's most charming city.

Visit the Fauna of Manu National Park

There is probably no other trip that better illustrates how Peru's diverse ecosystems are stacked on another than the rapid transition from the chilly Andean heights of Cusco to the lush Amazonian jungle of Manu National Park. This biosphere, whose preservation was made possible by its remoteness, is just a 45-minute plane ride away from Cusco (or by road, 8 to 24 hours or more—weather permitting—plus a 45-minute boat ride). Most travel within Manu is done by boat, which allows for eye-level views of one of the world's greatest preserved swaths of rainforest, one that includes more than 15,000 species of plants. Manu is best known for its superlative variety of animal life: jaguars, tapirs, giant otters, 13 kinds of monkeys, and at least a million different insect species. Manu is in particular a must-see for bird-watchers, since more than a thousand avian species (10 percent of the world's total and more than can be found in the United States and Canada combined) live within its borders.

Fly Over the Nasca Lines

A trip to Machu Picchu almost always requires connections in Lima, Peru's vibrant coastal capital, while arriving and departing. It's also a good place to arrange a short flight to view the Nasca Lines, which rival

OPPOSITE: The Alto Madre de Dios flows through the southern section of Manu Park. ABOVE: A mountain biker spins along terraced hills near Cusco.

Machu Picchu as Peru's greatest ancient wonder. Why the need for an aerial perspective? Because of the immensity of the geoglyphs that appear as if they've been etched into the ground below: spiders, llamas, fish, monkeys, and more, some of them stretching more than 600 feet (183 m) across. (Their extent was unknown until the 1930s, when pilots began flying across that Nasca Desert.) The original purpose of the images remains one of the world's greatest mysteries—extraterrestrials are sometimes cited as their source—but the lines are generally believed to have been created by the Nasca people between one and two thousand years ago as part of a religious ritual.

Bike the Andes

Two things are never in short supply in the Andes, dirt trails and steep descents, which is why the area near Machu Picchu and Cusco is a prime spot for mountain biking. It's possible to arrange your own two-wheel tour, but using an outfitter will give you access to a support vehicle (crucial in an area where bike shops are virtually unknown), local knowledge of Peru's often confusing road system, and, should you want it, a vehicle to portage your bike up the area's brutal ascents so that you can enjoy your vacation instead of playing Lance Armstrong. Some of the best trips include the peaceful Lares Valley; the Inca ruins–rich Sacred Valley, which runs from Pisac to Ollantaytambo; and a one-day, altimeter-busting one-mile (1.6 km)-plus descent starting with the Abra Malaga pass at 13,000 feet (3,962.4 m). Some outfitters offer back roads trips from Cusco to within shouting distance of Machu Picchu.

HIGHLIGHTS

• Soar above the ancient Nasca Lines carved into the earth as early as 100 B.C.

• Climb mountains on your way to a new view of Machu Picchu and through the Lares Valley.

• Raft through the glacial waters of the Urubamba River and Class IV to V rapids on the Apurimac River.

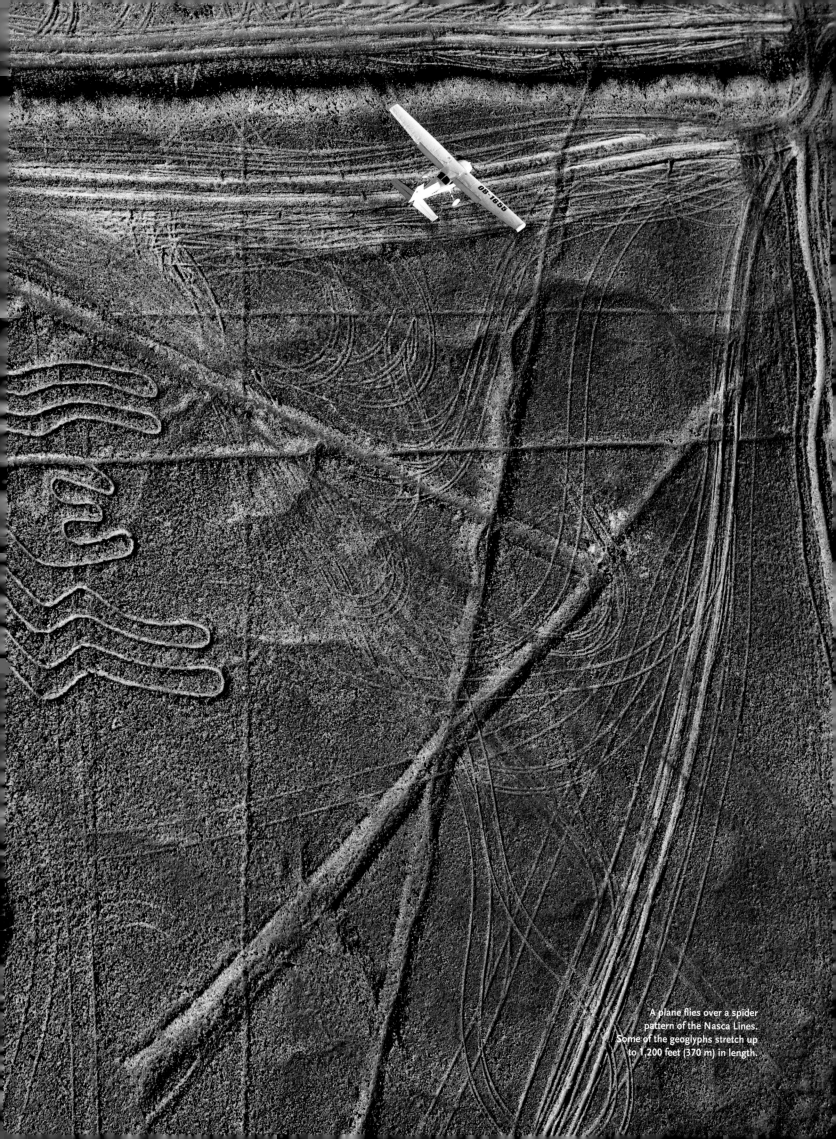

A plane flies over a spider pattern of the Nasca Lines. Some of the geoglyphs stretch up to 1,200 feet (370 m) in length.

TREKKING THE HEART OF COLOMBIA

Jump into limitless adventure, from jungle hiking to shark diving.

With its soaring Andes peaks, lush rainforest, and miles of Pacific and Caribbean coastline, Colombia is an adventurer's paradise. There are feats here for every level of ability, from experienced mountain climbers and advanced open-water divers to day hikers up for an afternoon trek.

Bogotá, the capital, is a gateway for high-altitude activities, even within the city limits: The hill of Monserrate dominates the metropolis, rising to 10,341 feet (3,152 m). Visitors can join pilgrims climbing to the historic church at its peak or take a comfortable cable car ride . For serious mountaineers, El Cocuy, lauded for its little-explored glaciated peaks rising over 17,000 feet (5,182 m), is an eight-hour drive from Bogotá.

In Colombia's interior, you'll find less taxing but equally stunning sights: the Valle de Cocora, a surreal landscape of sky-high wax palms, and the "liquid rainbow" river of Caño Cristales in Macarena National Natural Park, where sunlight striking an underwater plant creates an explosion of color.

Descend to the coasts for high-flying jaunts around seaside cities. Below the surface, some of the best dive sites in the world await, including Malpelo Island, located in a marine reserve that constitutes the largest no-fishing zone in the Eastern Tropical Pacific. Whatever your fancy, Colombia can deliver.

Travel Tips

WHEN TO GO: April to September offers the best diving conditions; avoid January to February, which tends to bring strong currents and rough seas around Malpelo Island. Hiking to Ciudad Perdida is closed during September to allow indigenous communities to visit the site.

PLANNING: Ten-day Malpelo liveaboard trips can be booked out of Buenaventura through PADI Travel. Treks to Ciudad Perdida must be booked through an authorized operator, such as Wiwa Tour, Turcol, or Expotur.

WEBSITES: colombia.travel; travel.padi .com; wiwatour.com; expotur-eco.com

The Clock Tower Gate in Cartagena's old city

WHAT TO DO

Take Flight Over Cartagena

Known as the "jewel of Colombia," Cartagena de Indias, a 90-minute flight from Bogotá, enchants with its colorful homes wreathed in tropical flowers and horse-drawn carriages that rumble over cobblestoned lanes. It's even more beautiful from the air. Motorized paragliding tours (with an instructor) commonly take off from the beach of La Boquilla, while parasailing boats depart from Playa el Laguito on the peninsula of Bocagrande. While flying high over the sparkling blue Caribbean Sea, spot the colonial rooftops, cathedral spires, and more than seven miles (11 km) of stone walls and ramparts that surround Cartagena's Old City, founded in 1533.

Explore a Historic Shipwreck

A 30-minute boat ride from the town of Bahía Solano—located an hour flight from Medellín in the sparsely populated Chocó province on Colombia's Pacific coast—brings divers to the *Sebastián de Belalcázar* wreck. The World War II ship U.S.S. *Jicarilla* won two medals before being acquired by the Colombian navy and renamed after a 16th-century Spanish conquistador. It was purposely sunk in 2004 on the Negritos shoal to create an artificial reef. Resting about 100 feet (30 m) below the surface, the *Belalcázar* plays host to reef sharks, grouper, pufferfish, olive ridley turtles, and more. Come June to October you may even spot humpback whales as they migrate to the area for breeding season. More regularly, divers can spot other big fish including tuna and giant trevallies—and trumpetfish and lobsters can be found in nearby rocky reefs.

OPPOSITE: **A hiker takes in the fantastic scope of the Cocora Valley. ABOVE: Malpelo, a UNESCO World Heritage site, is home to massive schools of silky and Galápagos sharks, as well as hammerheads.**

Hike Through the Valle de Cocora

The wax palm, the world's tallest palm tree, which grows up to 200 feet (60 m), is a national symbol of Colombia. A relaxed day hike through the Valle de Cocora in Eje Cafetero, Colombia's coffee region, offers close-up views in their native habitat. Most visitors start in the town of Salento, where residents readily provide rides to the trail entrance for a small fee. The three-hour loop rises through verdant cloud forest before opening onto a clearing filled with hundreds of towering wax palms, their quirky shape—a spindly trunk topped by a few dark green leaves—looking straight out of a fairy tale. Ringed by green hills shrouded in mist, the valley forms a beguiling landscape.

Dive With Sharks in the Pacific

Experienced divers with advanced open water certification can take a liveaboard trip to Malpelo, a small, rocky islet 300 miles (506 km) off the Colombian coast. A UNESCO World Heritage site, Malpelo has been called "shark heaven" due to the massive schools of hammerhead and silky sharks that congregate here, along with whale sharks, Galápagos sharks, giant grouper, and billfish. It's also one of the few places in the world where the short-nosed ragged-toothed shark has been sighted, so keep your eyes peeled. Malpelo's equally astonishing marine topography includes underwater caves and tunnels woven into steep walls that plunge to 11,155 feet (3,400 m).

Discover the Lost Cities

Ciudad Perdida, the Lost City of the Tayrona people, lay hidden beneath dense rainforest for hundreds of years until treasure hunters stumbled across it in 1972. Now, hikers can embark on a four- or five-day trek through the Sierra Nevada de Santa Marta mountain range to reach its ruins. The 14-mile (23 km), one-way trail crosses several rivers and streams, providing ample opportunity to cool off in the steamy jungle heat. It's an arduous trek, but the reward is worth it: The circular stone terraces of Ciudad Perdida, constructed some 650 years before Machu Picchu, around A.D. 800, sit on a ridge 4,265 feet high (1,300 m) overlooking thickly forested mountains and a valley cut by the Buritaca River.

HIGHLIGHTS

- View the Caribbean coast and walled Old City of Cartagena from a paraglider.

- Dive with hammerhead sharks and explore underwater caves in the Pacific.

- Trek through jungle-covered mountains to find the 1,200-year-old Lost City.

PADDLE THE BEST RIVERS

WHAT TO DO

Go on a Stargazing Tour

San Pedro is the launchpad for nightly stargazing excursions. Two of the best are offered by long-standing tour operators Atacama Desert Stargazing and San Pedro de Atacama Celestial Explorations (SPACE). Both offer sharp, vivid views of planets, galaxies, and stars through different telescopes. You'll learn how to read a sky map and identify constellations. Tap your guide's astrophotography expertise to elevate your Instagram with star-studded Atacama backdrops. The small group tours range from a few hours to Atacama Desert Stargazing's overnight camping excursions.

See Where Solar System Secrets Are Revealed

Discover how stars and galaxies are born on a tour of the operations center at the Atacama Large Millimeter/submillimeter Array (ALMA). Hidden high above the Atacama Desert on a protected plateau, ALMA's 66 ginormous radio telescopes collect data from invisible reaches of the universe. The project, a cooperative effort of 22 nations, focuses on the high-frequency sliver of the electromagnet system found between far infrared waves and radio waves. While the telescope array is off-limits, free guided tours offer an inside look at the science of astronomical observation and the antenna control room. Tours are offered only on Saturday and Sunday mornings and fill up quickly. Register online.

Stay Under a Blanket of Stars

At the Tierra Atacama Adventure and Spa Hotel, a National Geographic Unique Lodge of the World, guest rooms are designed with sliding glass doors and private outdoor showers, letting the stars shine through on

clear, moonless nights. Nearby, the luxurious Explora Atacama hotel boasts its own domed observatory, housing an advanced optics, high-resolution telescope. Nightly viewings offer Explora guests out-of-this-world opportunities to see astronomy A-listers, such as Jupiter, Venus, and the Southern Cross. Less than three miles (4.1 km) north at the Alto Atacama Desert Lodge and Spa is an open-air hilltop observatory with swivel viewing chairs and an astronomical telescope.

Tour the Very Large Telescope

Open to visitors on Saturday mornings, the European Southern Observatory's (ESO) Paranal Observatory, the planet's most advanced visible-light astronomical observatory, houses a high-tech optical instrument with a decidedly low-tech name: the Very Large Telescope array (VLT). The VLT is a giant eye on the sky that allows astronomers to focus in on details up to 25 times finer than with a single telescope. Guided tours (register online) include a visit to the VLT platform, where you can enter the dome of one of the large telescopes.

Climb to the Licancabur Volcano Crater

Dominating the horizon east of San Pedro de Atacama is Licancabur Volcano. Snow covered and classically conical, the 19,409-foot (5,915.8 m) dormant volcano straddles the border between Chile and Bolivia. Seeing Licancabur from a distance is easy. Hiking up to its 13,000-foot-wide (3,962.4 m) crater, however, takes serious high-altitude climbing skills. If you're up to the challenge, making a guided trek up Licancabur offers sky-high stargazing possibilities. The ascent on a typical two-day, one-night expedition begins before dawn, meaning you'll be climbing toward the stars (or the moon, depending on the lunar phase) and can watch the sunrise from the side of a volcano.

HIGHLIGHTS

• See distant stars and galaxies in some of the world's clearest night skies.

• Visit the world's largest ground-based astronomical observatory.

• Reach for the stars on a two-day sky-high volcano hike.

OPPOSITE: Due to limited light pollution, constellations are easy to spot from the rock- and cactus-strewn Atacama. ABOVE: Seen from Toco Hill, the Licancabur Volcano looms large.

Bottoms Up on Chile's Cape Horn

By Norie Quintos

It's the dawn of a new year, January 1, and I'm at the end of the world on Chile's Cape Horn. It's the southern tip of the habitable world: Land's End, tailbone of the Americas, the planet's last lick of land beyond which Earth's two great oceans—the mighty Atlantic and the misnamed Pacific— clash in a not-so-friendly mash-up. Beyond the Cape lie the forbidding shores of Antarctica, 500 miles (806 km) away.

At coordinates such as these, prosaic thoughts often give way to the profound. (It helps that I am far beyond the tentacley reach of Wi-Fi, and thus liberated from the neurotic, neuronic blips that pass for thinking in the Age of Hyperconnection.) This is the perfect time and place for a Big Think.

The Chilean luxury expedition cruise ship *Via Australis* has deposited me and 130 fellow passengers on this island in a manner far more cushy than previous travelers wended their way here—among them Francis Drake, whose storm-tossed detour led to the accidental discovery of the Drake Passage directly to the south; the Dutch merchant-explorer duo of Jacob Le Maire and Willem Schouten, who named the Cape after the latter's home town of Hoorn; and English naturalist Charles Darwin, who rounded the Cape on his celebrated ship, the *Beagle,* on his way to the Galápagos Islands and eventual fame.

The carcasses of countless ships and steamers litter the

BELOW: The *Akademic Vavilov* plies rough seas crossing the Drake Passage en route to Antarctica. OPPOSITE: A rustic chapel at the end of the world on Cape Horn, Chile

ocean floor around these parts. The "furious fifties," as the winds of the 50th parallel southern latitudes are called (Cape Horn is at 55° 58′ 47″ S), are legendary. Squeezed by the Andes and the Antarctic Peninsula, they give rise to equally fearsome waves. Throw in the odd iceberg to make things more interesting. Even now, only sailors who have "rounded the Horn" are by tradition and honor permitted to wear a gold loop earring and to dine with one leg on the table.

Landing on or rounding the island remains enough of a dicey proposition today that the cruise line, Australis, takes pains not to guarantee it in its promotional materials. (Queasy types shouldn't worry too much. The rest of the ship's route is through the sheltered passages of the Beagle Channel and the Magellan Strait.) The captain tells me that the ship manages a rounding of the Horn only about 50 percent of the time.

But the first day of the year turns out to be a lucky one: calm seas, the lightest of breezes, a hazy sun. It is summer in the Southern Hemisphere, and the temperature is a relatively balmy 50°F (10°C). We make landfall, clamber up a steep set of stairs, greet the lonely Chilean Navy sailor at his guard post, and snap the requisite photos. Eventually everyone scatters to explore the lighthouse, pop into the one-room chapel, and visit the monument to mariners, leaving me, briefly alone, to gaze at the Cape. (The actual point is about a mile/1.6 km away on a spit of land, protected from the erosive tread of visitors.)

For one brief shining moment, I'm the southernmost human in the Americas. At such times as these, I whip out my Moleskine notebook. (Hemingway famously used one, and therefore so do all the writers I know; interestingly, so did Bruce Chatwin, whose musings about Patagonia and Cape Horn I have just read.) I jot down deep thoughts, burning questions, fervent wishes, and firm resolves. I visualize

them rising to the heavens, carried on the wings of the albatrosses—the souls of sailors perished according to sea lore.

It doesn't have to be New Year's Day on Cape Horn. Any combination of place and time that takes you away from the incessant demands of daily living, that places you in direct contact with Nature's majesty or civilization's crowning glories, throws open the window on your essential self so you can get a hard look. These auspicious times and places can be truly enabling, in the best sense of that much-maligned word.

So when and where is it going to be for you? Valentine's Day in Tuvalu? April in Paris? Post-divorce in Bali? Your birthday on Machu Picchu? Christmas on the Equator?

At the small lighthouse cum souvenir shop, I sign the guestbook (Page 1!) and buy an "El Fin del Mundo" postcard stamped with today's date. Then I scale down the steps, hop on the Zodiac, take one last lingering look, and rejoin friends old and new back on the boat.

The end, come to think of it, makes a fine beginning.

• *Norie Quintos is an editor at large for National Geographic.*

OPPOSITE: A boardwalk paves the way down the slopes below the Cape Horn Lighthouse in Cape Horn National Park. ABOVE: Expedition boats anchor on the Beagle Channel in front of the Cordillera Darwin range.

BOLIVIA

HIKING THE CORDILLERA REAL

Take in sky-high views of the Andes from soaring peaks.

The Cordillera Real is the South American mountain system you've never heard of but need to experience. Running less than 80 miles (128.7 km) through west-central Bolivia, the narrow, subrange of the Andes forms an imposing barrier between the Amazon River Basin in the east and the Altiplano, the high plateau in the west. It was from the Altiplano that 16th-century Spanish conquistadors got their first glimpse of the mountains they christened the "royal range." The name comes from the Cordillera Real's series of majestic snow-crowned peaks: several over 19,685 feet (5,999.9 m) above sea level, hundreds topping 16,400 feet (4,998.7 m), and one, Illimani, soaring above 21,000 feet (6,400 m) and dominating the skyline of sky-high La Paz, the gateway city to backpacking adventures in the range.

The Cordillera Real has been traversed by the indigenous Aymara people since pre-Columbian times. Hiking trails regularly follow pre-Inca footpaths, sections of the Inca Trail network, and age-old llama paths across mountains and valleys and through the history of this breathtakingly scenic slice of South America.

It's not only the scenery—cobalt blue Lake Titicaca, herds of llamas and alpacas, and endless glaciated peaks—that can take your breath away. Acclimatize to the high altitude for at least three to five days in La Paz before hitting the trail.

Travel Tips

WHEN TO GO: May to September (late fall to winter in the Bolivian Andes) for dry weather and mild daytime temperatures. Overnight temperatures can dip near freezing.

PLANNING: Going as part of a small group tour led by an English-speaking guide is the safest and most convenient due to the altitude, language barrier, and challenging terrain. Trekking outfitters such as Mountain Kingdoms and Bolivian Mountain Guides take care of all the logistics.

WEBSITES: mountainkingdoms.com; bolivianmountainguides.com

The North Yungas Road from La Paz

Cordillera Real Traverse

Considered the mother of all Cordillera Real treks, the Cordillera Real Traverse (CRT) takes high-altitude hiking to the extreme. Most of the route is above 14,700 feet (4,480.5 m), and most days on standard 14- to 21-day through-hikes include climbing at least one mountain pass topping 16,000 feet (4,876.8 m). Mining roads and other industrial intrusions have marred the classic, or east side, CRT trekking route, so choose a tour that primarily follows the new, or west side, trail, from the colonial town of Sorata south to Botijlaca.

The breathtaking scenery you signed up for begins before you ever take a step. A portion of the three- to four-hour ride from La Paz to Sorata hugs the shores of cobalt blue Lake Titicaca, the highest navigable body in the world, sitting at 12,500 feet (3,810 m) above sea level. The actual hike begins high in the valley (elevation 13,038 feet/3,973.9 m) above the lake, where epic views await, following a wide ridge below the monumental massif formed by Jankouma (elevation 21,080 feet/6,425.1 m) and Illampu (elevation 20,769 feet/6,330.3 m) mountains.

Expect to trek at least four or five hours every day and camp out overnight, regularly at sites over 15,000 feet (4,572 m) above sea level. On this less developed west side of the CRT, you're more likely to regularly encounter shepherds and llamas than fellow trekkers. Sections of the route are narrow, steep, and rocky paths better suited to the padded, cloven hooves of llamas than to the crampon-compatible trekking boots you'll be wearing. Stay upright and on course by religiously following in the footsteps of your guide.

The first full day of trekking delivers what you signed on for: strenuous ascents (16,000-foot/4,876.8 m-high Sarani Pass)

and jaw-dropping views, including Jankouma and its sky-scraping neighbors, 20,336-foot (6198.4 m) Wakana, 19,211-foot (5,855.5 m) Kasiri, and 18,778-foot (5,723.5 m) Janko Piti. As the days unfold, there's no letdown (except for one rest day woven into most group itineraries) in the intensity or awe-inspiring scenery.

Arguably, the CRT is at its best on the last full day of trekking. The day before the descent to the southern terminus in Botijlaca features a climb between the rocky peaks of 17,721-foot (5,401.3 m) Cerro Ventanani and Janchallani. From here, you can see the glaciers of snowcapped Ala Izquierda (elevation 18,149 feet/5,531.8 m) and Cabeza de Condor (elevation 18,530 feet/5,647.9 m) and can trek to even higher views by hiking—what by now will seem an easy path—up to the rocky summit of 17,698-foot (5,394.3 m) Pico Austria.

Bolivia Mountaineering School

Adventure travel outfitter Mountain Madness's Bolivia Mountaineering School puts the Cordillera Real within reach of beginner climbers. Itineraries range from 13 to 18 days and start with expert instruction in essential high-altitude trekking skills, such as snow and ice climbing, ice axe positioning, and rappelling. Practice newfound abilities—including ones you hope never to use, like team crevasse rescue—on the relative safety of glaciated Tarija Peak (elevation 17,533 feet/5,344 m), a popular ice climbing spot near La Paz. Then, under the guidance of your experienced mountaineering guides, successfully tag the southern Cordillera Real's two most magnificent summits: 19,968-foot (6,086.2 m) Huayna Potosí and 21,193-foot (6,459.6 m) Illimani.

El Choro Trek

For a taste of the Cordillera Real without the technical ascents, take a three-day trek on the popular El Choro trail. The 35-mile (56.3 km) route is a pre-Inca path incorporated into the Qhapac Nan, Andean Road System, an Inca Trail network and UNESCO

With snowcapped peaks behind them, trekkers make their way toward a glacial lake nestled in the Cordillera Real.

World Heritage site. The trailhead (look for the statue of Christ marking the path) is at La Cumbre Apacheta pass, elevation 15,501 feet (4,724.7 m), in the southern section of the Cordillera Real.

The starting point, La Cumbre, the highest part of the road from La Paz to Coroico, is also the origin spot for North Yungas Road, nicknamed El Camino de la Muerte ("Road of Death"). No need to worry about the narrow gravel road's legendary drop-offs, fog, rock slides, and fatalities. You're only starting your three-day hike at the pass, not attempting a death-defying ride down the road by car or bike.

At the trailhead, follow the jeep track to the El Choro's highest point: 15,912-foot (4,849.9 m) Abra Chucura. From here, the entire trek is primarily downhill, with the scenery gradually changing from snow-capped mountains in the top section, to misty cloud forests and waterfalls in the middle, and subtropical banana and coffee plantations near the end. As you descend, watch and listen for the parrots, butterflies, hummingbirds, monkeys, and other wild things in the increasingly dense and colorful vegetation. Keep your eyes peeled for pre-Columbian and Inca ruins, which can be hidden off the trail or in the greenery.

Take caution: The El Choro trail's pre-Columbian paving stones can get slick, and there are multiple water crossings—sometimes on bridges, sometimes on tree limbs, and always an adventure—and potentially slippery suspension bridges along the way. To be safe, go slowly, use trekking poles, and take at least three days to complete the full route from La Cumbre to Chairo.

RAINFOREST AND REEF IN BELIZE

A dazzling gem on land and underwater in the Caribbean Sea

Belize's natural beauty knows no depths. To be more precise, its appeal lies at least 400 feet (122 m) below the sparkling surface of the Caribbean Sea. That's how far it is to the bottom of the cobalt abyss known as the Great Blue Hole, a massive sinkhole in the Belize Barrier Reef. A UNESCO World Heritage site that's second in size only to Australia's Great Barrier Reef, Charles Darwin crowned this mesmerizing place "the most remarkable reef in the West Indies."

More than 180 miles (290 km) of coastline add to the country's allure. In 2018, Belize made waves when it became the first country in the world to put a moratorium on offshore oil exploration and drilling. White-sand beaches fringe the shore, pristine islands dot the turquoise waters, and a tapestry of lagoons and atolls teems with marine creatures—from whale sharks and West Indian manatees to a kaleidoscope of tropical fish—that swim among fantastical coral and rock formations. Inland, thick tangles of rainforest harbor showy birds and other exotic wildlife, as well as a fascinating underground cave system revered by the Maya.

Adventure—whether by foot, flipper, or boat—awaits at every turn. In between it all, there are hammocks aplenty for soaking up the brilliant Caribbean sun.

Travel Tips

WHEN TO GO: February to April is dry season. Spring brings high humidity and triple-digit temperatures, while rain and wind are common in the summer and fall. Whale sharks swim near southern Belize in May and June.

PLANNING: International flights land in Belize City in the north, with connections to smaller airports throughout the country. Malaria and dengue fever are rare but endemic, and the Zika virus is a risk.

WEBSITES: travelbelize.org; belizehowlermonkeys.org; ambergris caye.com; belizeaudubon.org

A skull in Tunichil Muknal

WHAT TO DO

Glide Past Monkeys

The jungles of Belize are the domain of the howler monkey. Cruise inland along Monkey River through the cacophonous southern Belizean jungle in search of toucans, green iguanas, and tropical birds that coexist alongside the noisy primate. Or, west of Belize City, head to the New River, where howler monkeys populate the surrounding jungle. And for an up close encounter with wild black howler monkeys (known as baboons by local villagers), visit the Community Baboon Sanctuary, co-founded by five-time National Geographic grantee Robert Horwich.

Sea-Kayak the Coast

Ply the turquoise waters, mangrove swamps, secluded white-sand beaches, and pristine nature reserves on a sea kayak. Choose your own paddle adventure: Embark on an island-to-island journey along the Belize Barrier Reef or enjoy the shallow waters of a trio of fascinating coral atolls located just beyond the reef. Glimpse a beguiling array of marine life—including the endemic white spotted toadfish and playful dolphins—among the mangrove islands of Turneffe Atoll and Glover's Atoll. Or observe a colony of rare red-footed boobies at Lighthouse Atoll's crescent-shaped Half Moon Caye National Monument, Belize's first protected marine area.

Snorkel the Belize Barrier Reef

The Belize Barrier Reef provides myriad opportunities to swim and snorkel with colorful fish and aquatic creatures. Wearing mask and fin, you will find the undersea realm that awaits along the shallow fringing reefs inside the lagoon of Half Moon Caye (known in the diving world as "6,000 feet of vertical

abyss"), along palm-fringed Tobacco Caye, and elsewhere on the planet's second longest barrier reef. Encounter parrotfish, angelfish, and grouper; see otherworldly coral formations, and keep an eye out for sea turtles, dolphins, and spotted eagle rays. In the crystalline waters of Ambergris Caye's Hol Chan Marine Reserve and Shark Ray Alley, swim among stingrays and nurse sharks.

Take Wing to Superlative Bird Spots

With roughly 550 bird species in Belize, it's no wonder that birders flock to the country's avian hot spots, including six designated Important Bird Areas identified by BirdLife International, a global conservation consortium. Near Belize City, the lagoons and tropical forests of Crooked Tree Wildlife teem with 330 bird species, including kingfishers, jabiru storks, endangered yellow-headed parrots, and ospreys, which can be glimpsed from boat rides across the lagoon and on strolls along the boardwalks. On Half Moon Caye, some 4,000 red-footed boobies can be found among the orange-flowered ziricote thicket. Down in

the foothills of the Maya Mountains, scarlet macaws congregate near the village of Red Bank to nest each winter.

Plunge Into the Blue Hole

Off the coast of Belize, within Lighthouse Atoll, the massive marine sinkhole known as the Great Blue Hole has beckoned seasoned divers since the 1970s, when Jacques Cousteau declared it one of the planet's best diving spots. In its dark depths, explore thousands of stalactites and other geological formations left over from when it was a limestone cave above sea level, which began forming around 150,000 years ago. Water lovers without the requisite diving experience can snorkel the perimeter of the 1,000-foot-wide (305 m) pit, which teems with nurse and reef sharks and other marine life that hang out closer to the surface.

Go Cave-Tubing Through the Maya Underworld

Belize's western Cayo District harbors a fascinating system of remote cenotes and

subterranean caverns believed to have been the gateway to the mystical Maya underworld. Hire an outfitter for an unforgettable experience exploring the surreal limestone landscape by inner tube or canoe. Drift along the Caves Branch River in the Sibun Valley, keeping an eye out for wildlife, and gape at glittering stalactites and stalagmites along the way. Examine skeletal remains and Maya artifacts at the region's pièce de résistance: Actun Tunichil Muknal, or Cave of the Stone Sepulchre.

Hike the Verdant Jungle

The lush rainforests of Belize, protected by a tapestry of more than 100 nature reserves and other protected areas across the country, offer big payoffs for intrepid hikers. Venture into the Maya Mountains and feel the mist of the Thousand Foot Falls, which actually plummets 1,600 feet (488 m) into the gorge below. Visit the world's first jaguar preserve, Cockscomb Basin Wildlife Sanctuary, in southern Belize, which offers, along with the wildcats, a pristine wonderland of waterfalls and tropical forest, and neotropical birds. (If luck is not on your side at the reserve, the Belize Zoo offers a chance to see the elusive spotted cat.) Go for a hike on one of the reserve's nature trails where you can follow the tracks of tapirs, pumas, and ocelots, and scan the tree canopy for avian activity. Footpaths at the Mayflower Bocawina National Park lead to waterfalls and natural swimming holes. No matter the trail, look up to spy colorful birds—think toucans and kingfishers—in the tree canopy and enjoy the sound track of howler monkeys and other jungle life. Join a guided night hike for a glimpse of Belize's nocturnal creatures, from armadillos to kinkajous.

HIGHLIGHTS

• Dive the Blue Hole, part of the planet's second longest barrier reef.

• Follow the tracks of an elusive wildcat at the world's first jaguar nature preserve.

• Float through the cathedral-like chambers of a subterranean Maya cave.

Jaguars are often elusive, but these majestic big cats can easily be seen at the Belize Zoo.

ECUADOR

THE TREK OF THE CONDOR

The ultimate five-day route through the wilderness of the Andes

Y ou don't necessarily need two years and legs of iron to get a good look at the Andes. You just need a sense of adventure, a little training, and a plane ticket to Quito, Ecuador, to tick off the Trek of the Condor, a five-day route between the Ecuadoran town of Papallacta and Cotopaxi National Park.

"There's wild horses, 14,000-foot (4,267 m) passes, different kinds of deer than we had ever seen before. It was amazing," says conservationist Gregg Treinish, who traveled the route on his journey across the Andes. "There's volcanic ash everywhere, and we were walking by peaks rising more than 16,000 feet [4,877 m]."

The trek is open to anyone with the training—perhaps a better word is *courage*—to walk at more than 10,000 feet (3,048 m) for several days. The landscape is harsh, marked by rain, fog, and wind, but its wildness is a large part of what makes it so undeniably striking. While walking on the *páramo,* the high-altitude grasslands, trekkers encounter villagers herding their animals as their ancestors have for centuries, lagoons dotted with birds, a glacier, and the looming peaks of some of the highest active volcanoes in South America. At the trek's culmination in Cotopaxi National Park, climb to the refuge base center of its eponymous volcano—or if you're feeling up for another challenge, hike beyond to its glacier-topped summit.

Travel Tip

WHEN TO GO: Visit during the dry season (mid-July to early October) when windier weather means less cloud coverage and clearer views of Cotopaxi and the other peaks along the way.

PLANNING: Weather along the trek changes rapidly, and you are almost guaranteed constant cloud cover. Come prepared with layers, as well as rubber boots for the muddy areas and river crossings along the way.

WEBSITES: ambiente.gob.ec/ parque-nacional-cotopaxi

The Trek of the Condor's namesake bird sweeps through the sky.

5-DAY ITINERARY

Day 1

It's nearly a two-hour ride from Quito to El Tambo, a quaint village sitting 11,154 feet (3,400 m) above sea level. This is where the trek begins—but the journey starts easily enough. Depending on the tour, you can hike the muddy trail ahead—rubber boots are essential—or travel over the swampy terrain by horse. The four-hour day includes a few small river crossings, traveling over Potrerillos Pass, and a descent into a densely covered valley. Here, you'll make camp on the shore of Laguna del Volcan.

Day 2

Get an early start to the day because six to seven hours of hiking are ahead of you. After crossing more muddy terrain and small forests, you'll finally reach drier land as you spend the day trekking through a broad valley. This is the part of the trip that earns the hike its name; you're most likely to spot condors here. Another view to behold: the Antisana volcano and the lava peaks of Antisanilla. Just past the Santa Lucía lagoon, make camp at the foot of the mountains near the ruins of a hacienda that housed geographer and naturalist Alexander von Humboldt during his visit to Ecuador in 1802.

Day 3

Today's hike is a feast for the eyes with views of the Ecuadoran páramo as you leave the foot of Antisana and continue toward Sincholagua mountain. Keep your eyes peeled for more condors, as well as caracaras and Andean foxes, as you continue through the highlands. The seven-hour trek will take you to the valley of La Mica Lake, a water reservoir for Quito,

OPPOSITE: As clouds roll in to the Andean plateau, ichu grass and huamanpinta plants bend in the wind. ABOVE: A hiking group crosses a valley in Cotopaxi National Park toward the Ruminahui volcano.

and through the moraine of the old glacier. The day ends at the foot of Sincholagua mountain.

Day 4

Regularly covered in mist and a thin layer of snow, Sincholagua fittingly translates to "steep upward," the perfect description for your hike today. The pass over Sincholagua at 14,800 feet (4,511 m) offers sweeping views of the surrounding valley, Western Cordillera, and the Cotopaxi—an active, glacier-topped stratovolcano. After nearly five hours of hiking, camp at Río Pita, located at the base of Cotopaxi National Park, elevation 12,647 feet (3,800 m).

Day 5

At 19,347 feet (5,897 m), Cotopaxi is Ecuador's second tallest peak and the highest active volcano in the world. Make a 45-minute climb to Jose Ribas, the refuge center at 15,750 feet (4,800 m), where you can stop for lunch and a warm cup of tea.

Intrepid climbers can don crampons and continue to higher points (the air is thin, so be sure you're properly acclimated). Otherwise, make your descent and hike to Laguna Limpiopungo, the final spot of your journey. Birders will enjoy spotting the nesting Andean gulls, as well as hummingbirds, waterfowl, and wrens. Wild horses are known to graze by the trail. On a clear day, take in the view of Cotopaxi reflected in the waters as you walk the circumference of the lake (about a 90-minute jaunt). Explore the rest of the park before heading back to Quito.

Ecuadoran *chagras*, or cowboys, take an overnight ride for an annual cattle round-up with Mount Antisana behind them.

EPIC
SHOT

Clay cliffs just outside Manú National Park in Peru form a natural salt lick that attracts various animals, including these red and green macaws. More than 1,000 species of birds—10 percent of the world's total—live in and around the park.

At 6,627 square miles (17,164 sq km), the park—a biological wonder—covers the entire watershed of the Manú River, from grasslands on the eastern flank of the Andes, down through moss-draped cloud forest to the lowland rainforest of the westernmost Amazon Basin. In addition to the macaws, the region is traversed by tapirs and snakes, 92 species of bats, 14 species of primates, and harpy eagles with their six-foot (1.8 m) wingspans. And then there are the butterflies: scarlet knights, giant blue morphos, glasswings.

IMAGE BY **CHARLIE HAMILTON JAMES**

CKWISE FROM TOP LEFT: A courtyard
osaics in Marrakech; Egypt's Pyra-
of Giza; a double rainbow lining the
e over Victoria Falls; a chimpanzee
ganda's Kibale Forest National Park

CHAPTER 2

AFRICA

Discover the riches of vast and varied landscapes on wildlife safaris, breathtaking desert dunes, and thrilling rafting excursions.

TANZANIA

CLIMBING KILIMANJARO

Take in the heavenly views from the roof of Africa.

Alone, flat-topped massif towering above the wildlife-filled savanna near the Tanzania/Kenya border, Mount Kilimanjaro has for centuries enticed climbers to push their limits and stand on the roof of Africa. The Uhuru Peak summit lies at 19,341 feet (5,895 m) above sea level; it's the world's tallest freestanding mountain, and with well-trodden routes requiring little more skill than putting one foot in front of the other, hikers of all ages and experience levels can achieve it. Nearly 75 percent of the 30,000 to 50,000 people who tackle it each year achieve the summit.

Formed around a million years ago, Kilimanjaro is three dormant stratovolcanoes smooshed together. Six main trekking paths march through five distinct climate zones marked by morphing scenery. Banana and coffee croplands give way to towering moss-blanketed sycamore and juniper trees, ferns, and flowering plants in misty rainforest. Smaller trees and shrubland of the semi-alpine region, including Dr. Seussian giant groundsel trees, shrink to closer-to-the-ground vegetation in a moorland and heath incline. Here, hardy protea flowers attract curve-billed sunbirds and lichen color old lava rock. Finally, a barren gravel summit region, dominated by striated blue-white glaciers, hints the top is near. The final push, often aided by headlamps, climaxes with a spiritual above-the-clouds view at sunrise.

Travel Tips

WHEN TO GO: Wet weather compromises comfort and difficulty, as well as the views, so it's best to go in the dry (and cooler) season from January to March. The second dry season, from June to October, is also Kili's peak season, but routes are crowded.

PLANNING: All climbers must go with an outfitter. Research in advance to find one that treads lightly on the environment and employs well-trained and well-paid English-speaking guides.

WEBSITES: mountainexplorers.org; tanzaniatourism.go.tz/destination/mount-kilimanjaro-national-park

A hiker passes a Kilimanjaro sugarbush.

The Lemosho Route

This newer and lesser traveled route covers more distance and takes seven to nine days to complete. Said to be the most scenic of the trail options, it's also pricier to traverse because of its length and more remote starting point. The hike begins on a narrow path that winds through pristine jungle from around 8,694 feet (2,650 m). Here, you'll have better-than-average chances of sighting black and white colobus monkeys and hornbills. On day three, after a steep climb, you'll be rewarded with sweeping Shira Ridge views before heading up the western slopes of the Kibo Massif. Summit via the Western Breach.

The Shira Route

Another infrequently traveled trail departing from the west, the Shira route's start follows a 4x4 track, allowing driving access to a higher elevation start point—almost entirely bypassing the rainforest zone—at around 11,482 feet (3,500 m). At the end of day one, you'll follow the Ngarenairobi River into the moorland and heather region; day three includes a steep climb to Lava Tower, a 300-foot-high (91 m) lava formation. The final stretch either joins the popular Machame route for the summit attempt or follows the more precarious Western Breach.

The Machame Route

Easy to access, this is the most scenic route serviced by budget operators. Machame starts in the southwest and intersects the Shira Plateau before taking a sharp right past Lava Tower across the Southern Circuit below the summit. Lasting either six or seven days, this route has much more up-and-down hiking than the comparable Marangu or Rongai routes. However, likely

OPPOSITE: **The view from inside a tent at Lava Tower Camp in Kilimanjaro National Park** ABOVE: **Snowcapped Kilimanjaro rises into the clouds.**

because of the easier acclimatization these elevation changes offer, operators report higher summit success rates here than on the Marangu. The Barranco Valley, traversed on days three and four, affords scenic views of the plains below, and its challenging wall requires some scrambling.

The Marangu Route

With gradual slopes to the point of final ascent, en route concession stands, and hut accommodation featuring sleeping bunks, flush toilets, and solar-powered lights, the Marangu is the most established path up the mountain. It's the only route that uses the same trail for ascent and descent, and it can be crowded. Trips can be done in as few as four days. Outfitters estimate only a third of hikers on this route reach the summit—the lowest of any route—likely because of a shorter acclimatization period and early misperceptions about the difficulty of summiting overall.

The Rongai Route

The lone northern route, Rongai, starts around 6,400 feet (1,950 m) near the border with Kenya. With a gradual slope and fewer trekkers, it can be accomplished in a five- to seven-day trek. The northern slopes receive less rain, so the scenery is less varied on the ascent, but since it's drier, it's one of the easier paths to tackle during the rainy months of October and November. You'll pass features not seen on other routes, including several caves on days one and three and a small lake at the Mawenzi Tarn Camp.

The Umbwe Route

The shortest distance on the ascent, traversing just 17.2 miles (27.7 km) from the trailhead to the summit, the Umbwe route, the most demanding, has the fewest climbers. Following bare trail with tree roots for purchase, this steep route reaches Barranco Camp, the same campsite used on the third or fourth night of the Machame Route, in the first night. This ascent, only for experienced climbers able to acclimatize quickly, can be done in just four days.

HIGHLIGHTS

• Conquer Africa's highest peak with top-of-the-world sunrise views.

• See the iconic melting summit glaciers before they vanish.

• Wind through five climate zones as you climb in elevation.

RAFTING THE ZAMBEZI

Paddle the world's wildest ride.

n 1855 when David Livingstone first glimpsed Victoria Falls, he called the unbridled curtain of water the most wonderful sight in all of Africa. Today the UNESCO World Heritage site (and one of the Seven Natural Wonders of the World) is an adrenaline junkie's paradise—its torrent of water washing away inhibitions. Here, the Zambezi pours millions of gallons in a curtain more than a mile (1.6 km) long—an expanse two and a half times the width of Niagara Falls— landing spectacularly in a narrow gorge just 130 feet (40 m) wide. There the river earns the nickname "Slam-bezi" from rafters who have followed it through one of the densest concentrations of Class IV and V rapids—the highest ratings given for commercially raftable routes.

Rafted since the 1980s, the Zambezi is surprisingly accessible, even to novices. Here, rubber refuges are whisked along in bumpy chaos, dwarfed by canyon walls. And it's relatively safe: The warm water mitigates exposure issues, and its series of calm pools that follow the rapids ensure rafters can be retrieved quickly after almost-guaranteed flips. Crocodiles and hippo sightings are not uncommon, though interactions are rare. Most rafters take single- or half-day trips on the first stretch, but those who embark on multiday excursions are rewarded with more rapids and wildlife and the opportunity to experience the Zambezi's rarely seen reaches.

Travel Tips

WHEN TO GO: Peak conditions—and usually the only time multiday expeditions are offered—are from mid-August to December. Upriver rains in April and May bring the falls to full force but can close the river to rafting.

PLANNING: Bring a swimsuit, rash guard, insect repellent, waterproof sunscreen, water bottle with clip, and sturdy shoes that can get wet. Cameras should be waterproof and securely tethered.

WEBSITES: safpar.com; bundu adventures.com; zambiatourism.com; zimbabwetourism.co.zw

Rafters take on the Zambezi's rough rapids.

6-DAY ITINERARY

Day 1

Start on the Zambia side, where a larger tourism infrastructure and a diversity of reputable rafting guides may mean a smoother ride. Get your bearings at Mosi-Oa-Tunya National Park, gateway to Victoria Falls in Zambia, in the early morning when the sun's angle makes for a likely chance of seeing rainbows. Walk the Knife's Edge trail over a narrow footbridge to view the entirety of the Eastern Cataract, part of the Main Falls, as well as the Boiling Pot—the starting point for river rafting journeys. Spend time observing this wild curtain of water as it throws off musty, sweet spray on its journey into the Batoka Gorge below. In the local language, the falls are known as Mosi-Oa-Tunya or "smoke that thunders," and its towering mist plume can be seen for up to 12 miles (19 km). While both Zambia and Zimbabwe have unique views of the falls, the largest expanse is visible from Zimbabwe. You can cross the border on the Victoria Falls Bridge and walk through the rainforest past a statue of Livingstone to various lookouts, culminating at the aptly named guardrail-less Danger Point. Or if you don't want the hassle of a border crossing, take a helicopter or microlight flight over the falls for a full, international vantage. Afterward, head to one of the many craft stores in Livingstone and choose a *nyami nyami*. Worn on necklaces by virtually all rafting guides and crafted in stone, bone, or metal, the spiralized pendants represent a serpentine god said to inhabit the Zambezi. These serve as protective talismans (though it's said they have to be a gift to work) and make great souvenirs.

Day 2

It's time to tackle the river, and the first day is the wildest—it's what gave the river its tagline "the wildest one-day white-water run in the world." Hike the 750 feet (229 m) down on steep wooden planks into the Batoka Gorge, and if water levels are low enough, explore beneath the falls before embarking near the base. Then take off along the meandering route from the Wall (Class IV) to the bumpy Class V Stairway to Heaven, which drops you down the terrifying equivalent of a two-story building. Then it's through the Devil's Toilet Bowl to the next bucking Class V, Gulliver's Travels.

You'll have to portage at Commercial Suicide where the water gets a bit too dicey for rafts, but you can watch more experienced kayakers take it on. It's a smooth ride from there, interspersed with a spin through the Gnashing Jaws of Death, after which operators often pull over to the riverbank for lunch. There are five more Class V rapids that follow, with names like the Washing Machine and Oblivion (it's said only one in four rafts makes it through this one without a flip). All told, the 15-mile (24 km) trip on this day two includes some 21 named rapids, each between 330 feet (100 m) and 1.2 miles (2 km) apart.

Day 3

Prepare for another wild ride on the next 15-mile (24 km) stretch of river. This lesser visited lower half of the river has a handful of Class V rapids to test your fortitude. In the Narrows 1-4 section, rapids bounce and swirl off both sides of the canyon as the gorge shrinks to just 900 feet (274 m) wide. Later in the day, intervals between the chaos become longer, and calmer pools require more paddling. Now you can let your guard down and look for creatures—including the huge and toothy tiger fish below and fish eagles above—that call this impressive basalt gorge home. In the afternoon, the huge Upper Moemba rapid presents four long waves and a serious drop to navigate before landing in the calm, protected waters fronting a white-sand beach. Build an evening bonfire on the shore, and sleep under the stars.

Day 4

After a short hike around unraftable Class VI rapid Lower Moemba, a scenic series of

OPPOSITE: **A bridge connects the Zambia and Zimbabwe sides of Victoria Falls.** ABOVE: **Rafters make their way through the rapid-filled gorge amid waterfalls and rainbows.**

waterfalls dropping 26 feet (8 m), it's back on the river for about an hour's ride to Dam Site. There, a cooperative hydroelectric project between Zambia and Zimbabwe, some 33 miles (53 km) from Victoria Falls, threatens to flood the gorge and eliminate the white-water rafting experience to this point completely within the next few years. Portage around the site—now a Class VI falls—and prepare for the largest commercially run Class V rapids of the entire river, and the last of the trip: Ghostrider. On this stomach-flipping series, three huge waves seem to swallow rafts whole. Good luck! Scenic gorge views unfurl along the riverside until you find a good beach to set up camp for the final night on the river.

Day 5

A much calmer Zambezi continues from here as the river finds its way toward Lake Kariba. With only a few small rapids to navigate, you can spend the day fishing for the toothy tiger fish, looking for crocodiles and hippos, and watching the changing scenery as islands crop up in the river's widening path. In the evening, leave the river for the drive back to civilization.

Day 6

In Livingstone, take an early morning boat ride to tour Livingstone Island, a spit of land atop the falls. If conditions are right and you're brave enough, dip into popular local swimming spot, Devil's Pool. This calm, natural infinity edge pool allows you to sit on the heart-pounding precipice of Victoria Falls. Look down! Spend the rest of the day scoping out other adventures on offer, including bungee jumping or zip-lining a 400-foot-high (122 m) canyon swing. Or, of course, just relax. You've earned it!

HIGHLIGHTS

• Feel the adrenaline rush while conquering some of the world's best rapids.

• Hear the thunderous roar of Victoria Falls, and look for rainbows in its mist.

• Marvel at wildlife from sandy beaches along remote reaches of the Zambezi.

Green islands dot the wide Zambezi
River as it crosses a savanna plain.

Not So Easy Rider in Zanzibar

By Andrew McCarthy

THE SCRAGGLY TREE BESIDE my fallen motorcycle provides no relief from the African downpour. The rain sounds like machine-gun fire as it pelts the plant's few tattered fronds. I look back over the sandy dirt lane I've been riding until a deep rut threw me to the ground. The potholed road has turned into riotous little pools of water. There are no buildings in sight, no other signs of life. I bend over to inspect a deep scrape on my knee. What was I thinking?

I am roughly halfway across the island of Zanzibar, about 20 miles (32 km) out from its main city, Stone Town, on my way to the island's more remote and idyllic eastern beaches. I've never ridden a motorcycle before. What made me think that this small island off Africa's eastern coast was the place to begin acting like an extra in *Easy Rider*?

This morning, the kid behind the desk at my modest hotel mentioned he had a friend who rented motorcycles. "The beaches in the east," my impromptu concierge said, "are beautiful." I had already spent a few days wandering, following my nose, getting lost amid the warren of narrow lanes that make Stone Town so alluring. The distinctive doors with their brass studs made me feel far from home in the way that I search out while traveling. My afternoon was free, and I didn't really want to join a tour to Prison Island

BELOW: **Stone Town is the cultural center of the island of Zanzibar.**
OPPOSITE: **A motorcyclist parks at the Fukuchani ruins.**

just offshore. *It'll be fun, an adventure,* I blithely told myself. And so I said, "Yes. Get me a bike!"

He came back with a 250cc Honda. After about a half-dozen failed attempts to get it started, I turned to the young man, who jumped on the starter once and revved the throttle, then held the purring beast upright for me as I haltingly swung a leg over.

I should have reconsidered my journey then and there. Instead, looking back as I stand drenched under a tree, I am amazed to have gotten this far. I somehow managed to navigate the twisting, cluttered, one-way lanes of Stone Town, and then the traffic-choked outer parts of Zanzibar City. I zipped over roads swarming with schoolchildren in uniforms who waved and shouted as I passed.

And I successfully outmaneuvered a police barricade. Or, rather, I simply didn't know how to downshift quickly enough to stop when a guard stepped from a small hut by the side of the road and raised his hand for me to halt. I raced past him, not certain which of our faces registered greater shock. The gravel road gave way to dirt. The wind blew. Then it began to rain.

With my vision obscured by the monsoon wash, my progress slackened considerably. By the time I fell off the motorcycle, I had slowed to such an extent that I'm not sure if the road conditions or my lack of momentum had caused me to spill.

As I stand against the tree in the steamy rain, I see that the eastern sky has brightened. I think of the night before. I was in a crowded, outdoor bar amid groups of people who were laughing, drinking, touching, having a memorable night under the African sky as music throbbed. It seemed I was the only one alone. I couldn't seem to bridge the gap between myself and others. Why was I unable to do anything about my feelings of separateness when I was surrounded by so many? I slunk back to my lonely hotel, feeling impotent, defeated by my lack of social expertise.

So the next morning when the young man offered up the two-wheeled chance at redemption, I tossed timidity to the wind and leaped at the opportunity to prove my virility, if only to myself.

Eventually the rain lets up and the sun slips through. After a dozen increasingly panicked attempts, the Honda roars to life. I'm back! In short order, I make it to those glorious beaches and discover their posh resorts. At one, couples are drinking around a poolside bar. A few people eye the sopping figure who squishes onto a nearby stool, and yet I speak to no one. Again.

No matter. I've made it. Against the odds, I have traversed the island. Triumphed over adversity. I will be able to live with myself, even perhaps accept my shortcomings. I am okay. It is then that a woman approaches, saying something about the "mysterious" quality I possess sitting there all alone.

OPPOSITE: A man bends to touch the water at a shallow beach in Kizimkazi, Zanzibar. ABOVE: A colobus monkey steps out onto the roadway.

• *Andrew McCarthy* *is a writer, actor, director, and an editor at large for* National Geographic Traveler.

ETHIOPIA

THE CRADLE OF MAN

Uncover humanity's roots in the Lower Omo Valley.

Southwestern Ethiopia's Lower Omo Valley holds the distinction of being both a cradle of humankind and one of Africa's most intact cultural landscapes. A trove of hominid and animal fossils and stone tools have been excavated from the age-old sedimentary deposits of this remote, prehistoric region, designated as a UNESCO World Heritage site in 1980. The discoveries helped shape our understanding of human evolution by illuminating the earliest stages of the origins and development of our species, *Homo sapiens.* The Lower Omo Valley is also home to more than 200,000 people who live near the river and are members of largely intact tribes. Traditions like the body painting artistry of the Karo and the famous ornamental clay lip plates worn by Mursi, or Mursu, women still exist, yet are under extreme threat.

Since the 2017 opening of the 800-foot-high (243.8 m) Gibe III hydroelectric dam, the natural twice-yearly flooding cycle of the Omo River—and the life the cycle sustained for subsistence cattle herders, farmers, fishermen, and crocodile hunters—has been disrupted. In addition, the Ethiopian government has leased tribal lands to cotton, sugar, and oil production. No longer isolated, the Lower Omo Valley still is considered Ethiopia's most culturally and linguistically diverse region. Experience it now, before the tribes and their traditions disappear.

Travel Tips

WHEN TO GO: June to September and November and March to coincide with the Lower Omo Valley dry seasons; June to November to visit the Omo Delta, home of the Dassanech people

PLANNING: Find responsible guides to tour this part of the world. Sustainable tourism outfitters Journeys by Design and Wild Frontiers offer custom and small group tours designed to tread lightly and responsibly through the Lower Omo Valley.

WEBSITES: journeysbydesign.com; wild frontiers.com; wildexpeditionsethiopia .com; sabanalangano.com; paradise lodgeethiopia.com; buskalodge.com

A woman carries fruit in Addis Ababa.

9-DAY ITINERARY

Day 1

Make Ethiopia's capital city, Addis Ababa, more than a quick arrival and departure stop by visiting the National Museum of Ethiopia, home of Lucy, the 3.2-million-year-old hominid uncovered in northwestern Ethiopia's Afar Triangle in 1974. Lucy's bones are preserved in the museum archives, but you can view extraordinary casts of the bones in the basement paleontological exhibit.

Day 2

From Addis Ababa, ride three hours south through a portion of the East African Rift Valley, a 3,700-mile-long (5,954.5 km) lowland region produced by the ongoing geological splitting of the African continent. Called the "cradle of humanity," the region has yielded key archaeological finds, such as the 1.5-million-year-old "Turkana boy" hominin skeleton uncovered in Kenya in 1984. Overnight in a cliff-top bungalow at the Sabana Beach Resort overlooking Lake Langano.

Day 3

Continue south to the city of Arba Minch, situated just west of the "Bridge of God" isthmus, which is covered by Nechisar National Park and separates Lake Abaya and Lake Chamo. See crocodiles, hippos, and some of Nechisar's more than 350 recorded species of birds on a Lake Chamo wildlife-watching cruise. Spend the night overlooking the park and the lakes at Paradise Lodge, outfitted with furniture, decorations, and linens from Omo Valley tribal artisans.

OPPOSITE: **The Omo Valley inside Ethiopia's Mago National Park** ABOVE: **The Buska Lodge hotel and restaurant in Turmi in the lower Omo Valley**

Day 4

Ride south on the Konso-Jinka road through the relatively isolated homelands of the Ari, Banna, and Tsemai peoples. Tours typically time visits to coincide with the town of Key Afar's buzzing Thursday market, a multicultural gathering of tribal members trading and selling livestock, produce, crafts, and other goods. From here, it's roughly 25 miles (40.2 km) south to Jinka and isolated Mago National Park, home to multiple tribes, including the Mursi, best known for the ornamental clay lip plates worn by women as symbols of beauty. Outside Jinka, settle into the Eco-Omo Safari Lodge for a two-night stay.

Day 5

Spend the day touring Mago National Park, established in 1975 on the east bank of the Omo River to help protect the dwindling populations of elephants, buffalo, and giraffes from poachers. Game viewing is difficult due to the thick acacia shrubs

and dense woodlands; however, you'll likely see baboons and wattled ibis, a bird species endemic to the Ethiopian highlands. Make your way west across the park to the Mago River for a guided tour of the Mursi village.

Day 6

From Jinka, continue south 73 miles (117 km) through the Omo Valley to the remote market town of Turmi. On the way, stop to visit the Saturday market in Dimeka, home of the Hamar, or Hamer, people, best known for their male rite-of-passage ceremony—bull jumping. If you're considering buying souvenirs, the market typically offers original tribal pottery, woodcarvings, and other pieces crafted by Omo Valley artisans. Just outside Turmi, check into your private *tukul,* a round thatched hut, with en suite bathroom, at the Buska Lodge, your base for the next two days of exploration.

Day 7

From Turmi, travel into the surrounding region for village visits with the Hamer people and the Dassanech, or Dassenetch, the southernmost tribe living in the Omo Valley. The Dassanech ("People of the Delta") live where the Omo River delta enters Lake Turkana, the world's largest desert lake and a 2018 addition to the UNESCO World Heritage site "in danger" list. Primarily located in Kenya, the lake's far northwestern end is in Ethiopia, where the disruption of the natural flow and flooding cycle of the Omo River (which feeds the lake) has severely threatened the Dassanech way of life, as well as water quality and wildlife habit in Lake Turkana. Learn about the threats to the lake and to the cattle-tending Dassanech on a guided tour.

Day 8

Take a day trip to Murulle, home of the Karo, a highly aesthetic people who famously adorn their bodies with self-inflicted scars; piercings; and intricate designs drawn with pulverized white chalk, yellow mineral rock, red iron ore, and black charcoal.

Day 9

From Turmi, head northwest across the Stephanie Wildlife Sanctuary to the Konso Cultural Landscape, a UNESCO World Heritage site covering 21 square miles (54.3 sq km) of stone-walled terraces and settlements. Take a guided tour of a Konso village to observe cultural traditions kept alive for 400 years and counting. On the tour, you will see traditional Konso family compounds intentionally designed with low gates so that visitors (and any potential intruders) have to crawl on all fours to enter the property. The site also features carved wooden *wakas* (memorial statues) arranged in groups, representing an ancestor, his wives, and heroic events, such as the killing of a lion. Spend the night at the Kanta Lodge, overlooking the town of Konso (also known as Karati).

• *A note about responsible travel*

Visiting the Lower Omo Valley can promote wider awareness of how development is changing age-old tribal traditions. To respectfully and authentically experience the local cultures and communities, review the World Tourism Organization (UNWTO) "Tips for a Responsible Traveller" before your trip. The tips include asking permission before photographing people, learning words in the local language, and hiring local guides with knowledge of the area.

HIGHLIGHTS

• Visit Mago National Park to meet the Mursi people.

• Walk through town markets where tribal members trade and sell.

• See the ancient Konso Cultural Landscape, a UNESCO World Heritage site.

Pelicans flock together in Lake Chamo.

EGYPT

THE PYRAMIDS AND BEYOND

From sand to sea—and from the Nile Valley to Giza

From Moses to Tutankhamun, the luminaries of Egypt loom as large as its ancient stone pyramids. Encounter their immortal stories on a modern tour of this cradle of civilization—and add a few plot twists of your own as you chart an active adventure through this captivating country.

Among the most fabled destinations on the planet, the Nile Valley has captivated centuries of explorers, and yet this fertile region remains an enigma. Uncover some of its secrets as you drift down the world-famous river like a pharaoh aboard a traditional felucca (a wooden sailboat)—or paddle a kayak—under the watchful eye of falcons. Gaze down on the Valley of the Kings as you float over sandstone cliffs in a hot-air balloon. Rev your quad bike's engines in the imposing shadow of the Great Sphinx.

On the shores of the Red Sea, dolphins frolic in the warm water, and dazzling marine life awaits below the surface. Trek the rugged trails of the Sinai Peninsula, ascending its mystical mountains and communing with Bedouins amid the landscape's rich (and often contentious) religious legacy. Get immersed in the shape-shifting landscape of the Western Desert on the back of a camel or while soaring down its dunes on a sandboard.

In this eternal place, the sands of time are a force to be reckoned with.

Travel Tips

WHEN TO GO: Spring and autumn feature more moderate temperatures. Avoid the midday heat.

PLANNING: As of early 2019, the U.S. State Department advises against travel to the Sinai Peninsula (with the exception of air travel to the beach resort of Sharm el Sheikh) and the Western Desert due to terrorism threats. Check the State Department for updates (travel.state.gov), and hire a reputable private driver.

WEBSITES: egypt.travel; dailynews egypt.com

St. Catherine's Monastery sits below Mount Sinai.

WHAT TO DO

Ply the Nile

There's no denying the romance and time-honored allure of the Nile Valley. This storied river is the world's longest and has served as the lifeblood of Egypt since ancient times. A camel or donkey ride to the famed Pyramids at Giza is a classic way to explore the oldest of the Seven Wonders of the World, or you can take in the ancient site and surrounding Saharan sands from the saddle of an all-terrain, motorized quad bike. From the village of Saqqara, ride to the Step Pyramid, which dates to 2650 B.C., the oldest pyramid on earth.

Or take in the Valley of the Kings and Queens from the sky. Board a hot-air balloon and float over the collection of elaborate underground tombs nestled in desert cliffs. After enjoying a bird's-eye view of this sprawling spectacle, set off on foot to explore the ancient necropolises, which include the legendary tomb of King Tutankhamun.

From here, the calm waters of the Nile River await. Travel them as people have since the age of the pharaohs: in a felucca. Sail between Luxor and the bustling market town of Aswân, and glide around Elephantine Island, an archaeological treasure trove. For a more adventurous take on the classic Nile River cruise, the Cairo-based Nile Kayak Club offers weekend kayaking excursions, as well as multiday tours connecting temples. Watch for birds such as egrets, buzzards, and falcons as you paddle.

Dive Into the Red Sea Coast

Tourism along the Red Sea coast of the Sinai Peninsula has faltered in recent years due to safety concerns and flight bans following a 2015 plane bombing. Things are getting safer now, and the tropical fish and coral gardens dazzle as brilliantly as ever off the

coast. On the Gulf of Aqaba, snorkeling and diving sites remain world-class gems near the Bedouin village of Dahab, and the white sand still glistens at the sheltered Naama Bay of Sharm el Sheikh.

To add to your water world adventure, ride a camel hauling your gear to remote sites including the perilous Blue Hole, a massive sinkhole in the Gulf of Aqaba Reef. Water sports lovers follow the wind to Ras Sudr for wakeboarding, parasailing, and kite surfing.

At the coral headland of the southern tip of the peninsula, the crystalline waters of Ras Mohammad National Park teem with life, from thousands of migratory white storks to sea urchins and barracudas. The warm waters of Hurghada make it possible to swim with dolphins, and farther down the coast, the lagoon of Abu Dabbab offers the chance to swim with giant green sea turtles

and rare dugongs, an elusive cousin of the more familiar manatee.

Walk the Desert of the Sinai Peninsula

Linking Africa and Asia, Egypt's wild Sinai Peninsula sets a rugged backdrop for unforgettable desert and mountain treks. Intrepid hikers can set their sights on the Sinai Trail, a 143-mile-long (230 km) network of old caravan routes that became Egypt's first long-distance hiking path in 2015. Navigate this wild region from the Gulf of Aqaba to Mount Catherine, the so-called Roof of Egypt, with the help of local guides and their camels. Experience Bedouin hospitality, and traverse the sandstone plains and gorges of these desert landscapes and oases, including fabled stopovers for Christian and Muslim pilgrims en route to Mount Sinai and

OPPOSITE: Camels make their way through the desert with pyramids behind them.
ABOVE: A felucca sails along the Nile.

Hot-air balloons hover over the
Luxor West Bank Theban Mountains
and the Valley of the Kings.

Mecca. Wind through apricot and pomegranate orchards that were planted by early Christians, now tended by Bedouins. Discover the brightly painted cerulean rocks of the Blue Desert, which stand in contrast to Sinai's iconic red-rock mountains as an artistic symbol of peace.

Follow in the footsteps of the biblical prophet Moses and centuries of religious pilgrims on a climb to the 7,497-foot (2,285 m) granite summit of Mount Sinai, crowned by a chapel and mosque. (Spot rock etchings by 13th-century Crusaders along the way.) Plan to visit St. Catherine's Monastery on the mountain's lower slopes, a UNESCO World Heritage site considered sacred in Christianity, Islam, and Judaism. Here, Moses is said to have seen the burning bush of God. Climbers also flock to this historic area to scale its rock faces.

Western Desert Sands

Spanning roughly the area of Texas, the Western Desert of the Sahara sprawls from the Nile River west to Libya and from the Mediterranean coast to Sudan in the south. Embark on a camel trek or jeep ride across sweeping dunes and wadis, and venture to the mesmerizing White Desert, a surreal landscape of swirling white chalk and crystal peaks, and the nearby dark volcanic cones of the Black Desert. Hire a donkey-drawn taxi cart to explore one of the desert oases, such as the settlement of Siwa, with its natural springs, salt lakes, and mud-brick fortress.

For an adrenaline-pumping immersion in the desert landscape, try the emerging sport of dune surfing in the Great Sand Sea of western Egypt. Hire an outfitter, and glide down epic dunes at lightning speeds, gazing out at the undulating landscape.

HIGHLIGHTS

• Float down the Nile River on a traditional felucca sailboat.

• Ride a camel to the Pyramids at Giza or among the Western Desert dunes.

• Climb to the storied granite summit of Mount Sinai.

WILDLIFE SPOTTING IN AFRICA

1 BWINDI, UGANDA

Bwindi Impenetrable Forest National Park is 80,000-plus acres (32,375 hectares) of steamy mountain jungles, which suit the resident gorillas just fine. To preserve Uganda's oldest forest, gorilla treks are limited to eight people per gorilla troop per day. This also means less crowded experiences with chimpanzees and forest elephants.

2 LOWER ZAMBEZI RIVER, ZAMBIA

One of the best ways to experience the Zambezi is on safari, cruising to spot rhinos, buffalo, antelope, spoonbills, kingfishers, and elephants. National Geographic's 11-day "Zambia Private Expedition" offers canoeing, riverboat cruises, and fishing trips.

3 DZANGA-SANGHA SPECIAL RESERVE, CENTRAL AFRICAN REPUBLIC

Home to the second largest rainforest in the world, Dzanga-Sangha Special Reserve offers medicinal plant foraging with Ba'Aka nomads and observing traditional Ba'Aka net hunting. An elevated platform inside the reserve allows visitors to watch upwards of 75 elephants as they gather to drink mineral salts from the Dzanga Bai.

4 TARANGIRE NATIONAL PARK, TANZANIA

Lucky visitors driving along the Tarangire River in September and October can sometimes see more than 1,000 elephants in a single day, plus wildebeests, zebras, giraffes, impalas, elands, warthogs, and buffalo.

5 MASAI MARA NATIONAL RESERVE, KENYA

Few other safari destinations compare to the Mara River, especially during the annual migration when thousands of wildebeests and zebras join the reserve's resident Big Five—lions, African elephants, Cape buffalo, leopards, and rhinos.

6 ZAKOUMA NATIONAL PARK, CHAD

Ideally situated just below the Sahara and just above the rainforest, Chad's Zakouma National Park is an off-the-beaten-track fusion of traditional nomadic and Islamic culture, unique wildlife, and truly inspiring conservation. Zakouma is home to tiang, hartebeest, ostriches, leopards, lions, newly reintroduced black rhinos, and the largest population of endangered Kordofan giraffes. Once poached by the thousands, the park's elephant herds are now some of the largest in Africa.

7 MANA POOLS, ZIMBABWE

While many African safaris are restricted to vehicles, national parks in Zimbabwe still offer walking excursions, a unique chance to discover elephants, elands, leopards, baboons, and lions, sometimes from barely yards away. Scout rhinos and ancient rock art in Matobo Hills. Or head to Mana Pools National Park on a multiday canoe safari, falling asleep to the sound of hippos and restless hyenas.

8 OKAVANGO DELTA, BOTSWANA

A biodiverse refuge for some of the most endangered large species in the world, like cheetahs, rhinos, wild dogs, and lions, the Okavango Delta is the world's largest freshwater marsh ecosystem. Go horseback riding alongside wild giraffes and wildebeests with guides from Okavango Horse Safari. Established in 1986, Okavango restricts groups to eight riders at a time.

9 RAS ABU GALUM, SINAI PENINSULA, EGYPT

At Ras Abu Galum, rugged mountains give way to sand dunes, gravel beaches, and turquoise blue water harboring coral reefs, barracudas, sea turtles, pufferfish, blue-spotted stingrays, and lionfish. Camp with local Bedouin families, go for a night dive, and keep an eye out for hyrax, Rüpell's foxes, striped hyenas, snakes, and lizards.

10 KIRINDY FOREST, MADAGASCAR

Eighty percent of the wildlife seen on safari in Madagascar can't be seen anywhere else in the world. This includes more than 100 species of birds and lemurs (including indris, sifakas, and aye-aye). After swimming with the sharks in Nosy Be and spelunking past crocodiles in Ankarana's underground rivers, go on a night walking safari through Kirindy Forest to see fork-marked lemurs and stealthy fossa, Madagascar's largest carnivore.

OPPOSITE: A male and female giraffe cross necks at Chief's Camp in Botswana. ABOVE: A fortunate lion sighting on a safari drive in Masai Mara National Reserve

MOROCCO

THE BEST OF MARRAKECH

A palatial city with natural beauty just waiting to be discovered

Morocco is known for its diversity of traditions, religions, and landscapes. Boasting with life, Marrakech, its major economic center, offers a unique glimpse of it all.

This is the city of legends—today more than ever before. A former imperial city dating back to the 12th century, it is home to mosques, palaces, and gardens, and just a day trip away from the Atlas Mountains. Often called the "red city" for its beaten clay buildings built in the time of the Almohads (part of the Berber Muslim dynasty), it's truly a wonder to behold.

In and around the city you can experience an enticing labyrinth of centuries-old souks; taste the flavors of a cuisine that is a unique mix of African, Middle Eastern, and European; or enjoy lounging by a palm tree–lined swimming pool.

There's a little bit of everything in Marrakech—lively markets, wildlife adventures, nature parks, and bathhouses, to name just a few—making it an easy choice for travelers who want something a little out of the ordinary. For adventurers, there is downhill skiing just outside the city limits. For culture seekers, historic sites like Dar el Bacha and the Mellah spice market offer a glimpse into history. Shoppers will have no problem finding markets to fill their suitcases with unique souvenirs. Whatever your wishes, Marrakech delivers—and then some.

Travel Tips

WHEN TO GO: Summer can be oppressively hot and winter rainy. Aim for fall (October and November) or spring (May and April), when you'll have milder temperatures and sunny skies.

PLANNING: Work is being done to combat exploitation of animals including macaques, snakes, donkeys, and horses in the region. Do your part: Don't photograph the animals, and make a point to visit refuges like Jarjeer Mules.

WEBSITE: jardinmajorelle.com/ang/; jarjeer.org; nationalgeographic.com/expeditions

Colorful shoes on sale in a grand bazaar

WHAT TO DO

Ride Camels in the Desert

Camel rides are popular in Marrakech, but choose your ride wisely. For a more ethical experience, visit an Agafay Desert camp where the owners aren't after mass tourism and take better care of their animals. There are no rolling sand dunes to be found, but against the backdrop of the High Atlas Mountains and stone desert landscape, you may not miss them. On your ride, you might encounter mules, sheep, and goats.

Toubkal National Park

Outside Marrakech, Toubkal National Park is home to the largest mountain in North Africa, as well as seven other peaks. In the winter, expect weather that changes rapidly and drops below freezing with heavy snowfall. During this time, you can downhill ski at Oukaimden. In warmer summer months, enjoy a short walk along trails dotted with waterfalls, or hire a guide for a few days to summit Mount Toubkal at 13,671 feet (4,167 m). Macaques, gazelles, and wild boars often make an appearance in these ranges, so be on the lookout.

The Medina of Marrakech

The entire medina of Marrakech is a UNESCO site, boasting several architectural and artistic features such as the Bahia Palace (built in the late 19th century), Kotoubia Mosque (finished in 1199), and the Saadian Tombs, discovered in 1917 and dating back to Sultan Ahmad al-Mansur. While the medina played an important historical role in medieval urban development, today it exists as an example of traditional Moroccan lifestyle. By walking the streets and alleys, visitors to Marrakech can experience life in much the same way they would have centuries ago.

Explore the City at Night

Nighttime in Jemma el-Fna is an iconic Marrakech experience. The square was once the central trading hub of caravans crossing the Sahara. Visitors today experience musicians, aromatic food stalls, snake charmers, and, of course, shopping. Hate crowds? Head to one of the rooftop cafés before sunset to see the sun go down but also witness the bustle below without being in the middle of it.

Go Off the Beaten Path

Instead of battling the crowds at the popular Majorelle Jardin, head out of town to the Anima Gardens, where local flora and fauna are mixed with modern sculpture art and a fraction of the people to contend with. Each of the sculptures is thoughtfully woven into the natural landscape, and an on-site café provides refreshments when it's time to take a break.

An Iconic Experience

Visit a hammam. The traditional Moroccan

OPPOSITE: The ornate courtyard of Ben Youssef Madrasa college ABOVE: The Atlas mountains sit just beyond Marrakech in the Asni Valley.

bathhouse is a must-have experience. You'll be scrubbed top to bottom with a soap made of ground olive pits, a mitt to exfoliate, and copious amounts of warm water. Whether you're after a luxury spa experience or would rather head to the neighborhood version, hammams are everywhere. This truly is a part of Moroccan culture that hasn't disappeared in centuries.

Walk Into History

Pay a visit to Dar el Bacha, once home to the sultan of Marrakech, Thami el Glaoui, and today a museum with rotating exhibits featuring topics such as the coexistence of faiths in the Mediterranean region. Or head out of town to the Tin Mal Mosque near the village of Ourigane. This mosque from the 12th century is where the Almohad dynasty began its conquest of Marrakech. It then became the spiritual and artistic center of the new capital.

Recently renovated, the Mellah area of Marrakech was once the Jewish quarter and worth a visit. Stop by the Mellah spice market for tasty souvenirs. You can also visit the Lazama Synagogue to learn a little bit about Morocco's long Jewish history.

Celebrate With the Locals

It often feels as if there's always something happening in Marrakech so it's truly worth checking events scheduled in the city before you book. One of the newest festivals is the Oasis Festival located just outside Marrakech. If you love music and dancing, visit in mid-September when the three-day event kicks off. Live DJs and music acts, as well as champagne and hookah bars, great food, and an on-site spa bring the gathering to life under the Moroccan sun.

HIGHLIGHTS

- Explore the sights, smells, and delights of city's bustling souks.

- Find a nature reprieve right outside the city limits in Toubkal National Park.

- Visit a 12th-century mosque on an exploration of the city's unique history.

Crowds gather at sunset in
Jemaa el Fna Square.

BOTSWANA

EIGHT BOTSWANA ADVENTURES

Geological oddities, traditional crafts, and starry skies await in this African safari destination.

Botswana is a unique landscape, home to salt plains, baobabs, and a rich cultural heritage celebrated through art and craft by local artisans. Before heading out on one of the country's renowned safaris, experience its other offerings: the untouched wilds of Kubu Island, the crafts found in markets in Maun, fly-fishing, cosmic delights on the salt plains of Makgadikgadi, and the vibrant local artistry at two museums in the city's capital.

And then there's the Okavango Delta, Botswana's pride and the ideal wildlife sanctuary: a far-reaching network of floodplains and shimmering lagoons nearly devoid of human presence. Discover the region on hiking safaris, open-vehicle game drives, and *mokoro* (dugout canoe) safaris, seeking out rare and endangered species, including African wild dogs and blue wildebeests. Cap off your visit exploring thunderous Victoria Falls with a private guide. Botswana's Chobe National Park harbors more elephants than just about any other game park in Africa, along with massive herds of buffalo, zebras, and antelope. Bunk at the Zarafa Camp, a National Geographic Unique Lodge, in the Selinda Reserve, where you might hear lions roar outside your tent. After you've had your fill of wildlife encounters, visit the northwestern edge of the Okavango to find ancient rock paintings at Tsodilo Hills that date back to A.D. 800 to 1300.

Travel Tips

WHEN TO GO: The best time to visit the Okavango is from June to September; visit drier camps from March to May. Some lodges close during low season, from December to April. July to October sees the most crowds.

PLANNING: Visiting Botswana can be an expensive experience; prices are high to keep preservation efforts ongoing. Though there are budget options, be prepared for expense, particularly in the Okavango Delta.

WEBSITES: nationalgeographic.com/expeditions; wilderness-safaris.com; kubuisland.com

A woman weaves baskets in Shorobe.

Day 6

See what morning stirs up for your final Ruaha game drive. Then board a flight to Selous Game Reserve, one of the largest and oldest protected areas in all of Africa. Relax in natural hot springs; then take off on an evening boat safari along the Rufiji River, the lifeline for this massive reserve, which twists and branches into five sleepy lakes. Many creatures can be spotted as you drift by, including numerous hippos, bathing elephants, crocodiles, and 440 bird species. Around sunset, look for the charismatic auburn-colored and frog-eating Pel's fishing owls.

Day 7

Part of Selous is managed for big game hunting, but poaching is still a real problem here. Your tourism dollars in this lesser visited region are funneled back into its protection. Learn why that's so important by heading off-road in search of a park bright spot: wild dogs. Persecuted as scavengers and doomed by human encroachment, only 5,000 of these nomadic, pack-hunting canids remain in all of Africa; its estimated that more than 12 percent of the population thrives in Selous. It's also a good place to spot black rhinos. In the evening, hike to a remote campsite for fly camping.

Day 8

Rise early for a morning walk. This visceral experience puts you in the landscape in a way game drives and boat safaris can't, the perfect culmination to your journey. Learn from expert guides how to identify tracks, scat, and birdcalls, all the while scanning for large shapes on the landscape: buffalo, elephants, and giraffes. Soak it all in.

HIGHLIGHTS

• Immerse yourself in some of the last wild large-mammal ecosystems.

• Experience the thrill of seeing predators up close.

• Sit under the stars; then fall asleep to the growls and grunts of African wildlife.

A Self-Driving Safari in South Africa

By J. Maarten Troost

IT PAINS ME TO SAY IT NOW, but for many years, I lived under the illusion that only the very rich could afford an African safari. My preferred strategy for wealth accumulation (Powerball) had yet to pay dividends, and sometimes I'd wonder if I'd ever see a lion outside a zoo. Fortunately, I was profoundly mistaken.

"Do you think South Africans spend thousands a night to see an elephant?" my friend asked. She had lived in Cape Town for many years and knew what she was talking about. "If you really want to go on safari, travel like a local. Rent a cheap car and drive yourself."

Which is how I find myself in the town of Mkuze in Kwa-Zulu-Natal, South Africa. I'd flown into Durban, where I rented the cheapest car I could find—a Ford Fiesta.

Impulsive travel, of course, is the best kind of travel. What every tourist yearns for is surprise and wonder, and nothing beats following the breadcrumbs of serendipity. As I thread my way north on smooth two-lane highways, I note the sweeping changes in the landscape, from the fields of sugarcane outside Durban to rolling hills of bushveld to the savanna of African lore.

After checking in to my room, I saunter toward the water. A troop of vervet monkeys scampers across the grass. The colors begin to melt across the sky, with flaring streaks of crimson merging into a darkening blue void. I head toward a dock that stretches invitingly over the water. *Perfect,* I think. *That's where I'll watch the sunset.* And that's when I notice the sign: "Beware of the Crocodiles."

For real? What to do? Should I make some noise, or

BELOW: **An African elephant is spotted in a car's side view mirror.**
OPPOSITE: **Cheetahs climb a tree in Kruger National Park.**

should I be stealthy? I tiptoe my way toward the end of the dock, my senses attuned to every ripple, every rustle of grass, when suddenly, about 20 yards (18 m) from me, there is an explosion of water as a hippopotamus thunders above the surface, its gaping, toothy maw glistening with threat. I stand stunned as I watch what many consider to be the most dangerous animal in Africa belch a stone's throw from my quivering legs. I think of the Ford Fiesta.

"So, what do I do if I encounter a rhino in the park?" I'm speaking to Jean, an experienced safari guide originally from Botswana who moved here 20 years ago. "The thing about rhinos," she says, leaning in conspiratorially, "is that they are nearly blind. So whatever you do, do not stop your car above a pile of rhino poo. A rhino could mistake you for another rhino. It will feel challenged."

Hluhluwe-iMfolozi Park, the former hunting grounds of the Zulu kings, is the oldest game reserve in Africa. I see not more than a dozen other vehicles. As I slowly drive in, the first critter I come across is a baby zebra suckling at its mother's teat. *Aww,* I think, *it's like a Disney movie.* That's when the snake appears. It slithers across the narrow road. Sadly, I cannot tell you what kind of snake it was because

I had to pull over and take a few deep breaths and go to my safe place.

The park is a rugged mix of topography with steep, forested hills interspersed with vast savannas. And then, through a clearing, I spot two black rhinos. I pause, making sure I select a spot clear of animal droppings of any kind, rejoicing that I had found the first of the Big Five.

I head through the Kingdom of Swaziland, a surprisingly alpine country, on what is the most direct route to 7,700-square-mile (19,943 sq km) Kruger National Park. I am beginning to feel at ease in my car. Perhaps too at ease. I pull into a spot next to the Sabie River. A South African couple in a weathered SUV is staring intently at something through their binoculars.

"It's a lion," the man informs me. "Want to have a look?" Yes. Yes, I do. I step out of my car and reach for the field glasses. There, a short distance across the river, is a lion, a male with a rock-star mane that suddenly perks up at the sight of a human walking freely in his domain. "You might want to get back inside your car," the man says, as I return his binoculars. That seems like the prudent thing to do, and as I settle into the Fiesta, I feel giddy.

I pat the steering wheel. Thank you, little car.

OPPOSITE: **A lion relaxes in the shade in Kruger National Park.** ABOVE: **You don't need a Land Rover to encounter giraffes and charismatic megafauna.**

• *J. Maarten Troost is the author of several books, including* Headhunters on My Doorstep.

THE ULTIMATE NAMIBIA SAFARI

A wild ride in Africa's big sky country

t's easy to feel humbled by Namibia. With hundreds of uninterrupted miles between human settlements, it's one of the least populated countries in the world. Even the animals in this endless space are spread out and different. Cloud-catching beetles eke out an existence on shifting sands, desert-dwelling elephants appear larger than their savanna cousins, and rugged, desert-adapted populations of rhinos and lions have longer legs and thicker skin.

The Namib Desert has been baking for 55 million years, its temperatures regulated by the cold water and rich nutrients upwelling along its coast, creating contrasts both visual and visceral. Red dunes tumble down to the blue-gray sea, and craggy mountains poke up unexpectedly amid open flatlands. Watering holes in inland parks teem with birds, antelope, predators, and large game, while the coastline is littered with whale skeletons, the rusting hulks of long-forgotten ships, and long-abandoned mining outposts reclaimed by sand.

With such vast emptiness and the push and pull between life and death, Namibia feels timeless. Dry conditions have wonderfully preserved ancient rock art, impressions of an era pressed into inland mountains around the time the Egyptian pyramids were built, and plants, like the rare welwitschia, grow so slowly, they seem to live forever. Namibia's wide-open spaces practically beg to explored.

Travel Tips

WHEN TO GO: Sunny and arid Namibia is extra dry in winter (June to October), making it the best time for wildlife-watching and clear night skies.

PLANNING: Advance bookings—as far ahead as possible—for Etosha and other wildlife parks in the dry season are essential. Pack moisturizer and lip balm to combat dry desert air and plan for temperatures that can swing from sweltering by day to freezing at night.

WEBSITES: joesbeerhouse.com; namib rand.com; balloon-safaris.com; savethe rhinotrust.org; etoshanationalpark.co.za

Two children run down the Sossusvlei Dunes.

9-DAY ITINERARY

Day 1

Arrive in Windhoek, Namibia's capital city and main transport hub. Before hitting the dusty red roads for NamibRand Nature Reserve, a five-hour scenic drive through barren moonscape to the southwest, stop for a *braai* (barbeque) and beer. Breweries and beer gardens in Namibia, a German protectorate for over a century prior to its independence in 1990, carry on colonial culinary traditions. Joe's Beerhouse, an eclectic local favorite, serves springbok, oryx, and kudu steaks alongside German dishes like schnitzel.

Day 2

Desert savanna interspersed with red sand meet inselbergs and distant craggy hills under big skies in NamibRand, one of the largest private nature reserves in southern Africa. Fences were removed from these former sheep ranch lands in the early 1990s, and now wildlife roams freely. Four-by-four vehicles depart from tented camps through its roadless expanse in search of spotted and brown hyenas, Burchell's zebras, Cape foxes, cheetahs, leopards, and the critically endangered Ludwig's bustard. Walking safaris are also an option. In the evening, bask under the Milky Way in Africa's first Dark Sky Reserve.

Day 3

Literally rise with the sun in a hot-air balloon for golden hour views over an already golden landscape. Scale up the scenery by trading in finely grained detail for a vantage that reveals larger ripples in the sand, the transitions between unique ecosystems, and tiny game on the plains. Namib Sky has been offering the experience for more than a quarter-century, landing far from civiliza-

OPPOSITE: **A giraffe stands alone in the plain at dusk in Etosha National Park.** ABOVE: **Sand meets water on Namibia's Skeleton Coast.**

tion at a table set with a champagne breakfast. In the afternoon, follow the ancient Namib Desert in Namib-Naukluft National Park past some of its most gorgeous and undulating sand peaks, including Dune 45 at Sussusvlei and Big Daddy Dune. Take time for exploring and photographs before heading to the striated dolomite Naukluft Mountains. There, amid scrubland and perpetually clear springs, it's possible to see Hartmann's zebras. More than 2,000 roam the desert here in small herds of around six individuals; it's the largest population of this threatened subspecies in a protected area in Namibia.

Day 4

It's a long, barren drive along the fringes of the desert into the port town of Walvis Bay. On the way, stop by the lagoon outside town. Part of a network of important coastal wetlands for migratory birds, the lagoon is often dusted in an ombre pink spectrum of nearly red lesser flamingos and the nearly white greater flamingos. It's also a refuge for migratory seabirds, including the elusive

desert-breeding Damara tern. A short drive farther brings you to Swakopmund.

Day 5

With its palm-rimmed, half-timbered buildings, Swakopmund is a seaside colonial relic. Explore the fringes of this outpost—along Swakop River, by the sea, and around the city—on a fat-tire bike designed for rugged terrain. In the late afternoon, when sands are cooler, head into the Namib Desert and see its towering ocher dunes undulating into the distance. Look for tiny desert-adapted geckos, scorpions, and snakes, like the Peringuey's adder, which buries itself up to its eyeballs in sand. Or hike up the windswept ridge of Dune 7, the highest in Namibia at 1,256 feet (383 m), to watch the sunset before gliding down.

Day 6

Take off on a Skeleton Coast overflight leaving from Swakopmund. Here, a series of parks protects a swath of Namibia's coastline larger than the entire country of

Portugal. Heading north over ancient river canyons to follow the foggy, craggy coast, you'll have aerial views of huddled seals, sun-bleached whale skeletons, and the rusting hulls of ships that succumbed to the region's violent storms. This landscape is as bleak as it gets. There's not another soul for miles.

Day 7

Continue on land north through Dorob National Park, where you'll find Cape Cross Seal Reserve, the (smelly!) haul-out spot for more than 100,000 Cape fur seals. The colony thrives off the teeming shoals of sardines and ancho-vies that flourish in the nutrient-rich Benguela Current just offshore. Afterward, head to Uis, the gateway to ancient settlements and plants. Mount Brandberg Nature Reserve surrounds the country's highest mountain and contains some 50,000 rock paintings made by San bushmen between 2,000 and 4,000 years ago. Another ancient relic, the strange welwitschia plant, lives in the nearby Messum River region. Found only in Namibia and Angola, the two-leafed desert plant is believed to be between 1,000 and 1,500 years old.

Days 8 and 9

Head inland to Kunene in Damaraland, home to the fog-gathering darkling beetle and Afri-ca's largest stronghold of free-ranging, desert-adapted, and critically endangered black rhino. Freshwater springs in the Palmwag Concession, inland from the coast but still influenced by its chilly mist, draw the rare rhinos and other big game, including ele-phants, zebras, various species of antelope, leopards, and hyenas. Spend time exploring the endless horizon on game drives, and track black rhinos on foot with a member of the Save the Rhinos Trust.

HIGHLIGHTS

• See desert-adapted wildlife including lions, elephants, and the rare black rhino.

• Feel the thrill of hovering over a desert expanse in a sunrise hot-air balloon ride.

• Roam an endless beach and experi-ence the Skeleton Coast.

A huge colony of pink-and-white flamingos feed during sunset at Walvis Bay.

UGANDA & RWANDA

AFRICAN PRIMATE SAFARI

Chimps in the trees and gorillas in the mist

There's something about coming face-to-face with our closest animal cousins that stirs the soul and reminds us of our place on the planet. To experience this for yourself, grab your hiking boots and head for the lush landscapes of Uganda and Rwanda. The western branch of the Great Rift Valley remains home to nearly two dozen primate species, including troops of chimpanzees and some of the last wild redoubts of mountain gorillas. They share diverse terrain—from low-lying savanna to mist-covered mountains—with a dizzying array of biodiversity: more than 1,400 types of birds (half of all bird species present in Africa) and 330 species of mammals.

Human population growth in the region, as well as political and social upheaval in recent decades, have threatened the habitats and populations of many of the region's primates, which makes encounters with them all the more precious. Scarcely more than 1,000 mountain gorillas remain in the wild, and some species of monkey—like the gray-cheeked mangabey—are found nowhere else. To protect the animals, tracking excursions here are carefully regulated. The groups you'll visit have been habituated to human presence affording safe interactions for both parties, while trekking permits to find them help fund anti-poaching and habitat restoration efforts. This is one family reunion you'll never forget.

Travel Tips

WHEN TO GO: It's possible to track primates year-round, but the June to August peak season affords the driest and best conditions for trekking.

PLANNING: Permits to see gorillas are capped, so plan to book a year in advance. Bear in mind that conditions are often wet and flash photography is not allowed during primate encounters.

WEBSITES: nationalgeographic.com/expeditions; bwindiforestnationalpark.com/gorilla-trekking-uganda-bwindi-safari.html

A hippo grazes near waterbirds.

9-DAY ITINERARY

Day 1

Arrive in Entebbe via Uganda's main airport, and get your bearings in this lakeside city before kicking off your whirlwind primate tour. Afternoon speedboats depart for Ngamba Island on Lake Victoria, home to 50 or so rescued chimpanzees from all over the country. Meet with caregivers who will share the chimps' stories, then help serve dinner from a raised observation platform. Before heading back to the city, look for fruit bats, sunbirds, hornbills, and rare orange weavers in the island's dense forest, and take a refreshing swim on the Equator.

Day 2

Depart for Kibale Forest National Park, a five-hour journey by car. An hour in, just outside Kampala, stop at the palatial thatched huts of the Kasubi Royal Tombs. This UNESCO World Heritage site and traditional village is an active religious site, spiritual center, and historic burial ground for kings of the Buganda tribe. Muzibu Azaala Mpanga, the impressive, circular main structure, is nearly 102 feet (31 m) in diameter, 25 feet (7.5 m) high, and was constructed in the late 19th century of entirely organic materials.

Day 3

Kibale Forest, a hot spot of primate diversity, is home to a dozen species, including the largest population of wild chimpanzees in Uganda (some 1,450 individuals). Spend the day exploring the forested national park for glimpses of olive baboons, bush babies, as well as the rarer L'Hoest's and red colobus monkeys. While trekking within the park and the adjacent Bigodi Wetland Sanctuary—a haven for birds like African gray parrots and

the great blue turaco—you'll likely encounter evidence of other residents too. There are strange, striped sitatungas (Africa's only true amphibious antelope), tiny duikers, the elusive 600-pound (272 kg) giant forest hog, otters, and, if you're really lucky, lions, elephants, African golden cats, and leopards.

Day 4

Get up early for the three-hour drive to Kyambura Game Reserve on the northeastern fringes of Queen Elizabeth National Park. Arriving midmorning, head into the 300-foot-deep (91 m) Kyambura Gorge, a verdant chasm in stark contrast to the surrounding flat and treeless savanna. Hike up the viewing platform for a stunning landscape photo op before heading into the forest for a nature walk. A dwindling population of chimpanzees, which give the gorge the nickname "Valley of the Apes," remains sheltered within its confines, but your chances of spotting them are low. Instead, listen for their screeches and look for signs of the other 12 resident primate species, including black and white colobus and vervet monkeys. Then make your way toward the three crater lakes, which sport huge populations of flamingos. Come darkness, listen for the nighttime call of lions in the surrounding savanna.

Day 5

In the morning, take a cruise down the Kazinga Channel separating Lake George and Lake Edward for close encounters with hippopotamuses, Nile crocodiles, and waterbucks. It's also possible to sight distant elephants and antelope from this watery vantage. Then relax on another five-hour drive to Bwindi Impenetrable Forest National Park.

Day 6

Dense, ancient, and mist-filled jungle await. Bwindi is home to half of the world's endangered wild mountain gorillas, and today you're going to get muddy. All permitted visitors are briefed and assigned guides who will take them to a habituated family group based on fitness level. Depending on where your gorilla family resides that morning, you could be hiking anywhere from two to eight hours for your one-hour visit with them. Some 20,000 visitors visit the park's seven habituated groups each year; the park's Rushaga region houses the largest in all of Uganda, with about 25 members. However long, it's worth it to see the intimidating saunter of a silverback, the playful antics of babies, and the group's interactions.

OPPOSITE: **A baby chimpanzee rides on its mother's back through the canopy of Kibale National Park. RIGHT: Anti-poaching patrollers make their way through Mount Visoke.**

Looking northeast to Mount Muhabura, one of the five volcanoes in Volcano National Park in northern Rwanda

Day 7

Cross the border into Rwanda, and head toward Parc National des Volcans (Volcanoes National Park). In Musanze, 30 minutes from the park boundary, stop at the Karisoke Research Center, the headquarters of a gorilla conservation society founded by zoologist and author of *Gorillas in the Mist* Dian Fossey. A contemporary of Jane Goodall in the 1960s, Fossey studied gorillas here, becoming the first person to habituate them to human presence, and bringing their plight at the hands of poachers under global scrutiny. Learn about her work before heading into the park for the one-hour trek to her final resting place next to that of Digit, her favorite gorilla.

Day 8

Explore the flatter topography of the bamboo forest to find a habituated troop of endangered golden monkeys. It's one of the few places in the world to reliably see this shy and beautiful species. Like gorilla trekking, the length of your hike is based on the location of the monkeys that day, but they are often found within an hour or two. If you have time afterward, check out the Musaze Caves, which run beneath the national park, or take a guided community walk through nearby Iby'Iwacu village to learn about local cultural practices and traditional forest medicines from residents.

Day 9

Your whirlwind journey completes with a drive to Kigali. Explore this bustling city: learn about Rwanda's dark and recent history at the Kigali Genocide Memorial, sit down for a frothy drink in one of the city's popular milk bars, and pick up some colorful agaseke baskets from Kimironko market.

HIGHLIGHTS

• Hike through dense jungle to find wild families of mountain gorillas.

• Navigate swampland, bamboo forests, and misty volcano tops.

• Feed rescued chimps on an island sanctuary in Lake Victoria.

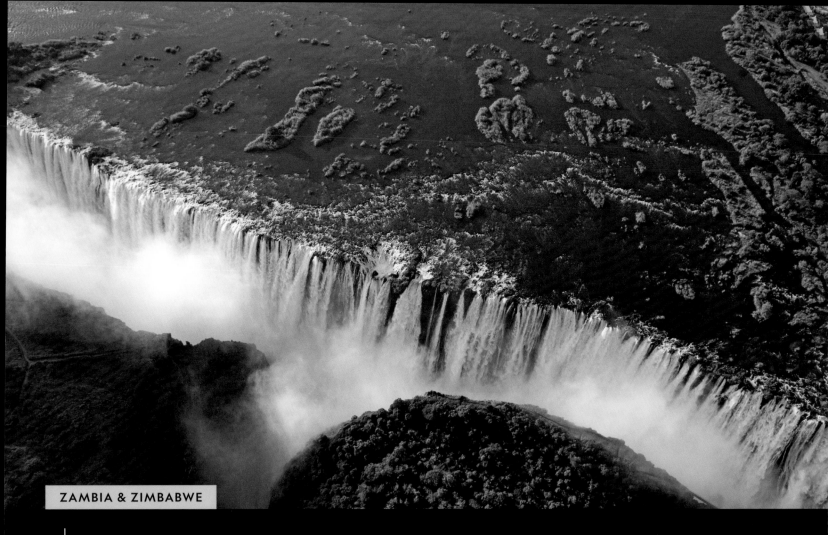

HOW TO VISIT VICTORIA FALLS

See—and hear—"the smoke that thunders" from all sides.

Victoria Falls is on almost everyone's bucket list, but few people know the best way to experience it. It's not the widest or tallest falls in the world, but it is without a doubt the most impressive.

Known by locals as Mosi-oa-Tunya, or "the smoke that thunders," it was first seen by Western eyes in 1855 when British explorer David Livingstone came upon it and named it after his queen. Reflecting on the experience of seeing Victoria Falls for the first time, he wrote, "Scenes so lovely must be gazed upon by angels in their flight."

The cataract still has that power to strike awe. It spans about a mile (1.6 km)—the entire width of the Zambezi River. Not only can you see it, but you can hear it (from about a mile away), feel it, smell it, and taste it.

The falls straddles Zimbabwe to the west and Zambia to the east. You can access it from either country via the town of Victoria Falls in Zimbabwe and Livingstone in Zambia. Zimbabwe has historically been the more popular entry point, but political turmoil and hyperinflation in the 2000s have made Zambia preferable. Zambia has been one of Africa's most stable and understated democracies; its safari lodges are known for old-fashioned hospitality and plentiful wildlife.

To see the falls, go to Zimbabwe; to feel the falls, go to Zambia.

Travel Tips

WHEN TO GO: Visit during the high flow (February to June) when you can feel the spray. Dry season offers new opportunities, but the falls may feel underwhelming.

PLANNING: There are national park entrances on both sides of the falls. If you book through a safari operator, your guide will drive you to the entrance. The per-person fee is $20 on the Zambia side and $30 on the Zimbabwe side.

WEBSITES: nationalgeographic.com/expeditions; zimparks.org/parks/national-parks/victoria-falls; zambiatourism.com/destinations/waterfalls/victoria-falls

Canoeing the Zambezi River

The Zambia Side

At high flow (February to June), the Zambia side is an exhilaratingly visceral experience; visitors walking on the other side of the narrow gorge can feel the spray (get drenched or rent a poncho). In the dry season, because the falls are at an incline, portions of land stay dry, which opens up other opportunities.

The Zimbabwe Side

The Zimbabwe side tends to offer the most picturesque views because the viewpoints are farther, offering perspective. Take note: If you go at the height of the dry season, say, in November, the water volume is at a low point and the falls can feel a little underwhelming.

Both in One Day

Get a multiple-country visa for your passport, and you can take in both sides of the falls in one day. From either Livingstone or Victoria Falls, visit the border-crossing office and get your passport stamped for exit. You can drive or walk across the bridge between the two countries, get your passport stamped for entry, and walk to the national park entrance. If you wish to return, make sure to get your passport stamped leaving the country and entering the other.

However, the most compelling experience may not require a park entrance at all: Stand on the bridge between the two countries, straddling Zim and Zam, and gaze at the world's most famous waterfall. You'll be joined mostly by cross-border drivers, hawkers selling souvenirs, and migrant workers rather than Western tourists.

Dine on the Falls

A luxury dinner train crosses from Zambia to Zimbabwe over the Zambezi River and stops in the middle for a view of the falls (though plans call for an additional departure in the other direction). The old-fashioned steam train crosses the Victoria Falls Bridge (completed in 1905) on a sunset journey to take in the falls. You'll be able to get off on the bridge and explore the landmark. The rest of the ride to Jafuta Siding includes a three-course meal and beautiful sights.

Fly Above the Falls

For an aerial view, microlight flights are a popular way to see the falls as Livingstone imagined angels do. Looking for more of a thrill, Zimbabwe outfitters offer bungee jumping from the Victoria Falls Bridge or a gorge swing, which drops you the width of the gorge from the edge of a sheer cliff. Zip-lining is another alternative, soaring 410 feet (125 m) above the valley floor, flying across the gorge at speeds over 62 miles an hour (100 kph).

The Devil's Pool

You've probably seen photos of people standing at the edge of the falls. Want to do that? The Devil's Pool is an experience you can have only on the Zambia side and only during the dry season (mid-August to mid-January). It involves a boat ride on the Zambezi to Livingstone Island, from which you can swim in a natural pool at the edge of the falls.

Breathe easy: An unseen lip prevents you from actually going over. Run by a well-regarded tour operator, the Devil's Pool is not a dangerous activity provided you follow the directions of the guides. There are other unofficial natural pools in which people have gone over the edge, so make sure your outfitter is properly licensed.

OPPOSITE: Victoria Falls is the world's largest sheet waterfall, double the height of Niagara Falls. ABOVE: A zip-liner zooms across the gorge for an up close view of the cascade.

HIGHLIGHTS

• Visit the world's most famous waterfall from two unique perspectives.

• Stand between two countries as Victoria Falls spills into the Zambezi beneath your feet.

• Soar above the roaring cascade on a microlight, zip line, or bungee cord.

The mist from Victoria Falls' rushing water creates a vibrant rainbow over the cascade.

TOP 10 **ADVENTURES FOR**

BIRD-WATCHING

1 OBUDU PLATEAU, NIGERIA

Take the aerial walkway of the Obudu Plateau to Becheve Nature Reserve's canopy platform for a rare glimpse of threatened species like white-throated mountain babblers and neon-yellow Bannerman's weavers. Trek along dense forest streams looking for spot-breasted ibis or spot red-headed picathartes living among lowland gorillas in the rainforest caves of Cross River National Park.

2 SANETTI PLATEAU, ETHIOPIA

From glacial lakes to waterfalls to the second highest mountain in Ethiopia, Bale Mountain National Park's remarkably diverse landscape is home to more than 300 bird species. Explore the park to search for golden eagles, lammergeier vultures, long-eared owls, wattled cranes, hornbills, plovers, and blue-winged geese.

3 NIOKOLO-KOBA NATIONAL PARK, SENEGAL

Niokolo-Koba National Park is Senegal's largest protected wilderness. Here, birders can tick Abyssinian ground hornbill, storks, ibises, lapwings, doves, kingfishers, bee-eaters, sunbirds, bushshrikes, and more than 360 other species off their life list. Although most of the park is vehicle only, it's worth getting a camp permit for Mount Assirik, a prime location for spotting giant elands, chimpanzees, and elephants.

4 KAKUM CANOPY WALKWAY, GHANA

Walk across 130-foot-high (40 m) rope suspension bridges in Kakum National Park to see turaco, drongo, blueheaded bee eaters, nine different species of hornbill, and over 600 species of butterfly. On the forest floor, the Sunbird Trail winds through three separate ecosystems, home to more than 200 bird species, as well as pangolins, gorillas, forest elephants, and striped bongos. Camp overnight in the park's treehouses to fall asleep to lullabies by nightjars.

OPPOSITE: Visitors follow canopy walkways through tropical rainforest in Kakum National Park. ABOVE: A Senegal parrot roosts at Parc National de Niokolo Koba in Senegal.

5 AZRAQ WETLAND RESERVE, JORDAN

What was once a popular watering hole for spice-hauling camel caravans is now a sanctuary for hundreds of birds. Visitors to Azraq Wetland Reserve's habitats can spy more than 40 species a day, from Palestine sunbirds to purple heron, crested larks, kingfishers, raptors, and graceful prinias—all best seen during spring migration (March through April).

6 IFATY, MADAGASCAR

Acoustic biologist and National Geographic Explorer Ben Mirin recommends birding the baobab-studded coastal town of Ifaty, "home to some of the most magnificent examples of spiny thicket, a habitat that cannot be found outside of Madagascar." In this unique enjoinment, endemic species like long-tailed ground rollers, subdesert mesites, and greater vasa parrots thrive.

7 SOCOTRA ISLAND, YEMEN

Birding on Yemen's Socotra Island offers not only a chance to spot endemic cormorants, Socotra buzzards, Jouanin's petrels, cream-colored coursers, flamingos, and Socotra cinnamon-breasted bunting, but also an opportunity to support ecotourism and preservation. Socotra's otherworldly dragon blood trees, stark white-sand dunes, granite cliffs, and spooky caves harbor more endemic species than almost any other archipelago in the world.

8 KUBU ISLAND, BOTSWANA

Mokoro dugout canoe trips throughout Kubu Island's surrounding marshes reveal African jacanas, weavers, majestic wattled cranes, coppery-tailed coucals, rosy-throated longclaws, and slaty egrets. The area is also home to ostriches, zebras, elephants, rhinos, giraffes, kudus, and impalas. Whether traveling by canoe, helicopter, 4x4, or horse, it's impossible to be disappointed.

9 UDZUNGWA MOUNTAINS NATIONAL PARK, TANZANIA

Getting to Tanzania's Udzungwa Mountains National Park is not easy, but the rewards are huge: unbroken forest canopy that shelters more than 400 bird species and Tanzania's largest variety of primates (including four species found nowhere else). Spot African marabou, Retz's helmetshrike, rufous-winged sunbirds, green-headed orioles, and more than a dozen Eastern Arc Mountains endemics, including the ultra-elusive Udzungwa forest partridge.

10 CAPE POINT, SOUTH AFRICA

In the southeast Atlantic surrounding Cape Point, trawling grounds are the perfect environment to see a wide range of pelagics, including albatrosses, petrels, and shearwaters. Chartering a small craft through the area also provides the opportunity to spot fur seals, whales, dolphins, turtle, and sunfish along the way. Book a tour with Avian Leisure during the austral winter season when pelagic seabirds travel north from their breeding grounds to Cape Town.

EPIC
SHOT

A great white shark follows marine biologist Trey Snow kayaking off the coast of South Africa. In 2003, an unusually large number of sharks were cruising the southernmost shoreline of South Africa. Photographer Tom Peschak was down to the last frames of his roll of film when he captured this spectacular moment. "Instead of the scientist tracking the shark, the shark is tracking the scientist," Peschak said.

With a GPS mounted on the bright yellow kayak, Snow and Peschak had been able to follow the shark into shallow water and observe its natural behavior. The two tracked sharks around Haaibaai, Afrikans for "Shark Bay," until one bold shark was brave enough to rise from the water and swim behind the kayak. The result: a viral picture that many thought was too good to be real.

IMAGE BY **THOMAS P. PESCHAK**

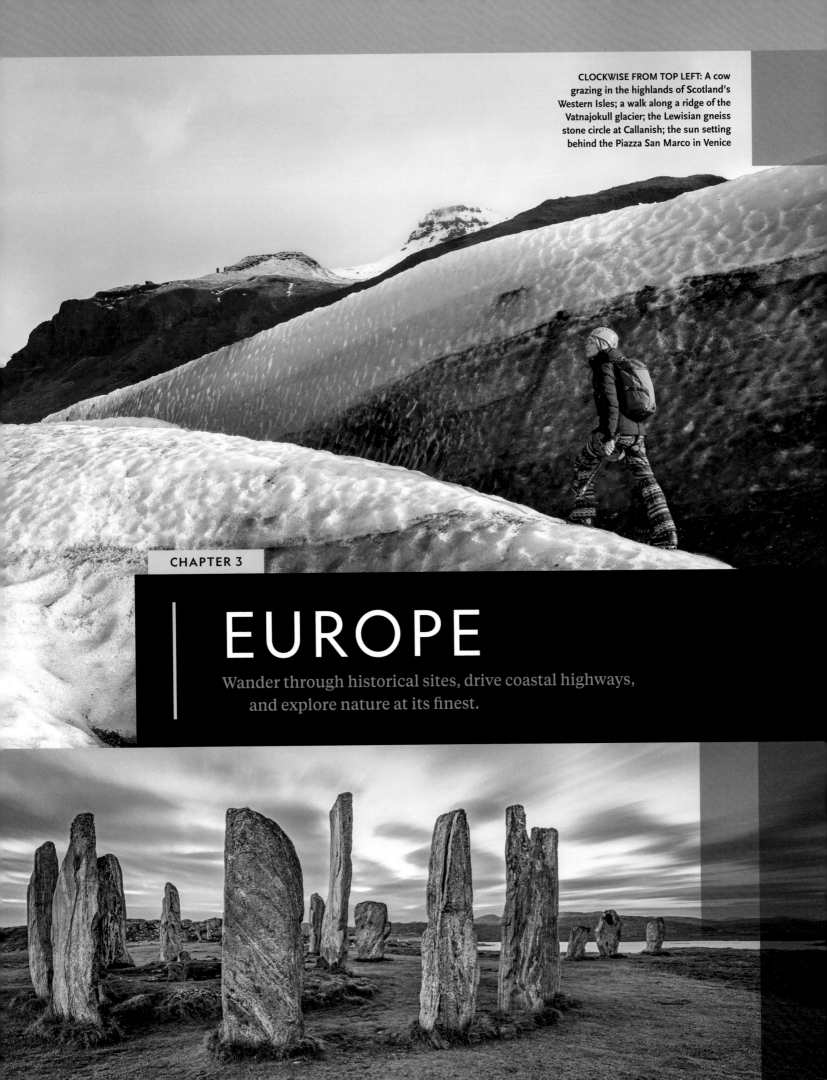

CLOCKWISE FROM TOP LEFT: A cow grazing in the highlands of Scotland's Western Isles; a walk along a ridge of the Vatnajokull glacier; the Lewisian gneiss stone circle at Callanish; the sun setting behind the Piazza San Marco in Venice

CHAPTER 3

EUROPE

Wander through historical sites, drive coastal highways,
and explore nature at its finest.

ROAD TRIP TO THE BURREN

From rocky cliff shores to delectable eats, this UNESCO Global Geopark has it all.

Framed by its mighty cliffs of Moher, the Burren region of western Ireland is a wonder of lunar landscapes, megalithic monuments, and beautiful botany. The 205-square-mile (530.9 sq km) UNESCO Global Geopark is one of the only places in the world where arctic, alpine, and Mediterranean plants grow side by side. A short drive through this remarkable landscape is like wandering into another time.

The name Burren derives from the Irish Gaelic for "stony place," and the dramatic rocky setting has captivated all sorts of creatives from J. R. R. Tolkien to Steven Spielberg. It'll take hold of you too, especially if you follow this route in the spring, when wildflowers paint the hillsides in hues of pink, yellow, and blue. (The best scenic overlook is at Corkscrew Hill on the N67.) There is plenty to do and see, including rocky wilderness, seaside villages, and delicious local delicacies to taste along the way.

The trip through this part of Ireland's County Clare will take you three days—depending on speed and how long you want to spend at each rest stop—to conquer the 55-mile (88.5 km) journey. Be warned: The narrow roads are more fit for grazing and wandering cows than cars, so drive slowly and practice the traditional one-finger salute—index finger, that is—with oncoming locals.

Travel Tips

WHEN TO GO: For spring blooms and hues, visit in March or April when temperatures are cool and comfortable (46°–54°F/8°–12°C). Warmer temperatures (high 60s Fahrenheit/low 20s Celsius) can be had from May to July.

PLANNING: Roads are narrow and are often taken over by cows and other local animals. Drive carefully, especially around tight curves. Instead of flying into Dublin, land at Shannon Airport—Ireland's second international gateway—a more direct departure point for your road trip.

WEBSITES: burrennationalpark.ie

A country road cuts through County Clare.

Ennistymon

Roughly 30 miles (48 km) from Shannon Airport, the Cheese Press in Ennistymon is the best place to stock up on road trip provisions and sample delicious bites from the Burren Food Trail. The specialty grocery stocks more than 40 varieties of Irish cheese plus Burren-roasted Anam Coffee, organic veggies from Moy Hill Farm, sandwiches with house-baked sourdough, and local kombucha.

Cliffs of Moher

Yes, there will be crowds, but this extraordinary escarpment is a must-see. Brave the tour buses to reach the Cliffs of Moher Visitor Centre, a concrete and stone edifice carved into a grassy headland. Displays themed around the local landscapes and culture fill the cavernous interior, while walkways lead to viewing platforms and the 19th-century O'Brien's Tower, which marks the cliffs' highest point (about 700 feet/ 213 m above the roiling sea). On a clear day, the vista extends from the puffin-peppered Great Sea Stack to the Gaelic-speaking Aran Islands. For more sights, explore the Cliffs of Moher Coastal Walk or take a boat trip with the Doolin Ferry Company.

Kilfenora

The birthplace of one of Ireland's oldest ceili dance bands, Kilfenora looks as if it's been petrified by the surrounding peat bogs. The gabled Kilfenora Cathedral is known for its high crosses, particularly the oversize Doorty Cross that depicts St. Peter blessing Kilfenora's upgrade from a monastic to a diocesan site in the 12th century.

OPPOSITE: **Paths edging the Cliffs of Moher provide some of Ireland's most spectacular views.** ABOVE: **Stone crosses mark a graveyard at Kilfenora Cathedral on the Burren.**

Agriculture is key here. Learn about it with Eva and Stephen Hegarty on a tour of their Burren Free Range Pork Farm, complete with samples of products made from the British Saddleback swine. A stay in the farm's Burren Glamping trailer comes with a breakfast of thick-cut bacon, tender sausage, eggs, and toast with homemade jam.

Carran

Tucked into the rocky highlands of the Carran, the Burren Perfumery distills the essence of the surrounding flora into small-batch fragrances, lotions, soaps, and candles. A perfume, launched in 2019, incorporates meadowsweet and wild ivy, which visitors can smell in the flourishing herb garden out back.

To get beneath the Burren's stone surface, however, book a tour of the Slieve Carran Nature Reserve with Heart of Burren Walks. Enthusiastic guide Tony Kirby shares facts and legends about the Carran Turlough (a disappearing lake), St. Colman's Hermitage, ancient monuments, and the

hardy wildflowers that somehow manage to bloom from cracks in the limestone.

Flaggy Shore

You can get your fill of local scallops, crab, lobster, and gigas oysters on the waterfront at Linnane's Bar, located in a centuries-old former cottage-pub-post office. A sweet spot for dessert is Café Linnalla Ice Cream. The most westerly ice cream parlor in Europe scoops creative flavors, from foraged blackberry to Baileys Irish Cream with sea salt to wild sea buckthorn (which tastes surprisingly like peach). Take your cone on a walk to the owners' eighth-generation dairy farm. Then amble out to the fossil-strewn Flaggy Shore, described by poet Seamus Heaney in "Postscript" as a place that can "catch the heart off guard and blow it open."

Ballyvaughan

As twilight falls, settle in at Gregans Castle Hotel, a luxe hideaway frequented by Heaney as well as Tolkien and Spielberg. The rooms are named after local wildflowers, places, and people. Tolkien fans should book the Martyn Suite, the former home's kitchen, where the owner, Frank Martyn, and the author gathered for drinks in the 1950s. For an end-of-the-road splurge, indulge in the restaurant's nine-course tasting menu, which features Irish delicacies such as spring lamb, rich cheeses, cherries, and wild mushrooms. Raise a glass of wine to the *craic* (good times), and say, "Slainte!"

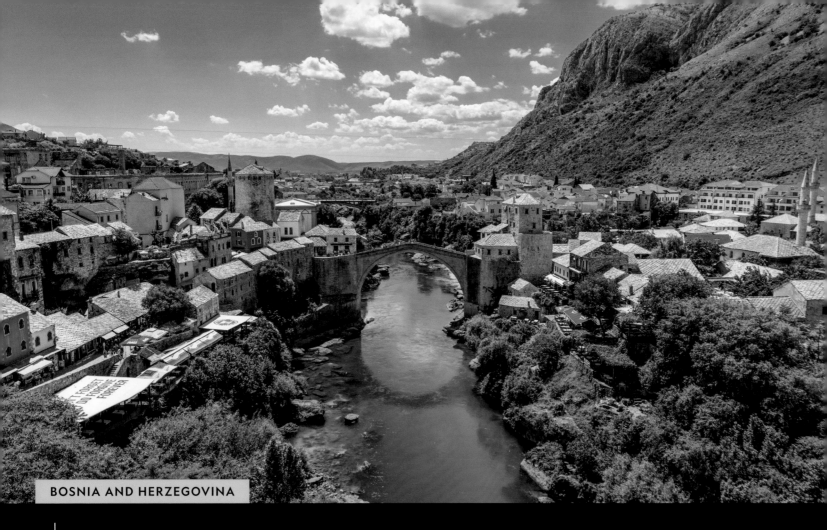

RAFTING FOUR RIVERS

Paddle world-class wild rapids on a four-river white-water adventure.

Bosnia and Herzegovina primarily owes its distinctive triangular shape, and maybe even its name, to water. The Sava River is the country's northern boundary with Croatia (the Dinaric Alps are the western boundary). The Drina River forms part of the eastern border with Serbia. The Tara River forms the southern border with Montenegro in multiple places. The Neretva flows into the Adriatic Sea on Bosnia and Herzegovina's tiny 12-mile-long (19.3 km) coast. Below the surface lie underground rivers and thermal springs that bubble up from the limestone plateaus of the country's south and southwest karst region. With water, water everywhere, one widely held theory is that the name Bosnia is a derivation of *bosana,* an Indo-European word meaning "water."

No matter the etymology, Bosnia and Herzegovina—one country composed of two autonomous entities, the Republika Srpska (Bosnian Serb Republic) and the Federation of Bosnia and Herzegovina—has miles and miles of clear, cold white-water routes on rivers you've likely never before heard of. And since adventure tourism is a relatively new concept here, you can still get the sense that you're venturing where few foreign rafters have gone before, adding a refreshing, next-frontier vibe to every adrenaline-pumping ride.

Travel Tips

WHEN TO GO: April to May for higher water levels and wilder rapids; June to September for warmer temperatures but typically lower water levels.

PLANNING: Sign on for a day trip or multiday tour on one river, or take on all four rivers in one epic rafting trip. The rapids can be challenging, so select an adventure commensurate with your skill and fitness levels.

WEBSITES: visitbih.ba/en; visitkonjic.com; neretvarafting.com; national park-una.ba/en

Chess opponents face off across oversize pieces in a park in Sarajevo.

Vrbas River

Host of the 2009 World Rafting Championships, northern Bosnia and Herzegovina's fast-moving Vrbas River boasts multiple Class III and IV white-water sections and pool drops. The rafting infrastructure here is relatively developed thanks to European Union–funded efforts to promote adventure tourism around the Vrbas. Rafting trips typically begin near 1,312-foot-deep (399.8 m) Tijesno ("tight") Canyon, a three-mile (4.8 km) route used for slalom kayaking competitions. Tijesno is one of two canyons (the other is 5-mile-long/8 km Podmilacje) on the 19-mile (30.5 km) wild romp down the Vrbas from the Bocac dam to the center of Banja Luka, capital of the predominantly Serb-led Republika Srpska. Sitting in the valley between the two canyons is Krupa na Vrbasu, a small-town adventure hub where you can join rafting tours, hike to waterfalls and the ruins of two medieval fortresses, and see ancient water mills still used to grind grain.

Neretva River

The Neretva River's 140-mile (225.3 km) path to the Adriatic Sea includes 126 miles (202.7 km) through the backcountry of central Bosnia and Herzegovina. Known for its clear, drinkable, and frigid emerald waters, it is reportedly the coldest river in the world, with temperatures as low as 44°F (7°C) in the summer. The Upper Neretva section, which flows through a mountainous and heavily wooded area near Konjic, south of Sarajevo, is the wildest. Four Class II to IV rapids await in the narrow Neretva canyon. Paddle them with an adrenaline-pumping group rafting trip led by a Konjic-based outfitter. Or take the exhilaration (and risk) up a notch on an all-day hydrospeed (riverboard-

ing) adventure, tightly holding onto a foam kickboard and steering clear of rocks as you hurtle, float, and flutter-kick down the river.

Una River

Forming a natural border with Croatia, the Una River travels some 130 miles (209.2 km) and is the centerpiece of Una National Park, Bosnia and Herzegovina's first, established in 2008. Travertine ledges create powerful Class II to V white-water stretches on the river's nine-mile (14.4 km) Štrbački buk–Lohovo section, which runs through the park. With a 77-foot (23.4 m) drop, Štrbački buk (a combination of several separate waterfalls and cascades) is the highest waterfall on the Una and a favorite of extreme sports enthusiasts craving the stomach-dropping rush of huge falls. Tamer water lies downstream in the eight-mile (12.8 km), Class II to III Costello-Grmuša section and in the lower 15-mile (24.1 km) Costello-Bosanska Krupa section.

Tara River

Cross into Montenegro and back, see Serbia, and float through a UNESCO World Heritage site on a three-nation, three-river rafting trip. Outfitter Rafting Centre Drina-Tara, located on the western Bosnian banks of the Drina River,

leads guided white-water excursions beginning on the Tara River in Montenegro and ending on the Drina in Bosnia.

Begin the trip by riding to the Montenegro launch site on the Tara, one of Europe's last remaining wild rivers. It's also home to Europe's deepest gorge—4,265-foot (1,299.9 m) Tara Canyon—formed by the river as it cuts through the mountainous northern edge of Montenegro's Durmitor National Park, a UNESCO World Heritage site. Local wildlife includes otters, eagles, bears, and wolves. The river's steep 11-mile (17.7 km) section from Brštanovica to Šćepan Polje is a white-water thrill ride offering 21 Class III to IV rapids. Float over the border from Montenegro to Bosnia at Šćepan Polje, where the Tara meets the Piva to form the Drina. From here, the northerly flowing river carries you back to the Rafting Centre Drina-Tara.

HIGHLIGHTS

• Paddle across borders on a rafting trip through Europe's deepest gorge.

• Take a wild hydrospeed ride in the emerald waters of the Neretva River.

• Tackle powerful Class II to V white water on the Una River.

ICELAND

HIKING ICELAND'S
EASTERN FJORDS

Trek across a primordial land of rumbling volcanoes, rhyolite mountains, and deserted inlets.

Most visitors to Iceland focus on its southwestern corner: the capital, Reykjavík; the Blue Lagoon, a tourist hot spot; and the Golden Circle of natural wonders—Gullfoss waterfall, Geysir and Strokkur geysers, and Þingvellir National Park.

Strike eastward, however, and you'll find yourself in another world. Austurland, Iceland's remote eastern region, covers a vast expanse of more than 8,770 square miles (22,721 sq km) but has a population of fewer than 11,000 people. The spectacular landscapes feature colorful rhyolite mountains, craggy fjords, geothermally heated waterfalls, and abandoned homesteads where even the hardy Viking descendants found the land too unforgiving.

It's no surprise that the Icelandic people consider Austurland the domain of the Huldufólk, the "hidden people"—elves and trolls. Splendid nonmythical creatures are in abundance as well. This is the only area of the country where you're likely to see herds of wild reindeer (introduced from Norway in the late 18th century) roaming the countryside and puffins nesting on islands in the fjords.

The largest town in the region, Egilsstaðir, makes an excellent jumping-off point for hikes in the area. This itinerary hits Austurland's greatest highlights, from the boulder-dotted valley of Stórurð to the colossal Vatnajökull ice cap.

Travel Tips

WHEN TO GO: Late summer and autumn, from July to October, is the best time for hiking in East Iceland, before heavy snows close many mountain trails.

PLANNING: The weather is highly changeable, and sudden rain showers are common. Come prepared with rain gear, comfortable waterproof hiking boots, and lots of warm layers. National Geographic Expeditions offers hiking trips that visit the eastern fjords.

WEBSITES: inspiredbyiceland.com; east .is; hallormsstadur.is; vatnajokulsthjodgar dur.is; nationalgeographic.com/expeditions

The largest puffin colony resides in Iceland.

Day 1

About an hour north of Egilsstaðir, in the Dyrfjöll mountains, is one of Iceland's most enigmatic places: Stórurð, or the "giant boulders." A moderately challenging 2.5-hour hike (five to seven hours round-trip) steadily ascends some 1,900 feet (600 m) from the trailhead on Vatnsskarð pass, traversing steep ridges and patches of snow—even in summer. The reward is breathtaking: a mystical valley filled with rippling meadows, blue-green glacial ponds, and enormous tuff boulders that look as if they've been tossed about by a giant.

Day 2

Spend the day wandering the delightful area of Borgarfjörður Eystri, just east of Stórurð. A 10-mile (16 km) loop begins in the seaside village of Bakkagerði (population 100), known for its summertime Bræðslan music festival. Behind the village, climb the nearly 100-foot-high (30 m) fortress-like rock formation called the Álfaborg ("city of elves") and believed to be the home of the Queen of the Elves in Icelandic mythology. Continue along the edge of the fjord to the islet of Hafnarhólmi, where a wooden walkway looks out over the nesting puffin colony. Then take the nearby trail over a pass to Brúnavík, a serene deserted inlet where waves lap against a black-sand beach.

Day 3

Reach the end of the Earth at Gerpir, the easternmost tip of Iceland. Marked trails constructed by the Ferðafélag Fjarðamanna hiking club run throughout the uninhabited peninsula. Pick up a trail map from the

OPPOSITE: **The village of Borgarfjodur Eystri lies below peaks in the eastern fjords.** RIGHT: **Hengifoss, one of Iceland's highest waterfalls, spills into a gorge famous in Icelandic legends.**

nearby fishing village of Eskifjörður, about a 40-minute drive from Egilsstaðir. Then strike out along the edge of the nearly 2,170-foot-high (661 m) sea cliffs, formed of rock more than 12 million years old and with dazzling views across the Norwegian Sea.

In the afternoon, bring a picnic to the nature reserve of Hólmanes, located just south of Eskifjörður on the edge of Reyðarfjörður, the longest (18 miles, or nearly 30 km) of East Iceland's fjords. Established in 1973, the reserve is noted for its intriguing rock formations and flourishing birdlife. Tramp over the tundra down to the fjord or up into the hills to spot seabirds and perhaps a herd of wild reindeer.

Day 4

At the southern end of Lagarfljót lake, a 30-minute drive from Egilsstaðir in the Fljótsdalur valley, a gently rising walking path leads to two spectacular waterfalls. During the two-hour, 1.5-mile (2.5 km) round-trip hike, first pause at Litlanesfoss, which pours between hexagonal basalt

columns lining a gorge. Then continue onward to Hengifoss, one of Iceland's highest waterfalls. The magnificent cascade plunges 420 feet (128 m) over black cliffs striped with bright red bands from layers of iron-rich clay. According to an Icelandic folktale, elves once inhabited the gorge around the waterfall and long-ago trekkers heard the singing of an Icelandic hymn coming from the rocks.

After finishing the hike, head to the other side of Lagarfljót lake to encounter one of the country's truly unusual sights: trees. Norse settlers chopping wood for fires, houses, and boats famously deforested Iceland centuries ago, leading to the land's barren volcanic appearance. Reintroduction efforts have produced some scattered woodlands, and the Hallormsstaðaskógur National Forest, protected since 1905, is the largest in the country. Well-marked trails wind through the rare brilliant green foliage formed by some 80 tree species—primarily native birch—that provide a sanctuary for birds including redwings, meadow pipits, and goldcrests.

Day 5

Iceland has countless waterfalls and hot springs, but the valley of Laugarvellir boasts a rare combo: a steaming hot waterfall. After driving to Hálslón Reservoir, about an hour and a half southwest of Egilsstaðir (4x4 required), walk along a 4.3-mile (7 km) trail over springy green turf. Despite the high elevation (more than 1,900 feet/600 m), there's considerable vegetation here due to the magma underground that warms the stream running along the valley floor. The alluring geothermal pool at the end of the hike is usually the perfect temperature for soaking weary muscles: about 102°F to 106°F (39°–41°C). Be sure to test the water with a fingertip before jumping in. Even better, the tumbling waterfall creates a natural hot shower.

Day 6

Journey to the southern reaches of Austurland, near the town of Höfn 2.5 hours from Egilsstaðir, to find 1,450-foot-high (454 m) Vestrahorn, one of Iceland's most scenic landmarks. The unusual gabbro mountain, estimated to be between eight and 10 million years old, rises above an otherworldly landscape of rolling tundra, vivid purple lupines, and jagged peaks on the edge of the sea. Walk along the black-sand beach of the Stokksnes Peninsula to photograph Vestrahorn reflected in the calm blue waters of the bay.

Afterward, stop by the Gamlabúð Visitor Centre in Höfn to pick up trail maps for Vatnajökull National Park, which covers nearly 14 percent of Iceland. The immense 3,127-square-mile (8,100 sq km) Vatnajökull ice cap is the largest glacier in Europe and is riddled with crevasses, volcanic fissures, and glittering ice caves.

HIGHLIGHTS

• Climb the Dyrfjöll mountains to the boulder-strewn valley of Stórurð.

• Hike through the Laugarvellir valley, and take a dip in a hot-spring waterfall.

• Walk along the towering sea cliffs of the uninhabited Gerpir Peninsula.

An onlooker peers into the majestic ice cave lying beneath the Vatnajokull Glacier near the Jokulsarlon Lagoon.

Traditional gondoliers and kayakers make their way past the historic Basilica di Santa Maria della Salute on the Grand Canal.

ROMANIA

ADVENTURE IN THE TRANSYLVANIAN ALPS

Venture off the beaten path in Romania's Southern Carpathian Mountains.

rish novelist Bram Stoker never visited the Transylvanian Alps, and yet the fictional sinister Count Dracula he created in 1897 lived or, more accurately, was "undead," there. The legendary story continues to draw visitors to the mountainous central Romania region where Vlad Tepes, the 15th-century inspiration for Stoker's creation, resided—and regularly skewered enemies on stakes. While Vlad, nicknamed the Impaler, wasn't a vampire and likely never lived in the 14th-century Bran Castle—now promoted to tourists as Dracula's castle—the landscape of his Transylvanian Alps does seem straight out of a dark fairy tale.

Bears and wolves roam deep, dark woods; Gothic churches and baroque buildings line sweeping central squares; and craggy peaks rise above meadows in the Alps, which form the southern section of the Carpathian Mountains. The Transylvanian Alps' three mountain ranges—Fagaras, Bucegi, and Paranag—run along a nearly continuous and largely impassable jagged limestone backbone.

For rock climbers, hikers, and mountain bikers seeking challenging terrain, the deep gorges, backcountry trails, and rocky outcrops remain a bit of a best kept secret. Isolation under Romania's communist regime (1947 to 1989) may have kept the mountains off outdoor adventure bucket lists in the past, but now is the time to discover the real Transylvanian Alps—no vampires but still legendary.

Travel Tips

WHEN TO GO: The best times are from June, when the Trasfagarasan Highway into the mountains usually opens after winter snows, to October.

PLANNING: Fly into Bucharest, rent a car, and drive two hours north to Brasov in the heart of the Transylvanian Alps. Operators such as MTB Tours offer adventure excursions in the area.

WEBSITES: romaniatourism.com; mtbtours.ro/en; facebook.com/BikeResort; uncover-romania.com; wildtransylvania.com; national geographic.com/expeditions

Peles Castle (1883) sits in the Alps.

WHAT TO DO

Rumble Down Mountain Slopes at Bike Resort Sinaia

Storybook Sinaia (home to the stunning Peles Castle, completed in 1883) sits at the foot of Mount Furnica in the Bucegi range of the Transylvanian Alps. A ski resort town in winter (with 11 miles/17.9 km of slopes), Sinaia, known as the "Pearl of the Carpathians," is a hub for summer hiking and biking excursions in the Bucegi Mountains and surrounding Prahova River valley.

Ride the gondola from town up to the lower station to tackle beginner-to-expert downhill, all-mountain, and cross-country tracks at Bike Resort Sinaia. The mountain bike park has 6.2 miles (9.9 km) of trails on four main routes: Happy Bear, Old School, Easy Breezy, and Fairy Trail. Rent a bike and helmet, or sign on with a guided tour, to ride the banked turns, boardwalks, forest roads, and other tracks down the slopes.

Tour the Transylvanian Alps by Mountain Bike

Village-hop through a rural Romanian highland region relatively untouched by technology or outside influences on a seven-day mountain biking tour led by Transylvania natives. Offered July to early October, the MTB Tours' Transylvanian Alps outing is designed for advanced to expert riders and covers more than 150 miles (241.4 km) on single tracks and trails.

Ride through high-altitude meadows and forests as you cross central Romania's main mountain ranges: Ciucas, Baiului, Bucegi, Piatra, and Craiului. Retreat to a local village each night to rest, raise a celebratory glass of *palinka* (plum brandy), and feast on mouth-watering Transylvania dishes like *ciorba de perisoare* (pork and rice meatball soup) and *mititei* (skinless grilled sausages).

OPPOSITE: **A cyclist makes his way down the Carpathians. RIGHT: Hundreds of caves, filled with Ice Age fossils, are scattered through Apuseni Natural Park including Scarisoara Cave.**

Climb the Highest Limestone Ridge in Romania

Southeastern Transylvania's Piatra Craiului National Park, famously featured as a stand-in for the western North Carolina mountains in the 2002 movie *Cold Mountain,* is teeming with wildlife and dozens of hiking trails. The park's signature serrated limestone backbone, which stretches over 15 miles (24.1 km) and tops out at over 7,345 feet (2,238.7 m), is the longest and highest of its kind in Romania.

From Zarnesti, the gateway town to the national park, expert hikers can cover the entire length of the Piatra Craiului ridge over two days, overnighting in a *cabana* (mountain hut). For a strenuous day hike, trek up to the highest point in the massif, La Om, or Piscul Baciului (Shepherd's Peak), and back. Watch for bears, wolves, deer, and lynx in the beech and pine forests as you climb. An easy day-hike loop is the three-hour (round-trip) journey into the Zarnestilor Abyss, or Zarnesti Gorge. Rock walls rise up 650 feet (198.1 m) or more along the 2.5-mile-long (4 km) canyon. As you make your way through the gorge, watch for Spider-Man–like rock climbers on the high-wall technical routes.

Drive Romania's Highest Paved Road

Thanks to a world's best road shout-out from BBC-TV's immensely popular *Top Gear* series, driving the serpentine Trasfagarasan Highway connecting Sibiu, Transylvania, Pitesti, and Walachia can be more of a bumper-to-bumper commute than an exhilarating run through a series of S-curves. Avoid the traffic by hitting the two-lane road south of Sibiu at sunrise. With fewer tourists on the road slowing to a crawl to gawk and snap selfies, you'll have a smoother ride through the long curves and sharp descents.

While the Trasfagarasan could double as a test track for sleek driving machines, the road was built in the 1970s as a defense against any Soviet-led invasion. The idea was that the Romanian military could transport troops and tanks over the Fagaras range of the Carpathian Mountains in case

of attack. Driving the highway north to south brings you up across a barren, alpine landscape and into a tunnel (Romania's longest) at Lake Balea. Emerging from the south side of the tunnel to descend the vibrant green southern slopes is a bit like the middle of a movie switching from black-and-white to color. Park at the viewing platform at Vidaru Dam to see mirror images of the mountains reflected on Vidaru Lake.

Go Caving in the Apuseni Mountains

While in Transylvania, make a side trip to the western Carpathians to explore what lies beneath the limestone surface of Apuseni Natural Park. Fossils of Ice Age animals and rare bat populations are among the treasures that have been discovered in the hundreds of caves scattered across the park. Spelunking skills and gear are required to explore most of the caves; however, two—Scarisoara Glacier and Bears' Cave—can be visited without climbing, crawling, or using ropes.

The 2,300-foot-long (701 m) Scarisoara Glacier is the world's most explored ice cave and the oldest cave glacier, estimated to be at least 10,500 years old. Ice cores drilled in the cave offer scientists a glimpse into how European weather and climate patterns have fluctuated over the past 10,000 years. Although Scarisoara is a show cave (open to the public), it has been protected since 1933 as a natural monument (the first karst area in Romania given the designation). Bears' Cave has an equally impressive backstory. It is named for the bones of the cave bear (*Ursus spelaeus*), classified as extinct 15,000 years earlier, discovered here in 1975. Some stalactites in the two-level cave are estimated to be 22,000 years old.

HIGHLIGHTS

• Mountain-bike down the rugged terrain of Bike Resort Sinaia.

• Go hut hiking through the deep green forests of Piatra Craiului National Park.

• Drive the winding Trasfagarasan Highway, Romania's highest paved road.

Vidraru Lake, created by a dam built in 1966, stretches more than six miles (9.7 km).

TRAIN TRIPS ACROSS EUROPE

1 Switzerland's eight-hour Glacier Express connects the ski towns of Zermatt and St. Moritz and winds past the Rhône River, the Matterhorn, the "Swiss Grand Canyon," Landwasser viaduct, and countless alpine panoramas. Board the vertigo-inducing Bernina Express from St. Moritz to see Morteratsch Glacier and Piz Bernina peak on your way to Tirano, Italy.

2 SEMMERING BAHN
Austria's 19th-century Semmering Bahn, Europe's first single-gauge track mountain railway, has been designated by UNESCO as one of the world's greatest feats of civil engineering. Train cars begin in Glognitz and travel 14 tunnels, 16 major viaducts, and 118 arched stone bridges to the popular ski town of Semmering. From Semmering, the Bahnwanderweg hiking trail parallels the train tracks across scenic mountainside and railway structures.

3 LYNTON AND LYNMOUTH CLIFF RAILWAY
Built in 1888, this kelly green funicular is the highest and steepest water-powered railway in the world, climbing the 500-foot (152 m) cliff between seaside Lynmouth and the Victorian town of Lynton (England's "Little Switzerland"). From Lynton, take the narrow-gauge Lynton & Barnstaple Steam Rail to Exmoor's National Park.

4 FLÅMSBANA
Norway's Flåm railway runs from Myrdal through the Aurlandsfjord dazzling passengers with misty vistas of river gorges, waterfalls, snowy mountains, sloping farms, and dreamy Norwegian fjords.

5 BALKAN EXPRESS
The twelve-hour "Balkan Express" conquers 254 tunnels and 435 bridges between Bar, Montenegro, and Belgrade, Serbia. Riders cross one of the world's highest rail-way viaducts over Lake Skadar, river gorges, and the Dinaric Alps. The trip is neither climate controlled nor first class, but it does pave the way for sharing tea in Macedonia's Old Bazaar in Skopje and canyoneering Medjurečje in Montenegro.

6 SAXON STEAM RAILWAY ROUTE
This German narrow-gauge railway tugs through Saxony, the Elbe region, Upper Lusatia, Lower Silesia, the Vogtland, and the snowy Erzgebirge Mountains. Hop off in Saxon Switzerland to free-climb your way to the top of medieval castle bridges and 1,000-plus free-standing sandstone rocks. Bathe in the Ore Mountains' soothing thermal springs. Tour the Moritzburg Castle. Or take the oldest cable car in Germany up to skiing and cycling trails in Fichtelberg.

7 AL ANDALUS
Al Andalus dances in and out of Sevilla, Córdoba, Granada, Ronda, and Cádiz. The belle époque train cars are just as glitzy as when they first enchanted passengers in the 1920s. Stops reveal the rich nature and history of Andalusia, from the Umayyad Mosque (one of the world's oldest and largest) to Monfragüe National Park, a Mediterranean oak forest thick with black storks and Spanish Imperial eagles.

8 ROYAL SCOTSMAN
The Belmond Royal Scotsman's train tours include a seal-watching boat trip, whisky tastings at Glen Ord Distillery (one of Scotland's oldest), clay-pigeon shooting, waterfall hiking, fishing in Cairngorms National Park, a round of golf at Ballindalloch, and plenty of castle gallivanting. Evenings on the train feature leisurely dinners and lavender massage treatments.

9 BOHINJ RAILWAY
After kayaking around Slovenia's Lake Bohinj, rush through the country's longest railway tunnel on the Bohinj Railway. The sleek locomotive runs through 27 more tunnels and over 65 bridges, including River Soča's 1906 Solkan Bridge, the largest stone railway bridge in the world. Stop off in Brda Hills, the "Tuscany of Slovenia," to sip chilled orange wine.

10 TRANS-SIBERIAN RAIL
The Trans-Siberian Railroad traverses one-third of the world—traveling over 5,867 miles (9,442 km) from Moscow to Nakhodka and passing the Gobi desert, the Great Wall of China, Tibetan Buddhist monasteries, and 16 major rivers. Stretch your legs by scuba diving or exploring frozen caves on Lake Baikal or free-climbing the pillars at Stolby Nature Sanctuary.

OPPOSITE: The Flåmsbana Railway cuts through Norway's stunning Fjordland. ABOVE: Passengers relax as they take in the views aboard Switzerland's *Glacier Express*.

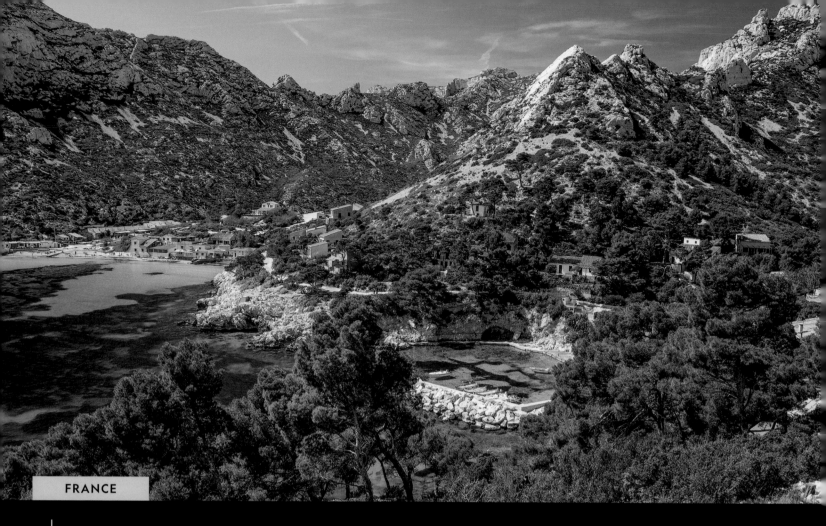

HIKING IN PROVENCE

Drink in the beauty of France's most magical region.

France enchants, and Provence enchants absolutely. The southeastern region of Provence-Alpes-Côte d'Azur spans some 12,100 square miles (31,400 sq km) of magnificent landscapes from the edge of the Alps to the Mediterranean Sea. Lavender fields, cypress groves, vineyards, and stony massifs cover the countryside, bathed in the wonderfully clear Provençal light. Most days welcome bright sunshine and blue skies thanks to the powerful northwesterly wind that blows away the clouds. People have cherished this land for millennia. You can view the ruins of Roman bridges, columns, and triumphal arches, and seven popes made the medieval city of Avignon their home in the 14th century.

Hikes here range from gentle village walks to coastal treks to difficult mountain trails. Paths are normally very well marked and maintained thanks to the Fédération Française de la Randonnée Pédestre, the official French body that oversees the management and safety of the trails.

The bustling port of Marseille, France's second largest city, provides easy access from Paris and other international destinations. For this five-day itinerary, base yourself in Avignon, crowned by the immense Papal Palace, or Aix-en-Provence, the birthplace of post-Impressionist painter Paul Cézanne and the site of Cours Mirabeau, considered among the most beautiful streets in France.

Travel Tips

WHEN TO GO: Spring and autumn are the best seasons for hiking in Provence, with bright sunny days, cool temperatures, and smaller crowds. Summer is when the lavender fields are in bloom, but the weather can get very hot and dry, and some trails close due to fire risk.

PLANNING: The cold mistral wind primarily comes in winter but can strike at any time, so pack layers. Hiking trips in Provence are offered by National Geographic Expeditions.

WEBSITES: aixenprovencetourism.com; nationalgeographic.com/expeditions

Flamingos gather in the Camargue.

5-DAY ITINERARY

Day 1

The Luberon massif contains some of Provence's most iconic scenery. Begin in Gordes, a hilltop village a half hour from Avignon noted for its white stone buildings clustered around a 10th-century château sitting at the peak. A roughly 2.5-mile (4 km) cobbled and dirt walking trail descends through oak forests to Sénanque Abbey, set in the base of a small valley filled with rows of blue-purple lavender in bloom from mid-June to mid-August. The 12th-century abbey is still in working order; you can even book a stay with the Cistercian monks to practice silent meditation.

Day 2

In the morning, take in the glorious views of the Luberon from Bonnieux, about 20 minutes outside Gordes. A 1.9-mile (3 km) loop begins above the village and winds through a luxuriant cedar forest first planted in 1860. From the highest point, you can gaze across the southern Luberon valley all the way to the foothills of the Alps.

Afterward, drive 15 minutes to Roussillon, a village of tawny buildings situated in the heart of one of the world's largest ocher deposits. The signposted Sentier des Ocres (also known as the Giants' Causeway) is an hour-long walking path through a former ocher quarry. At sunset, the exposed cliffs blaze with color, ranging from deep russet to crimson with brilliant yellow shining through.

Day 3

Known as the "Grand Canyon of Europe," the Gorges du Verdon, about two hours

OPPOSITE: Limestone cliffs line the aquamarine bays of the Calanques near Cassis in the south of France. ABOVE: Lavender fields guide the way to the Sénanque Abbey.

from Aix-en-Provence, wows with its turquoise river rushing between 2,000-foot-high (610 m) rock walls. The Sentier Blanc-Martel, named for the two explorers who first navigated the gorge at the turn of the 20th century, is considered one of the finest hiking routes on the Continent. This trek isn't for the faint of heart. The challenging 8.7-mile-long (14 km) trail traverses rough inclines, steep ladders, catwalks, and even two lengthy dark tunnels (be sure to bring a flashlight). Many experienced hikers begin at the Châlet de la Maline entry point, which leads into a long descent along the river before gradually rising to the Couloir du Samson canyon and the aptly named Point Sublime.

Day 4

Soak up the sun in the Côte d'Azur, France's own strip of paradise. The French Riviera town of Cassis, about 45 minutes south of

Aix-en-Provence, is a gateway to Calanques National Park, named for the alluring coves that etch the coastline. A 12-mile (20 km) trail leads all the way to Marseille, or you can walk shorter sections. Pack a picnic from the Cassis farmers' market for a 1.5-hour hike (three hours round-trip) that links three of the inlets, ending at the pebbled beach of Calanque d'En Vau, where you can take a dip in the aquamarine waters.

Day 5

See a different side of Provence in the Camargue, a rich marshland where the Rhône River meets the Mediterranean and forms Western Europe's largest delta. The ancient Roman city of Arles, about 45 minutes from Avignon, anchors this region of broad beaches, rice paddies, and rosy salt flats. Head for the historic village of Saintes-Maries-de-la-Mer to walk (or bicycle) along the stone *digue à la mer* (sea dike). Built in 1859, the 7.5-mile (12 km) dike stretches across the mouth of the Rhône, passing ponds filled with pink flamingos and La Gacholle lighthouse (built in 1882). Then saddle up for a ride on one of the Camargue's legendary white horses through the Domaine de la Palissade, a nature reserve aflutter with hundreds of bird species that roost in the grassy marshes and lagoons.

HIGHLIGHTS

• Wander through fragrant fields of lavender around 12th-century Sénanque Abbey.

• Navigate the daunting tunnels, catwalks, and cliffs of the Gorges du Verdon.

• Walk along the Camargue's sea dike past rolling sand dunes, grass marshes, and flocks of flamingos.

TOUR DU MONT BLANC

A classic hiking circuit on the roof of Western Europe

t's a distinctly American conceit to race up a mountain, reducing its majesty to a mere checkmark or merit badge. As is often the case, Europeans tend to take a different path, preferring to savor every crag and meander through meadows for the privilege of filling their lungs with alpine air.

The Tour du Mont Blanc exemplifies this slow-and-steady approach while still appealing to superlative chasers. High in both elevation statistics and joy potential, it's often considered the crème de la crème of the continent's trekking routes—and for ample reason. The 100-plus-mile (161 km) loop through the Alps circumnavigates Western Europe's highest peak, the 15,781-foot (4,810 m) Mont Blanc (White Mountain), as it passes through three countries: France, Italy, and Switzerland.

The route winds along scenic high Alpine passes and past picturesque villages on a circuit around the massif, traditionally going counterclockwise from France to Italy to Switzerland and back to France. Split into a series of stages, daily hikes clock in around 10 miles (16 km), with an average ascent of more than 2,500 feet (762 m), and are known to end with a mound of melted cheese and a generous pour of wine at cozy mountain huts—not to mention a hearty helping of culture and companionship with fellow hikers.

Far from the path of least resistance, it just may be a way toward revelation.

Travel Tips

WHEN TO GO: Mountain huts are open from mid-June until early September, with the highest traffic from mid-July to mid-August. The tour is at its loveliest early in the season, when smaller crowds can enjoy an array of alpine flowers.

PLANNING: Build physical endurance before traveling. If you'd like, arrange for baggage transfer between huts to lighten your hiking load.

WEBSITES: chamonix.com; visit-mont-blanc.com/en; chamonix.net/english

A train takes visitors up Chamonix-Mont-Blanc in France.

9-DAY ITINERARY

Day 1

Begin your trekking adventure at the foot of Mont Blanc in legendary Chamonix, France, the 1924 host of the first-ever Winter Olympic Games. Explore this charming alpine resort, cradled by dramatic rock pinnacles, and get an eyeful of the looming peak that inspired your journey. For a preview of the challenging hike that awaits, chug up the slopes of the Mer de Glace (Sea of Ice), the second-largest glacier in the Alps, in a historic red cog train. As you clatter up the mountainside, imagine 18th-century tourists tackling this terrain on the backs of mules. Upon arrival at the Montenvers station, walk through a cave carved out of the ice. There's plenty to consider here—from its brilliant shades of blue to the undeniable effects of climate change. The glacier has retreated more than a mile (1.6 km) since 1850. Back in Chamonix, rest and fuel up for the physical challenge ahead.

Day 2

Set out on foot following a trail beneath the Aiguilles Rouges (Red Peaks) to the rocky alpine path known as the Grand Balcon. Weave in and out of forest, watching for marmots along the way, and enjoy spectacular vistas of the massif from high above. Reach the small, glassy Lake Bleu and take in the panorama over the valley. Continue on to the Montenvers railway, perched above the Mer de Glace glacier, and return to Chamonix by the cog railway.

Day 3

Transfer to the French village of Les Houches and depart via cable car to Bellevue. Hike through pastures that pass by the Bionnassay Glacier and rhododendron

thickets that line the steep ascent to the Col du Tricot viewpoint, at 6,955 feet (2,120 m) in elevation. Descend to the alpine hamlet of Miage, perched on a glacial plain, and continue through scenic countryside to the delightful village of Les Contamines-Montjoie, where traditional chalets and acclaimed gastronomy await.

Day 4

Pay a visit to the brightly painted Notre Dame de la Gorge and its baroque chapel, where centuries of mountain travelers have paused to say a prayer for a safe journey ahead. Then follow an ancient Roman route—long a thoroughfare for mountain travelers—through the stands of evergreens and wildflowers that make up Les Contamines Nature Reserve, France's highest protected area, with a range in elevation from 3,608 to 12,769 feet (1,100 to 3,892 m). Climb to the Col du Bonhomme (7,640 feet/2,329 m), with sweeping views of the valleys below. Carefully pick your way down a vertiginous grassy trail to

the remote hamlet of Les Chapieux, or transfer to picturesque Bourg St. Maurice for the night.

Day 5

From the trailhead at La Ville des Glaciers, ascend through open meadows and across snow-covered fields to the Col de la Seigne at the Italian border. After taking in the panorama from up here, hike past shimmering glacial lakes to the southern slopes of the Val Veni, an emerald valley framed by jagged peaks. Finish the day's hike in the cobblestone-lined alpine town of Courmayeur in Italy's Aosta Valley.

Day 6

Marvel at Mont Blanc during the hike along the Mont de la Saxe to Rifugio Bertone, a mountain refuge that affords a particularly spectacular vantage. Follow the balcony path, which overlooks the ridge of the dramatic Grandes Jorasses peak, en route to the idyllic Val Ferret valley.

OPPOSITE: **Hikers make their way through the Swiss portion of the Mont Blanc route.** ABOVE: **In the French village of Chamonix, mountains frame cobblestone streets lined with shops.**

The iconic pink church in the Swiss village of Trient sits in the shadows of the Mont Blanc range.

Day 7

This morning, traverse a bucolic scene of alpine meadows and rushing streams, dotted with grazing cows and scurrying marmots. Then tackle the steep climb to the 8,320-foot (2,536 m) Grand Col Ferret, at the border of Italy and Switzerland and in the shadow of the towering Mont Dolent—the only peak in the Alps that straddles the three countries of Italy, France, and Switzerland. Enjoy close-up and long-range views of hanging glaciers and granite spires as you follow a grassy path through a pastoral alpine setting of chalets and cattle to the sleepy Swiss village of La Fouly.

Day 8

Departing from the village of Champex, go the way of the cows on a hiking excursion along the rolling hills of the Bovine trail, a route that herders once relied on to lead their herds across the mountains to these high pastures. Reach the summit of the Col de la Forclaz before descending between pine trees to Trient village, where a memorable pink-spired church greets hikers.

Day 9

Spend the morning zigzagging up the verdant hillside to the Col de Balme peak (7,172 feet/2,186 m), a sunny Franco-Swiss ski area on the border between the countries. With the Swiss countryside at your back, gaze out over the Chamonix Valley and Mont Blanc from a completely different angle from the one at the start of the tour. Embark on one final downhill stretch, soak up more incredible vistas, and revel in the sense of accomplishment of completing your Tour du Mont Blanc adventure.

HIGHLIGHTS

• Walk across the borders of three countries: France, Italy, and Switzerland.

• Traverse bucolic meadows, lush forests, and glacial valleys on foot.

• Discover legendary Chamonix, host of the first Winter Olympic Games in 1924.

FINLAND

SAUNA IN FINLAND

Steam away the chill in Ferris wheels, hockey rinks, in a gondola, and more (seriously).

n a country where there are likely more saunas than cars, a person doesn't have to go far to find a steamy room to warm away the winter chill. Devotees both young and old flock to saunas—essential to Finnish culture—to restore themselves mentally and physically with the hot *löyly* (steam). By some estimates there is about one sauna to every two people in the country. Don't be shocked to see people rolling around in the snow or taking a dip in arctic waters to cool down and elongate the healing practice.

The oldest sauna on record dates back to A.D. 1112. Originally earth pits covered with animal skins, they are part of a rich tradition that has lasted centuries and seen many evolutions from the Iron Age to today's luxurious versions. In Finland, the sauna, along with its restorative claims, has been used for religious ceremonies, cleansing, and healing illnesses and as a place to gather socially. The saunas we are familiar with around the world originated here. The first to hit the United States was brought by Finns who settled in what is now the state of Delaware in 1638.

Traditionally set in semidark rooms with temperatures often rising above 150°F (65.6°C), saunas can be found anywhere from inside the Parliament to private homes. But for Finns—and visitors feeling a little more adventurous—there are some even more surprising places to get your steam on.

Travel Tips

WHEN TO GO: Visit in January, when crowds have thinned, and you'll have the best chance of seeing the northern lights. February is the coldest month of the year in Finland.

PLANNING: Unlike American saunas, many Finns choose to relax in the nude, so don't be surprised. Stay hydrated, a key to handling the high temps in the sauna.

WEBSITES: varuste.net/en; hartwall arena.fi/en; vartiovene55.fi; yllas.fi/en; skysauna.fi/en; rukapalvelu.fi/en; rukansalonki.fi/en; kesansauna.fi; herrankukkaro.fi/en

Sauna at new heights in the Ylläs Gondola.

Maasavusana

Descend underground below the small fishing village of Herrankukkaro to experience one of the world's largest belowground smoke saunas. With enough space to seat 124 visitors across six levels, this sauna follows the ancestral tradition of burning birch wood. Occasionally, local bands perform live music for entertainment.

Kesän Floating Sauna

Drifting leisurely along the Gulf of Bothnia, the Kesän Floating Sauna is a rare find in the world of saunas. Completely run by volunteers, this sauna sits on a small wooden raft and is one of the few unisex public saunas, meaning bathing suits are required.

Rukan Salonki Ice Sauna

A perfect contradiction, the Rukan Salonki Ice Sauna combines the heat from the sauna and the cold from the ice found in surrounding lakes to create a unique steamy effect. To keep from overheating, the resort provides a hole in the ice for visitors to take a refreshing dip in the lake before jumping back inside to warm up. The sauna is open from late December to late March, depending on the weather, and can fit 10 people at a time.

Saunabussi

Elevate your sauna experience with the Saunabussi as you take in the sights along the open road. Travelers can custom-plan their own quests around the Kussamo area in this sauna on wheels (yes, a spa in a bus). When you need a break from the wood-heated sauna, break out the karaoke machine to keep the party going.

OPPOSITE: **There are more than three million saunas in Finland—about one for every two people.** ABOVE: **From the comfort of a private lounge and hot tub, take in views of Finland and the Baltic Sea aboard the SkySauna.**

Sky-Wheel Sauna

Enjoy epic views of modern Finland and the Baltic Sea on the Helsinki SkySauna. Snag unlimited rotations between the private lounge, hot tub, and Ferris wheel sauna. Added bonus: Brag-worthy selfies.

Ylläs Sauna Gondola

Gaze down on the winter wonderland of Lapland, Finland, during an Ylläs Sauna Gondola ride. Ideal for people who love heights and scenic views, the 20-minute ride starts at the top of Ylläs mountain before dropping off the group of three to four people to explore the resort's other saunas, fireplace, and outside hot tub. The fixed price of 1,350 euros (U.S. $1,558) includes a two-hour experience for up to 12 people.

Vartivene 55

Sauna at sea on the warship *Vartivene 55*. Built in 1959, the ship served in the Finnish Navy for 40 years before being renovated for private charter. Below deck, the sauna can accommodate up to 15 people at a time. Guests can combine their sauna experience with a cruise around Helsinki, a karaoke fiesta, or a dinner party.

Skybox 270

Whether you're a devout hockey fan, want to impress your business clients, or both, Skybox 270 at the Hartwall Arena in Helsinki provides a tasteful sauna experience everyone can enjoy. Prices range from 400 to over 2,500 euros (U.S. $400–$2,886) depending on the stadium's event calendar, and the box can hold up to 30 people at a time.

Sauna tent

If you find yourself needing a bit of sauna time in the Finnish wilderness or by the sea, consider purchasing a sauna tent. Compact and portable, they're ideal for mobile adventurers. Depending on the tent, the sauna stove can also be used to cook a hot meal before bedtime.

HIGHLIGHTS

• Indulge in a century-old tradition in a place where saunas rule the world.

• Take in the skylines from a gondola or Ferris wheel while you grab some R&R.

• Watch a game of hockey from a sauna skybox that can fit 30.

SAILING THE TURQUOISE COAST

Take a "Blue Cruise" through human history.

Turkey's southwestern Turquoise Coast harbors a veritable time capsule of human history. Beneath the surface of crystalline waters and on the pine-fringed shore lie a bounty of ancient Greek, Byzantine, and Roman ruins, as well as earthquake-shattered remnants of the ancient maritime kingdom of Lycia. Helping preserve the artifacts and protect secluded coves from development are the imposing limestone mountains and soaring cliffs that once made the rugged coast the domain of pirates.

Arguably the most idyllic stretch of the Turquoise Coast is the Lycian coast, which hugs the shores of the Tekke Peninsula. Turkey's first long-distance footpath, the 335-mile (539.1 km) Lycian Way, roughly covers the route on land, but the way to go is by sea on a chartered *gulet* (traditional wooden yacht) voyage, commonly called a "Blue Cruise." Perhaps the most idyllic Lycian coast blue cruise route is east to west from Demre to Fethiye.

Guided by a professional captain and crew, the nimble gulet effortlessly maneuvers in and around the coast's rocky nooks and crannies. Days are spent slow-sailing near shore, with frequent stops for land excursions or for swimming or kayaking. Devoting five days to a Blue Cruise allows you to reset and let life unfold at the leisurely pace in a timeless place inhabited for millennia.

Travel Tips

WHEN TO GO: April, May, or September are the best times to avoid the intense summer heat yet still enjoy warm water temperatures for swimming. The weather cools down starting in October and can be very cold November through March—many coastal areas close during this time.

PLANNING: Do your research because the quality, amenities, and costs of Blue Cruises vary widely. Private charters offer more luxury; cabin-only charters can be barebones but budget friendly.

WEBSITES: alaturkacruises.com; kekovatravel.com; petersommer.com

The abandoned fortress village of Kayaköy

Day 1

Start in Demre, the Mediterranean coastal town built on the site of Myra, a major Lycian city. Before embarking on the cruise, hike the hillsides to see ruins, including Roman columns and carvings and Lycian stone tombs, carved between the seventh and fifth centuries B.C. Stop at the small Santa Claus Museum to learn about the Turkish ties to St. Nicholas, who was born in nearby Patara and lived and worked in Demre in the fourth century.

It's a quick ride from Demre to the departure point in Çayağzı Harbor. Board the gulet and lounge on the deck for the cruise to Kekova, a region chockablock with rocky islands (including uninhabited Kekova Island), Lycian ruins, and sheltered bays and coves. On the northern side of Kekova Island, see the partially submerged remnants of Simena, a Lycian city destroyed by second-century earthquakes. Called the sunken city, the archaeological ruins are part of the Kekova area currently under consideration for UNESCO World Heritage site status as of spring 2019. Diving and swimming are off-limits, but kayaking around the relics is permitted. Anchor in Gokkaya Bay for the night. Take a dinghy ashore for a fresh seafood dinner in Üçağız, a traditional Aegean fishing village.

Day 2

Cruise across the bay from Üçağız to Kaleköy (castle village), built on the site of ancient Simena. Named for the Crusader-era castle perched above the town, Kaleköy is reachable only by boat or on foot. Explore the castle and the other Hellenistic, Roman, and Byzantine ruins, such as public baths and Lycian tombs, scattered around the hilly terrain.

OPPOSITE: Calm lagoons off the Aegean Sea provide picturesque anchorages for visiting ships. RIGHT: A tree-filled alley in the Old Town of Kas offers charming shops for tourists.

From the castle, you can see Kekova Island and the boats anchored in the turquoise waters of Kekova Sound.

Head back to the boat and set sail north to Kas for an afternoon of adventure. From the harbor there, take a diving or snorkeling tour to see reefs, caves, ruins, wrecks, and marine life, such as barracudas, sea turtles, and rays. Soar high over the coast on a tandem paragliding ride. Rappel down waterfalls and explore hidden gorges on a canyoning expedition. Return to the boat for the short sail to the overnight anchoring spot in Aquarium Bay.

Day 3

Aquarium Bay is nestled between two islands, significantly limiting wind and wave action. As a result, the water in the bay is typically calm and clear, ideal for swimming, snorkeling, diving, and kayaking. Look for octopus, sea urchins, and clown-fish among the ocean life easily visible in the sheltered bay.

Cruise north and anchor in the cove at Butterfly Valley. Accessible only by boat or a fairly treacherous hiking path, the secluded valley is tucked between soaring rock walls. Backpackers regularly camp on or near the beach, giving the place a low-key, bohemian vibe. Waves of the valley's eponymous flying insects once filled the air and blanketed the rocks and vegetation; today, butterfly sightings are sparse.

There's plenty to do here. Hike the dirt path to the back of the valley and clamber over big boulders to the base of a small waterfall. If you have serious rock-climbing skills, continue up the stones to a bigger waterfall and panoramic views of the valley and sea below. Head back to the gulet and cruise up the coast to drop anchor for the night just outside the Blue Lagoon at Ölüdeniz Beach.

Day 4

Named for its light aquamarine waters, the Blue Lagoon, or Ölüdeniz Beach, is the Turquoise Coast's signature swimming hole. Go ashore for a full beach day. Rent a chaise lounge and umbrella to read, nap, and relax on the sand. Swim and snorkel in the lagoon. Get a bird's-eye view of the beach and surrounding pine-covered mountains on a tandem paragliding ride.

Sail on to spend the night off the coast of uninhabited St. Nicholas Island, or Gemiler Adasi, thought to be the original burial site of St. Nicholas.

Day 5

Take the dinghy ashore to hike among the ruins dotting the hillsides of St. Nicholas Island. The empty tombs, remnants of rock-cut Byzantine churches dating to the fourth century, and crumbling stone arches and walls reportedly were part of a monastic community established by the saint. After exploring the ruins, hike away from the coast through the pine and olive trees in the island's peaceful, less visited interior.

From St. Nicholas Island, sail off for a series of swimming and hiking stops in the bays and on the islands off the coast of Fethiye. Tarzan Bay takes its name from the rope swing swimmers can use to launch into the blue waters. Visit the Red Island (Kizilada) lighthouse, which stands watch at the mouth of Fethiye Habor, at sunset when the rocky landscape glows a pale red. Spend one last night on board to watch the sunrise over the harbor in the morning.

HIGHLIGHTS

• See ancient Greek, Byzantine, and Roman ruins, and remnants of a Lycian sunken city.

• Anchor in secluded coves to swim, snorkel, and kayak through crystal-blue waters.

• Go hiking and paragliding to see out-of-the-way beaches, gorges, valleys, and waterfalls from above and below.

Ölüdeniz Beach is a popular spot for paragliding—the ultimate adventure for spectacular views.

The Easy Way Up Mont Blanc

By Mary Anne Potts

THREE GORE-TEX-CLAD MOUNTAINEERS are making their arduous slog up Mont Blanc, along the French/Italian border; it is Western Europe's tallest peak. Its 15,771-foot (4,807 m) summit looms still some 3,000 feet (914 m) above them. Their top-of-the-world vista takes in a snow-dusted Alpine massif that spans three countries: France, Switzerland, and Italy.

My friend and I share nearly the same epic view the intrepid climbers have, but not the same foot blisters or crevasse hazards. Unlike them, we have arrived at 12,395 feet (3,778 m) via a cushy 20-minute cable car ride from the French resort town of Chamonix to this observation deck on Aiguille du Midi, a peak neighboring Mont Blanc.

Gondolas, or aerial lifts using cables, have ferried passengers to surrounding heights from Chamonix since 1924. Holding the world record for the highest vertical ascent, the Aiguille du Midi cable car gives us a taste of what it's like to be an alpinist—but without the need for exertion and expensive hiking boots. It's a two-stage process, with the first taking passengers to the Plan de l'Aiguille, a setting-off point for off-piste skiing in the winter and rock climbing in the summer. The second stage goes to a complex of terraces with views of the French, Swiss, and Italian Alps.

Up here, it's bright, cold, and blustery, and we need our warm layers, sunscreen, and sunglasses on the observatory walkway. We step into a sheltered glass cube off the walkway and pull up Instagram on our phones to capture the obligatory "step into the void" shot. The spectacle of a sheer drop below our feet thrills and chills.

While the mountain climbers are refueling on energy bars, we order up strong coffee and chocolate cake at Le 3842, one of the highest restaurants in Europe. The Aiguille du Midi also has one of the world's highest museums. Located in a rocky chamber deep in the mountain, the Musée de l'Alpinisme Pointe displays photos and memorabilia from the early days of extreme sports—such as BASE jumping, for which Chamonix has historically been considered a top spot.

After mailing postcards from one of the world's tallest peaks with a souvenir shop, we hop on the cable car back into town, with a new appreciation of Alpine summits and the adventurous souls who explore them.

• *Mary Anne Potts is an adventurer and writer and the former editorial director of* National Geographic Adventure.

LEFT: **A path leads out of a snow tunnel at Aiguille du Midi in Mont Blanc.**
OPPOSITE: **Don't look down! A glass-bottom floor enables 360-degree views.**

No need for hiking gear. The gondola offers passengers their own views of Mont Blanc from soaring heights.

HIKING THROUGH EUROPE

1 PAKLENICA NATIONAL PARK, CROATIA

The Velebit Mountain trail through Paklenica National Park offers some of Croatia's most scenic hiking. Think wild horses, lush beech tree valleys, craggy peaks, and dolomite limestone canyons. Visit in May when paired climbers race up a 524-foot-high (160 m) cliff during the park's annual Big Wall Speed Climb.

2 HIGH TATRAS, CARPATHIAN MOUNTAINS

Straddling Slovakia and Poland, the High Tatras are home to more than 100 alpine lakes, waterfalls, old Slovakian mountain spas, Gerlachovsky štít (the highest peak in the Carpathian Mountains), and endangered Tatra chamois (similar to mountain goats). Trails are open to hikers June through September. Trek from hut to hut to explore Poland's highest waterfall, Rysy peak, and Kriváň, Slovakia's beloved "most beautiful mountain."

3 KING'S TRAIL, SWEDEN

Almost 250 miles (402 km) long, the *Kungsleden* (King's Trail) treks along stunning gorges, snowy summits, and meadows of purple mountain saxifrage in Swedish Lapland. Northern lights dance over cozy rustic cabins as nomadic Sami people herd reindeer along the path. Sweden's "Freedom to Roam" policy means hikers are permitted to hike and camp wherever they like, so long as they clean up after themselves.

4 GIANT'S CAUSEWAY, NORTHERN IRELAND

Northern Ireland's 40,000 interlocking basalt columns are a stunning hiking site that you won't find anywhere else on the planet. Begin by crossing the knee-shaking 100-foot-high (30 m) Carrick-a-Rede Rope Bridge, first woven by salmon fishermen in 1755. Then hike to Giant's Causeway for a bird's-eye view of ocean waves crashing into the columns.

OPPOSITE: The Carrick-a-Rede Rope Bridge, which dangles 98 feet (30 m) above the rocks below, links Ballintoy to the island of Carrickarede. ABOVE: A hiker makes her way through Picos de Europa National Park in Spain.

5 MONT BLANC, FRANCE

Mont Blanc is the highest peak in Western Europe, standing at a whopping 15,781 feet (4,810 m) above sea level. Risk warm weather avalanches and falling rocks while you crampon your way to the summit, then paraglide back down across the Chamonix Valley. Or opt for Tour du Mont Blanc, the peaks-and-valleys 105-mile (169 km) massif circuit that winds through Italy, France, and Switzerland (see page 134). The scenic three-country journey is a must-do for avid hikers and novices alike.

6 PICOS DE EUROPA CIRCUIT ROUTE, SPAIN

Be warned: Bears and wolves often make an appearance on Spain's central Picos Circuit in the Picos de Europa mountains. Steer clear of the wildlife as you handle the steep switchbacks, tunnels, and cliff-cut paths that lead to above-the-cloud vistas of tree-studded gorges and limestone massifs (quite popular for rock climbing). Cable cars along the way rise to remote trekking routes and even wilder views. Spring is the most pleasant and least crowded time to hike.

7 LAUGAVEGUR & FIMMVÖRDUHÁLS TREK, ICELAND

This 47-mile (76 km) six-day route begins with a hot-spring soak in Landmannalaugar, then wanders up and down through the Icelandic highlands to the otherworldly mountains of the Fjallabak Nature Reserve. Black lava fields, Iceland's unique rhyolite mountains, volcanic craters, glacial rivers, and the famous Skógafoss waterfall are only a handful of sights seen along the way.

8 VIA DINARICA

Via Dinarica connects more than 1,200 miles (1,931 km) of trails, darting in and out of seven countries: Slovenia, Croatia, Serbia, Bosnia and Herzegovina, Montenegro, Kosovo, and Albania. The Balkan hiking route climbs over 6,000 feet (1,829 m), crossing worn shepherds' paths, karst fields, and mountain trails to secret lakes, medieval forts, cave-clinging castles, the dreamy Kravice Falls, and Europe's deepest canyon, Tara River Canyon.

9 ST. OLAV WAYS, NORWAY

Norway's St. Olav Ways is the northernmost pilgrimage trail in the world. Eight separate routes lead to the Nidaros Cathedral in Trondheim, together a total of 1,864 miles (3,000 km) of trails. Hikers camp in mossy forests or stay with local farmers as they wander between traditional stave churches, ancient spruce forests, fjord shores, and Bronze Age ruins.

10 LOUSIOS GORGE MONASTERIES HIKE, GREECE

Trails tracing Greece's Lousios Gorge region on the Peloponnese Peninsula are remote, rugged, and heartbreakingly beautiful. The paths happen upon ancient Byzantine monasteries built into rock ledges. Cross a narrow stone bridge to Philosophou Monastery to see woodcarvings, intricate icons, and faded frescoes. Or visit the fourth-century B.C. temple and healing well at the Asclepieio of Gortys.

ENGLAND COAST TO COAST

Follow literary footsteps from the Irish Sea to the North Sea.

E ngland's beloved Coast to Coast Walk is less a long-distance route and more a testament to one man's love of the land. The man, Alfred Wainwright, turned his rambles across rural northern England into *A Coast to Coast Walk: A Pictorial Guide,* first published in 1973. His route, stretching 190 miles (305.7 km) west to east from St. Bees on the Irish Sea to Robin Hood's Bay on the North Sea, meanders along back roads and footpaths; crosses streams and fields; and winds through three distinctly different national parks: Lake District, home to England's highest mountains; Yorkshire Dales and its storybook villages; and the wild heather-covered highlands of the North York Moors.

Following in Wainwright's footsteps means stopping to tour historic sites and regularly venturing off course for a pint in a cozy pub or other similarly worthy endeavors. One of the many charms of the Coast to Coast is that even though Wainwright created hand-drawn maps and suggested day-by-day stages, the experience was more about being out in nature than completing a specific route.

"Oh, how can I put into words the joys of a walk over country such as this; the scenes that delight the eyes, the blessed peace of mind, the sheer exuberance which fills your soul as you tread the firm turf?" Wainwright wrote in his guide. "This is something to be lived, not read about."

Travel Tips

WHEN TO GO: Year-round, but May to October offers the best weather and walking conditions.

PLANNING: Carry a light daypack and use the Sherpa Van baggage service to transport luggage between stops. Lodging is limited in rural areas; book early or camp. National Geographic Expeditions offers a 13-day Hiking England Coast to Coast tour.

WEBSITES: wainwrightorg.uk; coast tocoastguides.co.uk; sherpavan.com; lakedistrict.gov.uk; nationalgeographic .com/expeditions

Sheep graze on coastal hills.

12-DAY ITINERARY

Day 1

Dip a toe in the Irish Sea and pick up a pebble to carry in your pocket (both are Coast to Coast traditions to mark an auspicious beginning of the journey) before setting out on a 15-mile (24.1 km) route that hugs the sandstone cliffs of St. Bees Head.

Day 2

Ramble through Lake District National Park, a UNESCO World Heritage site, where rolling mountains rise from glassy lakes. See the lakes, peaks, and pastures from Honister Pass, elevation 1,167 feet (355.7 m).

Day 3

Take a short drive to Grasmere to visit the home of William Wordsworth. Stop at the Grasmere Gingerbread Shop before the nine-mile (14.4 km) walk to Lake Ullswater.

Day 4

Board a historic steamboat and see Helvellyn (England's third highest peak) on a cruise across Lake Ullswater to Howtown. From the pier, walk to the 12th-century Shap Abbey.

Day 5

Get an early start on the 15-mile (24.1 km) trek from Shep to Ravenstonedale. The route passes limestone crags and stone-built villages on the way to Orton. Get dessert at Kennedys Fine Chocolates Coffee House.

Day 6

Walk five miles (8 km) across pastoral hills, stopping in the remote Yorkshire Dales market town of Kirkby Stephen for lunch. Hike 10

more miles (16 km) to Keld, the historic crossroads of three long-distance hikes: Coast to Coast, the Pennine Way, and the Herriot Way.

Day 7

Follow Wainwright's low-route option along the River Swale, discovering waterfalls and hamlets nestled among the dales on the 12-mile (19.3 km) hike to Reeth. At the five-mile (8 km) mark, take a break at Ghyllfoot Tea Room and Bistro in Gunnerside.

Day 8

Continue 10 miles (16 km) through the Yorkshire Dales on the way to Richmond. Tour the 11th-century Richmond Castle, considered England's best remaining example of an early Norman fortress.

Day 9

Take public transportation from Richmond to Osmotherley, on the western edge of windswept North York Moors National Park. From here, follow the Cleveland Way for 11 miles (17.7 km), crossing over five moors and passing the Wainstones, massive sandstone crags and pillars. The route ends in Clay Bank Top.

Day 10

Hike a high-level route across the melancholy moors to Blakey Ridge. The nine-mile (14.4 km) trek offers far-reaching views of the region's iconic heather: green in early summer and purple in August.

Day 11

On today's 13.5-mile (21.7 km) leg through the moors, the tradition is leaving a snack and taking one at "Fat Betty," a white boundary cross.

Day 12

The last day is a long one—15.5 miles (24.9 km)—but the cliff-top views will make you forget your blisters. Toss your pebble in the North Sea and soak your feet.

HIGHLIGHTS

- **Walk across the Lake District, England's largest National Park.**

- **Hike through Keld, the historic crossroads of three long-distance hikes.**

- **Visit the home of poet William Wordsworth.**

SOARING ALPS AND SPARKLING SEA

Central Europe's adventure-ready champion of sustainability

Slovenia is patiently waiting to be noticed and blissfully making the most of its low profile in the meantime. With travel heavyweights Italy and Austria as neighbors, this little republic-that-could sits happily at the majestic crossroads of the Alps and the Mediterranean, a veritable force of nature in central Europe.

Once you wake up to Slovenia's charms, don't be surprised if you find yourself falling head over heels in love. Explore plunging gorges and tumbling waterfalls, Roman-era vineyards and medieval villages, and emerald valleys and snow-frosted Alpine peaks. More than 9,000 karst caves dot the landscape, waiting to be discovered among thermal spas and the world's oldest grapevine. Lake Bled and its postcard-ready island church are as enchanting as any fairy-tale setting. Outdoor adventure here ranges from textbook classics—think hut-to-hut hiking in the Julian Alps—to the latest thrills, such as canyon jumping and stand-up paddleboarding.

More than a third of this compact enclave claims protected status, maintaining its place as Europe's third most forested country. In 2017, National Geographic named it the world's most sustainable country, after the European Union crowned its capital, Ljubljana, as Europe's Greenest Capital in 2016.

How green is the valley? Here in Slovenia, the question isn't rhetorical.

Travel Tips

WHEN TO GO: Summer is high season and often means crowds in Ljubljana, the coast, and the Julian Alps. Plan hiking trips during the spring and fall shoulder seasons when weather and scenery are at their most appealing. You'll also find fewer crowds on the trails and waterways.

PLANNING: The country's main airport is in the capital, Ljubljana; the major airports of Venice and Vienna are within a few hours' drive or train ride. Any of the airports are an easy starting-off point.

WEBSITES: slovenia.info/en; slovenia.si

Bikers cycle past vineyards near the quaint Fojana village.

WHAT TO DO

Trek the Julian Alps

Tucked along the borderlands of Slovenia, Italy, and Austria, the majestic Julian Alps remain one of Europe's best kept secrets and a favorite playground for hikers. The newly completed Julian Alps Hiking Trail network courses 186 miles (299 km) through mountainous terrain, beginning and ending at the village of Rateče in Slovenia's far northwest corner. Crisscross Vintgar Gorge on wooden walkways and bridges overlooking tumbling waterfalls and swirling pools. Climb to the panoramic summit of Mount Matajur, along Italy's border, to gaze out over the crystalline Adriatic on clear days. From Lake Bohinj, ride a cable car up Mount Vogel for spectacular vistas at the top—and to access footpaths along the ridge.

Hike Hut to Hut

Among Europe's oldest national parks, Triglav National Park envelops its namesake peak—Slovenia's highest, at 9,395 feet (2,864 m)—which appears on the country's flag. Follow old mule paths embedded in the limestone slopes, ascend steep paths using steel cables and iron rungs, and walk through verdant forests of beech and larch trees (during fall, these alpine beauties turn brilliant shades of yellow). Dotting the way are rustic mountain huts such as the Vodnik Hut, in the heart of the park, a favorite stop for trekkers set on summiting nearby Triglav.

Paddleboard on Lake Bled

Crystalline Lake Bled has attracted travelers for centuries. Today these tranquil waters are perfectly suited for stand-up paddleboarding. Glide across the lake on your own board—or ride in a traditional, gondola-like wooden *pletna*—to reach the tiny tear-

shaped island in the middle, which harbors the 17th-century Church of the Assumption. Climb its 99 stone steps and ring the storied bell inside its soaring clock tower before paddling back to your starting point.

Walk the Cliffs of the Adriatic Coast

With its Venetian Gothic architecture, labyrinthine alleyways, and mesmerizing sunsets, the picturesque fishing town of Piran offers plenty of reasons to stick around. Yet the coastal paths leading to the plunging Strunian cliffs also beckon. Breathe in the salty air of the Adriatic Sea and meander on foot past olive groves and vineyards en route to the pristine Strunjan Nature Park, a protected stretch of Slovenia's craggy shoreline.

Raft the River Soča

The emerald River Soča courses 90 wild miles (145 km) through the Julian Alps, carving out a dramatic valley of sheer rock walls, vivid forests, and cascading waterfalls on its path from the Trenta Valley, home to Mount Triglav, to the Adriatic Sea. Paddlers from around the world convene here for Class III and IV white-water rapids. For a more relaxed approach, fly-fishing enthusiasts come for a chance to catch the indigenous Soča trout.

Cycle to Vineyards

Tucked between the Julian Alps and the Adriatic Sea, the sunny Mediterranean climate of western Slovenia's Goriška Brda hills supports vineyards, cherry orchards, and olive groves. Winemakers here have worked the rolling landscape since Roman times. Join a cycling tour or head out on your own for a two-wheeled exploration of the region's winding country roads. Over in eastern Slovenia, the world's oldest grapevine (confirmed by the *Guinness Book of Records*) grows in Maribor, as it has for the past 450-plus years. Cyclists can choose from a trio of wine roads that lead from the Old Vine to neighboring vineyards, stopping for tastings along the way.

Descend into Karst Caves

Get immersed in subterranean splendor on a walk, crawl, swim, or even kayak or bike ride through one of the country's legendary karst kingdoms. At the Škocjan Cave system beneath the Karst Plateau in southwestern Slovenia, navigate a maze of tunnels to an epic limestone chamber that, in the words of its UNESCO World Heritage inscription, offers an "almost supernatural visual appeal." Not far away, a train descends deep into Postojna Cave Park's realm of stalactites and stalagmites and

OPPOSITE: A trail near Vrsic Pass opens to panoramic views of Prisank in the Julian Alps.
ABOVE: The Kozjak Waterfall in Triglav National Park tumbles into a stony amphitheater.

Lake Bled attracts swimmers and sailors for its crystal-clear waters and verdant scenery.

rare creatures such as the "human fish," an aquatic salamander. Built into the mouth of the cave is the Renaissance-era Predjama Castle, the world's largest cave castle. Climbers can tackle the narrow depths of a secret passage used by Erazem, a 15th-century knight known in legend as a Slovenian Robin Hood.

Go Canyoning in Narrow Gorges

The natural slides and cascades of the Soča Valley create an exciting playground for guided canyoning excursions. Beginners and seasoned adventurers alike find thrills here, from the approachable and pictur-esque Pršjak canyon to the wild series of cascades culminating in 50-foot (15 m) Kozjak Waterfall.

Paddle the Capital

Find a new perspective of Slovenia's ele-gant capital on a kayak trip down Ljublja-na's sacred lifeline, its eponymous river. A wide-ranging paddle starts or ends in the nearby town of Vrhnika and traverses the Ljubljana Marshes, an archaeological repository, as it winds through the historic city center—crisscrossed by 17 distinct bridges and lined with beautifully land-scaped promenades and artfully designed embankments.

Soak in Thermal Springs

Thermal water saturates Slovenia. Rejuve-nate adventure-weary bodies amid the purported healing powers of one of the country's natural spas, such as the thermal spa in the country's oldest town, Ptuj, inhabited since the Stone Age.

HIGHLIGHTS

• Glide across crystalline Lake Bled on a paddleboard or traditional boat.

• Climb Mount Triglav, the highest peak of the Julian Alps, staying at cozy moun-tain huts along the way.

• Go white-water rafting along the wild rapids of River Soča.

SLOVENIA, CROATIA, SERBIA, BOSNIA AND HERZEGOVINA,
MONTENEGRO, KOSOVO, ALBANIA & MACEDONIA

TREKKING THE VIA DINARICA

Walk the White Trail through six European countries.

I n a region historically splintered by bitter conflict, the Via Dinarica mega-mountaineering and hiking route is building connections and bringing visitors to peaks long off-limits to outsiders. Spanning some 1,250 miles (2,011.6 km) along three different trails—White, Blue, and Green—the Via Dinarica runs through the western Balkans, linking Slovenia, Croatia, Serbia, Bosnia and Herzegovina, Montenegro, Kosovo, Albania, and Macedonia.

The main and highest-elevation trail is the White, which hits the highest peaks of each country from Slovenia south to Macedonia. Under development since 2010 and still lightly traveled, the White trail is a cross-border network of new and existing hiking routes, military roads, and shepherd paths. Abandoned bunkers, stone castles, crumbling ruins, war memorials, medieval gravestones, and other remnants of Illyrian, Roman, Slav, Ottoman, Austro-Hungarian, and Serb kingdoms stand as testaments to the region's complex and highly contentious history.

The Via Dinarica is best approached in sections—mainly because there's so much to experience. Go slowly. Meander through karst (eroded limestone) fields, dense beech forest, and tall-grass meadows. Swim in a glacial lake and explore a network of underground caves. Sit and sip *rakija*, the region's ubiquitous home-made brandy, with the villagers who warmly welcome visitors.

Travel Tips

WHEN TO GO: Depending on snow, hiking season begins in late May or early June and ends in late September or early October. Avoid the midsummer heat and tourist traffic by trekking in June or September, when temperatures and crowds are milder.

PLANNING: To chart your own route, use the interactive trail maps, route planner, and lodging and mountain hut listings on the handy Via Dinarica information portal.

WEBSITES: trail.viadinarica.com/en; via-dinarica.org; vmd.hr/eng; peaks ofthebalkans.com

A traditional metal and copper tea service

Slovenia

Whether you are planning an epic Via Dinarica through-hike or are sampling sections, start at the beginning: Predjama, Slovenia. The first stage of the White trail commences near Predjamski Grad, a fairy-tale castle-in-a-cave built halfway up a 403-foot (122.8 m) cliff. Before setting out, tour the castle and the mind-blowing Postojna Cave system beneath it. The maze of caverns, halls, and passages is part of Slovenia's network of more than 9,000 underground caves. Sinkholes and underground rivers excavated the region's massive soluble limestone, creating these mysterious subterranean formations and the rugged, rocky karst landscape on the surface.

Emerge from the depths and start the hike by following the paved trail from the castle, under train tracks, over a highway, and up a hill. From here, the trail turns to gravel through thick pine forest. The karst terrain means surface water is scarce here, so pack extra drinking water. Overnight in guesthouses, villages, and on farms as you make your way southeast through the Dinaric Alps toward Croatia.

Croatia

Discover a kingdom of karst formations— peaks, towers, ledges, caves, and columns— on the Premužić Trail in North Velebit National Park. Part of the Via Dinarica White route, the 35-mile (56.3 km) stone trail is a marvel of engineering built in the early 1930s. Forestry engineer Ante Premužić designed the gently graded path to provide easy access into a previously inaccessible region of the Velebit, Croatia's largest mountain. In addition to the starkly beautiful karst landscape, the trail leads through rolling meadows, dense forests, mountain passes, and rocky terrain.

OPPOSITE: **Bled Castle sits high in the hills overlooking the town of Bled. RIGHT: Rowboats are docked on Lake Bled with the Santa Maria Church behind them.**

It offers sweeping views of the azure Adriatic and its sun-bleached islands. Side trails connect to the many mountain huts in the area. A popular Via Dinarica day hike is walking five to six hours on the Premužić Trail from the Zavizan mountain hut south to the Alan mountain hut.

Bosnia and Herzegovina

Called the "Yosemite of the Balkans," Sutjeska National Park in southeastern Bosnia and Herzegovina boasts several postcard-perfect day hikes on the Via Dinarica White trail. Among the easier treks is a six-mile (9.6 km) route beginning 4,800 feet (1,463 m) above sea level on Zelengora (Green) Mountain at Donje Bare Lake, one of area's numerous glacial lakes (known locally as "mountain eyes"). Near the start of the hike, you'll pass remnants of a stone hunting lodge used by Yugoslav dictator and "president for life" Josip Broz Tito, who died in 1980.

The trail leads across open mountainous terrain and down into a dense beech forest. Before turning to make the descent at the red sign pointing toward Kovačev Panj, hike a short distance ahead to an overlook. From here, you can see clear across the Sutjeska River Valley and marvel at two of

the park's peak performers—7,828-foot (2385.9 m) Mount Maglic and 7,664-foot (2,335.9 m) Volujak. You'll also see neighboring Montenegro's stunning Durmitor limestone massif, with its roughly 50 peaks towering 6,500 feet (1,981.2 m) or higher. Head back to the turnoff and hike down into the valley and onto the main road.

Montenegro

From Sutjeska National Park in Bosnia and Herzegovina you can (with the proper border-crossing permit) follow the Via Dinarica White trail into Montenegro's Durmitor National Park, a UNESCO World Heritage site. This section of the Via Dinarica was one of the first to be completed and leads through what regularly ranks among the most scenic stretches in the Dinaric Alps.

Durmitor is the place to experience Montenegro's top-of-the-world Via Dinarica views. Hike the country's craggy highest peak—8,277-foot (2,522.8 m) Bobotov Kuk—and you're rewarded with a three-nation panorama: Bosnia and Herzegovina, Albania, and Montenegro. The (relatively) easiest route up is an out-and-back trail from Sedlo Pass, elevation 6,256 feet (1,906.8 m), the highest paved road pass in

Montenegro. Making the winding, white-knuckle drive up to the pass is part of the adventure—and cuts the climbing time roughly in half, to about six hours round-trip.

The trail begins innocently enough, meandering across meadows and along lakes on a slow, steady climb. Heading into the last hour up, however, the grassy slopes give way to a steep ascent on a mainly dirt and grass trail. It is rocky at the top, but by then, all you're thinking about are those incredible views.

Albania, Kosovo, and Montenegro

Head to northern Albania's formidable-sounding Accursed Mountains, or Albanian Alps, for a 10-day trek of a lifetime on the Peaks of the Balkans circuit trail. Equal parts long-distance hike, Balkans' history lesson, and cultural immersion (lodging largely is with local families or in rustic mountain huts), the 119-mile (192 km) route loops through the isolated border region where northern Albania, western Kosovo, and southeastern Montenegro meet. Go with a guide since the trail is lightly traveled (you'll encounter more sheep than people), and it can be difficult to secure required cross-border permits and arrange family homestays online.

The classic start and end point is in northern Albania on an old mule path connecting the mountain village of Theth to Valbona Valley National Park. Most of the way, you're above the tree line, ensuring wide-open views of grassy alpine meadows, glacial lakes, and craggy, high-elevation (up to 8,694 feet/2,650 m above sea level) peaks that outsiders rarely see. Multiple abandoned military bunkers on the Albanian section of the route serve as tangible reminders of the not-so-distant Balkan Wars.

HIGHLIGHTS

• Hike through the western Balkans along the spine of the Dinaric Alps.

• Visit the "Yosemite of the Balkans," Sutjeska National Park.

• Explore a remote karst landscape on the Velebit, Croatia's largest mountain.

A river crossing in the
Accursed Mountains of Albania

Plunging in Cold Water: An Act of Joy

By Neil King

WHEN MY FIRST DAUGHTER WAS three weeks old, I dunked her into the Mediterranean, an hour's drive outside Rome. She squealed. When she was two, she would beg to go out stomping through the rain puddles in Brussels. I obliged. When she was seven, she pleaded for me to throw her into the frigid Roaring Fork River, in the Rockies outside Aspen. I did so with glee, then dove in myself.

Over the years we've dared each other to dive into Lake Michigan in late October and into alpine lakes at the foot of glaciers. A swim in the northern Atlantic three days after Christmas? Definitely. Nothing topped swimming; the more bracing, the better.

So I'm not surprised by Lilly's response to my college graduation gift of a father-daughter adventure anywhere in the world. She texts me: "Let's swim in the fjords of Norway."

The drive in the rental car from the tiny burg of Torvikbygd, across the shimmering Hardangerfjord, and along the fjord-veined western coast, speaks to the wondrous contrasts of Norway. In 10 minutes we've left the tall grass, buzzing bees, and grazing cattle of June and are well into a November moonscape of slate-gray rock fields and waterfalls plummeting into black lakes. Another 10 minutes, and it is a deep January of snow fields, scudding clouds, and—coming around the last bend—a ski area packed with people in parkas who haven't come to Norway to swim.

Imagine the shock, half an hour later and back into June, when we catch a glimpse along the shore of something truly remarkable: swimmers! There, just up from the

BELOW: **Surrounded by green hills and rocky peaks, cold water awaits in the lakes of Sørfjorden in Norway.** OPPOSITE: **A brave swimmer jumps from a wooden pier into Reinefjord.**

village of Jondal through an opening in the trees, we see a boy push two girls off a wooden plank that juts out over the fjord. They scream on the way down and scurry out within seconds of hitting water. But, hey, they survived.

By the time we are ready to swim, the kids are gone and we have the plank to ourselves.

Here I have a confession: In an act of caution—or, perhaps, utter weakness—we have brought neoprene tops and shorts. So our first swim, plunging off that plank to the slap of water on the face, is utterly fantastic, invigorating, and slightly unreal. We loll like seals, protected by the equivalent of a thin layer of blubber. We swim and dive and take a long float, examining the clouds, the silence, the breath.

Wet suits aside, we have, at this moment, truly arrived in Norway. That's the wonder of it, the beauty of traveling to swim. Nothing else puts you in a place quite like diving into it. Images flash of so many other immersions: off cliffs in Colorado, late-night beaches in Sumatra, from a dock in Switzerland's Lake Constance, that heart-stopping May swim off the tip of Nova Scotia's Cape Breton. Each, a punctuation point, a true moment of being there.

Still, nibbling smoked mackerel and crackers on the deck of our Airbnb in Herand that afternoon, we are ashamed. Real swimmers don't wear padding. Swim caps and swim shoes, sure. But that's it.

The next morning, we rise with the sun and take an unencumbered-by-neoprene swim from a gentle swoop of rock that makes for a perfect launch. Lilly rubs the sleep from her eyes and tiptoes, shivering, out to her waist before diving. I follow, with even more trepidation. Then the jolt,

the breathlessness, the whoops and laughter until calmness comes and the heart evens out.

We had no plans for swims in advance. If the perfect place arose, in we went. And so it happens later that day when we looped over to the Sorfjorden, a 24-mile (39 km) finger of blue-green water. Coming around a bend near Lofthus, I swerve to the shoulder, and there it is: an old fisherman's pier, weathered but firm, with a ladder coming up from the water.

We take turns diving from that pier, exulting in the cold smack of the water and the unexpected bath of sunlight. We should have a word in English for that moment right after the launch, when you are suspended in air but have yet to hit water, have yet to break the calm and descend into murk. We've traveled far for this moment of exhilaration distilled.

There will be other swims, each vivid and filled with delight. Between swims we'll scout places for improvised smorgasbords of salmon, cheese, apples, and wine, all while plotting futures— hers and mine—and debating the ingredients of a life well lived.

• *Neil King is a journalist, formerly with the* Wall Street Journal.

ITALY

ROAD TRIP THROUGH TUSCANY

A breathtaking drive through rolling hills and verdant countryside

Sure, it's possible to zip between Siena and Florence, two of central Italy's most beloved towns, in about an hour. But why rush the trip? The Tuscan countryside is like the wine produced there—meant to be savored rather than gulped. There are countless places to explore, each with something gorgeous or delicious to discover. Tuscany is Italy at its best. In Florence, it has the country's greatest Renaissance city; in Siena, one of its most perfect medieval towns; and in San Gimignano, its single most celebrated village. In addition, its landscapes fully embody the popular image of rural Italy. The region also offers beaches, lots of outdoor activities, and some of Italy's best food and wine.

This roundabout route is just a sampling of what's available. It links up fairy-tale castles, artistic treasures, picture-perfect vistas, outdoor adventures, and vineyards galore. What's not on the itinerary: mobs of tourists. In their place, you'll find quaint cobblestoned villages, museums with renowned collections from both local and foreign artists, and hot springs where you can rest your road-tired limbs. Should you need refreshments, there are plenty of stops along the way—including top-notch vineyards, truffle hunts, and delicious cheeses.

The route is breathtaking in scenery and welcoming for adventurers. Be prepared for curvy roads and some unexpected twists.

Travel Tips

WHEN TO GO: The best weather comes from April to June and in September and October, but that's also when crowds and prices are at their highest. Summer heat in July and August can be grueling. In spring you'll find fields of poppies to gaze at on your drive around the countryside.

PLANNING: Most cars in Italy are manual, so come prepared to drive stick shift unless you want to pay a lot more.

WEBSITES: castellodiama.com/en/; aziendaagricolalechiuse.it/index.php/en/; visittuscany.com/en

Eight million cases of wine are produced annually in Tuscany.

WHERE TO GO

Buonconvento

From Siena, drive about 18 miles (29 km) south to Buonconvento, a pristinely preserved medieval village that lives up to its name, derived from the Latin for "happy gathering place." Hikers on the Via Francigena, a pilgrimage route now popular with today's trekkers, routinely gather here. For folk history, visit Museo della Mezzadria Senese, which is housed in a centuries-old barn and tells the story of the area's sharecroppers.

Montalcino

Just 15 minutes away, in a landscape dominated by grapevines and olive groves, find a Montalcino farmhouse built in 1840. The rustic spot is Azienda Agricola le Chiuse, a winery and *agriturismo* that offers four apartments. Guests can splash in the pool and enjoy tastings led by owner Lorenzo Magnelli, whose great-great-grandfather created Brunello, the local wine celebrated internationally for its notes of licorice, tobacco, cherry, and chocolate.

San Giovanni d'Asso

In the Crete Senesi hills, San Giovanni d'Asso has a thing for white truffles. The town's castle houses the Museo del Tartufo, complete with a giant walk-in replica of a fungus. Up the street is Osteria delle Crete, which sells its own truffle-infused grappa. The restaurant arranges truffle hunts, accompanied by a lagotto Romagnolo, a specially trained dog. All truffled out? Wander around Bosco della Ragnaia, an artist-designed park with tranquil paths and quirky sculptures.

Rapolano Terme

Thermal hot springs bubble up all over Tuscany, and several famously steamy spots, such as Saturnia and Bagno Vignoni, are worth a detour. But the town of Rapolano Terme, where ancient Romans once relaxed, is conveniently on the route. Follow the whiff of sulfur to Terme San Giovanni, a reasonably priced, family-friendly spa that's open year-round for soaks in a series of pools with varying temperatures and enriched by calcium bicarbonate. (You'll feel the sediment squish between your toes.) A signature treatment? Naturally, the "mud ritual." Bring a bathing suit, towel, and flip-flops—plus a bathrobe to blend in with the locals. On weekends the spa stays open for dips after dark, which can be combined with Campari cocktails in the adjoining lounge.

Castello di Ama

In a quiet corner of the Chianti Classico region sits Castello di Ama, which attracts attention for more than just quality reds. For almost 20 years, the winery's owners have invited artists, Anish Kapoor and Louise Bourgeois among them, to create installations for the cellar and grounds, now an open-air museum. Some pieces stand out immediately, such as the telescope set up to spy on the countryside, but finding them all requires signing up for a guided tour and tasting. The kitchen at Il Ristoro di Ama uses veggies grown on the property; tuck into *pappa al pomodoro* (tomato-bread soup) and other Tuscan specialties before retiring to one of five lavish villa suites.

Sansepolcro

Neighboring Sansepolcro delivers a crash course on native son Piero della Francesca, the noted Renaissance painter. The Museo Civico's star attraction is the "Resurrection" fresco, featuring a strikingly buff Jesus standing above sleeping soldiers (one of them a self-portrait). A combo ticket also gives access to the artist's recently opened house museum, near a public garden dedicated to (who else?) della Francesca.

Poppi

The 13th-century Poppi Castle is the stuff of fantasies, starting with the deep moat that surrounds it. At the bottom is a prison that originally had no windows. (New prisoners were dropped in through a trap door.) At the top is a working bell tower, with 360-degree views of the lush Casentino Valley. Find more Instagram-worthy subjects inside the charming walled town lined with sidewalk porticoes.

HIGHLIGHTS

• Visit a wine cellar turned open-air museum with art work on display.

• Walk a charming walled town in Chianti outside a 13th-century castle.

• Taste your way through the countryside's best wine and truffles.

BEST OF THE DOLOMITES

Go inside, over, and through the Italian Alps.

Northeastern Italy's imposing Dolomites don't exactly roll out the welcome mat. The ancient range of the Italian Alps is a formidable rock fortress. Serrated steeples and pinnacles, precipitous cliffs, and steep faces covered with crags form an imposing backdrop to the surrounding alpine valleys. From a distance, the Dolomites appear to be impenetrable, but some of the fiercest battles of World War I took place on this ancient range, which served as the front line between Italian and Austrian troops.

The Dolomites' military past is a big reason why the mountains—a UNESCO World Heritage site boasting 18 peaks topping 9,800 feet (2,987 m) above sea level—are far more welcoming than first impressions would imply. The networks of bolted-down steel cables—called *via ferrata* (iron path)—ladders, and tunnels that soldiers originally built to transport supplies and move personnel up and down the mountains now make it possible for rock climbers and hikers of varying skill levels to explore otherwise inaccessible ridges and peaks. Cable cars and chairlifts whisk adventurers up to trails weaving through the mountains and connecting idyllic alpine villages in the surrounding valleys. Charming mountain huts perched on scenic overlooks serve as rest areas, making it possible to follow a hut-to-hut route for a long day hike or a multi-night trek.

Travel Tips

WHEN TO GO: Summer is high season for hiking. June and September are typically less crowded.

PLANNING: Some knowledge of one of the three official languages—German, Italian, and Ladin (a centuries-old Rhaetian language spoken in the Dolomite valleys)—will help with directions. Before attempting a via ferrata, rent a ferrata kit (helmet, harness, gloves, ropes, and carabiners).

WEBSITES: altabadia.org/en/italian -alps-dolomites; dolomiti.org/en; cortina express.it/en; laperlacorvara.it/en

World War II trenches built into the mountain

Day 1

From the Venice airport or train station, take the Cortina Express bus north to Cortina d'Ampezzo. The small alpine town (and host of the 1956 Winter Olympics) is a major gateway to the Dolomites and your home base for the next three nights. For 360-degree views of the jaw-dropping panorama you'll be exploring all week, ride the Tofana-Freccia nel Cielo cable car to the summit terrace of 10,643-foot (3,243.9 m) Tofana di Mezzo, Cortina's highest mountain peak.

Day 2

On your first full day in the Dolomites, take a seven-mile (11.2 km) hike on the western portion of the Alpe di Sennes Circuit. The trek begins six miles (9.6 km) north of Cortina d'Ampezzo at the Rifugio (mountain hut) Malga Ra Stua, elevation 5,472 feet (1,668 m). The route crosses marshlands, lush valleys, and barren alpine slopes, climbing to an altitude of 6,942 feet (2,116 m). Make a stop for lunch at Rifugio Fodara Vedla (try the barley soup with homemade spinach and cheese dumplings or *kaiserschmarren,* a kind of omelet with lingonberry jam), then follow a World War I mule track back to the starting point.

Day 3

Kick the altitude and distance up a notch by taking an eight-mile (13 km) hike from Rifugio Auronzo (elevation 7,650 feet/ 2,332 m) up to the rocky pass at Pian di Cengia (elevation 8,200 feet/2,500 m) and across to the foot of Tre Cime di Lavaredo, a trio of outsize rock plates jutting out of the massif. The trail winds steeply uphill in places and passes abandoned World War I

bunkers and barracks. If you want to try one of the Dolomites' famous fixed-rope via ferratas, the Via Delle Scalette (accessible from Rifugio Auronzo) is an excellent option. Rent a feratta kit to tackle the iron path, which offers stunning views of the towering Tre Cime peaks and a glimpse into the harrowing, high-elevation conditions experienced by World War I soldiers.

Day 4

Check out of your hotel and hop back on the Cortina Express bus to Falzarego Pass, starting point of the Lagazuoi cable car. Ride it up to the Rifugio Lagazuoi, one of the highest mountain huts in the Dolomites at elevation 9,000 feet (2,743 m). Hidden within the natural rock fortress of Lagazuoi is a network of military structures built during World War I. The site is maintained as an open-air museum. Walk downhill through the seemingly endless series of tunnels and trenches containing artifacts such as utensils and weapons. When you're done, catch a bus to your overnight stop in the village of San Cassiano.

Day 5

San Cassiano sits at the feet of two super-size Dolomite peaks: 10,023-foot (3,055 m) Piz Lavarela and 9,186-foot (2,800 m) Piz Conturines. Ride the chairlift up to Piz Sorega (elevation 6,570 feet/2,002.5 m) and follow a ridgeline trail through high mountain meadows to a lunch stop on the outdoor terrace at Rifugio Utia de Bioch. From here, hike down about 3.5 miles (5.6 km) to Corvara (elevation 5,120 feet/1,560.5 m), a popular tourist village nestled at the base of the imposing 8,743-foot (2,665 m) Sassongher. Splurge on a two-night stay at La Perla (closed October to early December and March 31 to mid-June), a family-run luxury mountain lodge.

Day 6

Enjoy big meadow and mountain vistas with little effort on an easy 3.7-mile (5.9 km) one-way walk from the base of the Boe cable car in Corvara to Colfosco and back. Colfosco (elevation 5,400 feet/1,646 m) is a charming Alpine village on the edge of Puez-Odle Nature Park, a UNESCO World

OPPOSITE: A climber makes his careful way along via ferrata, built into the peaks during World War I. ABOVE: Alpine hut Rifugio Auronzo sits 7,644 feet (2,330 m) above sea level surrounded by the Three Peaks.

The hike along Tre Cime Lavaredo (or Drei Zinnen)—three of the best known peaks in the Dolomites—offers sweeping views of the rugged landscape.

Heritage site. Stop for pizza at L'Tabladel before walking back to Corvara.

Day 7

Rent a ride—motorcycle, car, e-bike (electric-powered bicycle) or, if you have the lung capacity and leg strength, a road or mountain bike—in Corvara to experience the Dolomites' top scenic drive: the serpentine Sellaronda. The 38-mile (61 km) loop crosses four mountain passes—Campolongo, Pordoi, Sella, and Gardena—as it winds around the ginormous Sella Massif. An iconic ski-touring route in winter, the Sellaronda is easily accessible to cyclists in summer via chairlifts from towns in the four valleys below. The mountain bike trail is an off-road route roughly paralleling the main way. Drive or pedal the route in either direction, allowing ample time for stops at scenic overlooks and to pay homage to the "Queen of the Dolomites," the Marmolada glacier, elevation 10,725 feet (3,269 m).

Day 8

A bus makes the short hop south to Arabba, the starting point for your final Dolomites hike: a serpentine climb up the south face of the Sella Massif. From the Porta Vescovo cable car lift parking lot, follow the trail toward Passo Pordoi, crossing grassy meadows and hiking up a ski slope on the way. At Passo Pordoi (elevation 7,345 feet/2,239 m), zigzag up the steep path to the Rifugio Forcella Pordoi (open late June to September), base for several Sella Massif day hikes. From the mountain hut, follow the dry and rocky terrain along the massif's south face to your lunch stop at the Rifugio Franz Kostner (elevation 8,366 feet/2,550 m). Ride the gondola down to Passo Pordoi and retrace your steps back to Arabba.

CROATIA

THE RUGGED BEAUTY OF CROATIA

Venture beyond the views for adventure.

With the limestone cliffs and blue waters of the Adriatic coast to the west, the jagged peaks of the Dinaric Alps to the east, and countless cascades and dense forests in between, Croatia offers seemingly unlimited opportunities for tackling adventure on land and sea.

The rugged beauty of the country's 1,100-mile (1,770.3 km) Adriatic coastline rivals any others in the Mediterranean. Offshore, a collection of some 1,200 rocky islands and islets shimmer like pearls in the azure sea. On the northern Istrian Peninsula, vineyards, valleys, alpine meadows, and hilltop villages are set against the backdrop of snowcapped peaks. Protected within the growing number of national parks and nature preserves are vast expanses of Croatia's dominant karst landscape featuring caves, underground streams, and steep rocky cliffs.

With scenic vistas revealed around nearly every bend in Croatia's famously winding roads and indented main coast, it's easy to bask in the country's beauty. Venture beyond easy, however, and the views and the adventure possibilities go to the next level, often leading to more remote or less visited wild places. To help get you started, here are seven ways to explore—not simply see—Croatia's jaw-droppingly scenic and rugged landscape.

Travel Tips

WHEN TO GO: Avoid the high season prices and crowds by visiting in May, June, September, or October. Many hotels and attractions close from November to April.

PLANNING: Make Split, on the central Dalmatian coast, your base to take day trips or overnights via rental car, bus, ferry, or train. If you have the time, choose to travel by car—the small country's villages and scenic routes are worth taking detours for.

WEBSITES: croatia.hr/en-GB; np-plitvicka-jezera.hr/en; zipline-croatia .com; np-kornati.hr/en

The Square of the Radic Brothers just outside Diocletian's Palace

WHAT TO DO

A Drive Along the Dalmatian Coast

Driving doesn't get much more scenic than this: brilliant-blue Adriatic Sea waters on the right and the jagged peaks of the Dinaric Alps rising on the left. The jaw-dropping scenery means extra concentration is required to keep your eyes squarely focused on the Adriatic Highway, which snakes its way down Croatia's western coast about 220 miles (354 km) from the Slovenia border south to Montenegro. The mountain-hugging section of the road running along the Dalmatian Coast, Croatia's southernmost coastal region of Croatia, is a white-knuckle thrill ride. Channel your inner James Bond by renting a sleek sports car in Split, located about midway along the coast, and driving south to Dubrovnik, which fans of the HBO series *Game of Thrones* will recognize as King's Landing, capital of Westeros. Adding to the route's appeal for adventure lovers is a brief pass through Bosnia and Herzegovina along the country's 12-mile (19.3 km) coastline, the second shortest in the world.

Mountain-Bike Across Pag

Historically known for its Paški sir, or Pag (hard sheep's milk cheese), the northern Adriatic island of Pag is gaining ground as a mountain biking destination. Helping drive interest is the eerie, lunar-like terrain of the island's eastern side. Powerful Bura—sudden north-northeast to east-northeast—wind gusts infused with salty sea spray keep the rocky region devoid of vegetation. Rent a mountain bike or join a guided ride to rumble across the barren landscape. After touring Pag's moonlike landscape in the east, bike along narrow paths lined with stacked-stone walls to see sturdy Pag sheep grazing on the island's rocky, dry scrub hillsides.

OPPOSITE: Rocky cliffs line the shores of the Dalmatian coast. RIGHT: A zip line soars above the Canyon of Cetina River near Omis, a thrilling way to see the views from the sky.

See Waterfalls at Plitvice Lakes National Park

Choose the road less taken—Route, or Program, K—to make a challenging six- to eight-hour loop around Plitvice Lakes National Park, a UNESCO World Heritage site. Boardwalks, streams, and cascades connect the park's terraced lakes: 16 shimmering pools filled with waters in varying shades of blue and green. The lakes, divided into "upper" and "lower" sections, are connected by travertine dams, creating a series of glistening and gushing waterfall staircases. Start the hike at the upper lakes entrance to the park, working your way down to the base of Veliki Slap, the tallest (256 feet/78 m) waterfall in the park and in all of Croatia. The trail leads through a canyon, cave, and dense wild beech and fir forests and climbs to overlooks for a loftier perspective on the lakes.

Climb to the Vidova Gora Lookout

The highest peak in the Adriatic islands, Vidova Gora lookout, elevation 2,280 feet (695 m), is worth the seven-mile (11.3 km) climb for the 360-degree views. The peak is located on Brac, the largest island on Croatia's central Dalmatian coast, best known for its greatest natural resource: white limestone. Take the ferry from Split to Supetar on the north shore of Brac; then hop a bus to the south shore town of Bol. The trail begins on a road leading up to a limestone quarry and then gives way to a rocky path. Pack a lunch to linger at the top with the mesmerizing blue waters of the Adriatic and the white-pebble beach of Zlatni Rat, or Golden Cape, spread out below.

Jump Into the Adriatic Sea

Perched at the tip of Istria, the peninsula Croatia shares with northern neighbors Slovenia and Italy, is the rugged nature reserve, Cape Kamenjak, part of Kamenjak National Park. Sheer 70-foot (21 m) cliffs, rocky coves, and hiking trails retracing the footsteps of dinosaurs (with fossils and footprints to prove it) give the windswept cape an edge-of-the-world feel. There are designated cliff jumping sites where you can leap feet first into the Adriatic from

adrenaline-pumping heights up to 40 feet (12.2 m) or more. There are lower launching spots too, as well as windsurfing and kayaking outfitters at Skoljic Cove.

Adventure in the Cetina River Canyon

The stunning Cetina River canyon is southern Croatia's outdoor adventure hub. Make Omis, the Dalmatian coast port town at the mouth of the Cetina gorge, your base for a couple of wild play days. April to October is best for water sports like white-water rafting, rappelling down the 164-foot (50 m) drop of Gubavica waterfall, and rock hopping and swimming in the canyon. Spend the first day on and in the water, and the next in the air zooming over and through the canyon by zip line. The three-hour Zipline Croatia tour is a gut-churning descent across eight steel cables, the highest of which is 492 feet (150 m) above the ground.

Explore the Kornati Archipelago

Head off the beaten tourist track to Kornati National Park, the largest archipelago in the Adriatic. Located off the northern Dalmatian coast near Murter, an island and town connected to the mainland, the park is a protected maritime playground boasting some 90 small, shell-colored islands and more than 30 dive sites. Outfitters in Murter and Zadar offer guided sailing, snorkeling, and scuba diving trips. Among the treasures awaiting experienced divers are underwater cliffs, colorful corals and reef fish, the wreck of a German World War II military jet, and the wreck of the *Francesca da Rimini,* a German World War II cargo ship, sitting on the sea bottom at depths between 124 and 164 feet (37.8 and 50 m).

HIGHLIGHTS

• Leap off a limestone cliff into the azure waters of the Adriatic Sea.

• See 16 luminous lakes and dozens of waterfalls in Plitvice Lakes National Park.

•Soar down the Cetina River canyon on a three-hour zip-lining tour.

A boardwalk winds through
Plitvice Lakes National Park.

BICYCLING THE BALTICS

Pedal through three countries on an epic European adventure.

There's no shortage of reasons why northern Europe's Baltic states—Estonia, Latvia, and Lithuania—are ideal for a cycling adventure. Top of the list: The Baltics are basically flat. The highest peak is Estonia's Suur Munamagi at 1,043 feet (317.9 m) above sea level, and there are about 1,240 miles (1,995.5 km) of Baltic sea-level coastline.

Then there's the history and heritage. The medieval Old Towns of all three capital cities—Tallinn, Riga, and Vilnius—are protected as UNESCO World Heritage sites. Ancient ruins, fairy-tale-like castles, Russian Empire and Soviet-era remnants, and long-lasting folk traditions chronicle the diverse influences that shaped the region. This includes the large Baltic song and dance celebrations recognized on UNESCO's Intangible Cultural Heritage list.

The Baltics are also compact. It's only 375 miles (604 km) from Estonia's capital city south to Lithuania's capital, with the Latvian capital situated roughly in between. The close proximity, predominantly flat terrain, and cycle-centric cultures make it easy to visit all three countries on a 10- to 12-day biking trip, particularly since self-guided tours typically include transfer buses between longer stops. This 10-day tour begins in Estonia, rolls through Latvia, ends in Lithuania, and cruises close enough to the Russian border for bonus fourth-country views.

Travel Tips

WHEN TO GO: May to September; spring is less crowded than peak tourist times in July and August.

PLANNING: Several outfitters, such as UTracks, Baltic Bike Travel, Eurobike, and Exodus Travels, offer guided or self-guided Baltic cycling itineraries. Some operators offer a discount if you bring your own bike.

WEBSITES: utracks.com; bbtravel.lt; eurobike.at/en; exodustravels.com; latvia.travel/en; visitestonia.com/en; visitlithuania.net; 3s.ee; palmse.ee/en; visitestonia.com/en/otepaa-nature -park-2; pullmanriga.lv

A riverbed in Guaja National Park

Day 1

Pick up your wheels for the day to tour Tallinn, the capital of the smallest of the three Baltic states. Pedal the paths crisscrossing 173-acre (70 hectare) Kadriorg Park, named for its pink Kadriorg Palace, built by Tsar Peter the Great of Russia in 1718. Overnight in Tallinn's Old Town, a UNESCO World Heritage site.

Day 2

Take the tour bus from Tallinn east to Lahemaa ("Land of Bays") National Park, Estonia's largest, encompassing 280 square miles (725 sq km) of land and sea. Ride the Kasmu trail through the forested eponymous peninsula and out to the tip of the Palganeem cape, which overlooks the Gulf of Finland. Watch for resident wildlife, such as moose, foxes, and lynx, before pedaling south to the grand Palmse Manor museum.

Day 3

From Palmse, ride the bus 90 minutes southeast to Mustvee, a half Estonian-speaking and half Russian-speaking town on the western shores of Lake Peipus, Europe's fourth largest. Today's 30-mile (48.2 km) cycling route hugs the lakeshore from Mustvee south to Varnja, passing sandy beaches, pine forests, and small fishing villages. Meet the bus in Varnja to transfer for the night to a hotel in the college town of Tartu, Estonia's second largest city.

Day 4

Ride the bus 34 miles (54.3 km) south to the Kaariku Sports Center, an all-season recreation resort and park on the shores of Kaariku Lake and the starting point for

multiple hilly trails. Cycle the nine-mile (14.4 km) Kekkonen hiking track up and over 693-foot (211.2 m) Harimägi Hill. Climb the tower at the top for sweeping views of the Otepää Highlands. Then bike to 19th-century Sangaste manor and park, modeled after England's Windsor Castle. After a day in the park, take a cross-border ride (about 100 miles/160.9 km southwest) to Sigulda, Latvia. Stay in a hotel near Gauja National Park, the starting point of tomorrow's ride.

Day 5

Roll right from your hotel to Gauja National Park, Latvia's largest, protecting 348 square miles (901.3 sq km) of the picturesque Gauja River valley. Follow trails along the river, passing windmills, medieval castle mounds, castles, sandstone cliffs, rock formations, and caves. Picnic in the park before taking the bus about 35 miles (56.3 km) southwest to Riga, Latvia's capital. Spend the rest of the day biking around Riga's World Heritage–designated center and wander through the Central Market— Europe's largest, housed in old Zeppelin airship hangers. Overnight in the Pullman Riga Old Town, a restored 18th-century horse stable turned hip hotel.

Day 6

From Riga follow a flat route west to the Baltic Sea resort of Jūrmala. The 12-mile (19.3 km) bike ride passes through city and suburban neighborhoods, across open fields and forests, and onto the sandy beach. After lunch, retrace your route back to Riga to board the bus for the 82-mile (131.9 km) ride south to the overnight stop in Šiauliai, Lithuania. North of town, visit the world-famous Hill of Crosses, an earthen mound pilgrimage site covered with some 100,000 metal and wooden crucifixes. Thought to date back to the 1830s, the area was destroyed and rebuilt five times during the Soviet era. Now, pilgrims continuously add new crosses and other religious icons to the hill.

Day 7

Take the bus west to the seaside resort of Palanga, the starting point of a roughly 20-mile (32.1 km) ride along the Baltic coast to Klaipėda. Follow a section of the paved and car-free Lithuanian Seaside Cycle Route through the protected Seaside Regional Park, passing white-sand beaches and dunes, pine forests, and coastal cliffs as you pedal south. Walk to the end of the

More than 100,000 crucifixes and other religious icons cover the Hill of Crosses, a pilgrimage site of unknown origin in Lithuania.

L-shaped, 1,542-foot-long (470 m) Palanga pier for unobstructed coastal views. In Klaipėda, stay in the historic seaport at the Old Mill Hotel on the Curonian Lagoon.

Day 8

Ride the ferry across the lagoon to the Curonian Spit, a UNESCO World Heritage site. The 61-mile-long (98.1 km) sand-dune peninsula separates the Curonian Lagoon from the Baltic Sea and is split between Lithuania and Russia. Pedal the Curonian Spit section of the Lithuanian Seaside Cycle Route south from the ferry landing about 30 miles (48.2 km) south to Nida, located less than two miles (3.2 km) north of the Russian border.

Day 9

Watch the sunrise over Russia atop 170-foot (51.8 m) Parnidis Dune. Take a boat from Nida east across the Curonian Lagoon to the Ventes Ragas Peninsula, a main European migratory flyway hot spot where, during peak autumn migration, up to 300,000 birds fly over each day. Tour the peninsula and beyond by cycling routes through Nemunas River Delta Regional Park. From the park, ride the bus 120 miles (193.1 km) east to overnight in Kaunas.

Day 10

From Kaunas, continue east by bus to Vilnius, Lithuania's bike-friendly capital. Spend a full day exploring the city using designated cycling routes, which wind around locations such as the medieval Old Town, part of the Vilnius Historic Centre, a UNESECO World Heritage site, and Verkiai Regional Park, site of the 18th-century Verkiai manor complex and six emerald lakes.

HIGHLIGHTS

• Tour the medieval Old Town UNESCO World Heritage sites of three capital cities.

• See storybook castles like Kadriorg, built by Tsar Peter the Great of Russia.

• Bike along the Baltic and see Russia from the Curonian Spit.

HIKING CORSICA

Awaken all five senses on the Scented Isle.

Corsica, the fourth largest island in the Mediterranean, boasts the requisite regional sun-splashed beaches and turquoise waters. Yet adventure on this rugged island off the coasts of France and Italy is focused more on turf than surf. Most of Corsica's 3,352 square miles (8,682.6 sq km) are mountainous. Even Corsica's sole UNESCO World Heritage site—Gulf of Porto: Calanche of Piana, Gulf of Girolata, Scandola Reserve—which protects both sea and land, is best known for its rock star Scandola peninsula and its incandescent, purple-red–tinted cliffs and pinnacles.

A network of long-distance footpaths and hiking routes crisscrosses the island, providing access to wild coastal beaches; rocky ridges; alpine lakes; fertile fields; and scrubby, aromatic underbrush, known as *maquis,* which gives Corsica the nickname "Scented Isle." Most trails tend toward the challenging due to mountainous terrain; relatively easier routes run along the coast, however.

Whatever your fitness level, on foot is the best way to experience Corsica, which, while officially part of France, is fiercely independent. So when you stay at one of the *gites d'étape* (traditional rest houses) during your hike, thank the host in Corsu—the ancient Tuscan dialect still spoken by many residents—by saying *À ringraziavvi* rather than the French *merci.*

Travel Tips

WHEN TO GO: May, June, or early September are the best months to visit to avoid the intense sun, heat, and crowds of the July and August high season.

PLANNING: Some hikes are extremely challenging, so choose the route that matches your fitness and skill level and bring the right gear for the trip. You can plan a route on your own (remember that everything is in French), but going with tour operators on a guided or self-guided trek makes things simpler.

WEBSITES: corsica.forhikers.com; gr20 .co.uk/gr20-trips-holidays; visit-corsica .com/en; demeureloredana.com/en

Views await hikers on the GR20.

WHERE **TO GO**

The GR20

Considered the most challenging of the Grande Randonnée, or GR, long-distance hiking routes crossing Belgium, France, Germany, Spain, and the Netherlands, the GR20 winds 112 miles (180.2 km) along Corsica's jagged, granite backbone. If you're an experienced trekker who's tackled the Appalachian Trail in the eastern United States or the GR10 across the French Pyrenees, then you may have what it takes to meet the unrelenting physical challenges of the GR20. Only about a third of hikers who start the trek at Calenzana manage to conquer all of the lengthy ascents and descents over mountain passes and granite cliffs required to make it all the way south to the end in the village of Conca, near Porto-Vecchio.

The GR20 is divided into two sections, northern and southern, with the steepest, rockiest parts in the north. On the northern end (the typical starting point), red-and-white way markers dare hikers to defy gravity at times, leading across the type of sheer, rocky terrain normally reached only with ropes or by fixed-route via ferratas (iron paths). The somewhat easier southern section still requires some scrambling and climbs along the ridgeline of 7,001-foot (2,133.9 m) Monte Alcudina, yet also covers miles of mainly flat meadow and forest terrain on the lush, green Cuscione Plateau. If you don't have time (typically 12 to 15 days) to hike the whole GR20 or aren't sure you're up to the challenge, the southern section is a shorter, more doable option; it takes only about seven days to complete. Whether you attempt a section or the whole epic hike, go as part of a private or small group guided tour. Having someone else navigate (the signs are in French) and arrange meals and overnight stops along the way will

boost your chances of checking GR20 off the hiking bucket list.

_____

Tra Mare e Monti Nord

For a long-distance trek with fewer ascents, try the Tra Mare e Monti Nord (Between the Sea and the Mountains, North). The 75-mile (120.7 km) route crosses the G20 at the starting point in Calenzana, but that's about all the trails have in common. From Calenzana, the Tra Mare e Monti Nord winds southwest to the coast at the seaside village of Galéria and then primarily follows the coast the rest of the way to its end in Cargèse. The highest elevation point on the trail is near the beginning: 3,937 feet (1,199.9 m) above sea level in the mountainous Bonifatu Forest.

There is an option south of Galéria to veer inland through a forest via the Capu Tondo loop, a more shaded walk providing some relief from the intense summer sun. But it's the main coastal route where you'll be treated to the best views of Corsica's extraordinary Scandola Nature Reserve, a UNESCO World Heritage site and protected geological gem that's off-limits to the public. As you hike the trail south between Galéria and Girolata (which is accessible only by boat or on foot), pause to marvel at Scandola's stunning purple-red rock cliffs and arches. Formed more than 250 million years ago by lava flows, the hard rock is a rare form of granite called porphyry, highly prized for its decorative qualities by ancient Roman emperors, who used it for sculptures and architectural elements.

Plan to spend nine to 11 days hiking the entire Tra Mare e Monti Nord. Chart your route in advance so you can reserve rooms at the small gites d'étape along the route.

OPPOSITE: The ruins of the Genoese Tower at Mortella overlook the turquoise Mediterranean Sea. RIGHT: The pink and red Capo Rosso rocks make up Porto Gulf's coastline.

Désert des Agriates Sentier Littoral

The best way to experience Corsica's barren Désert des Agriates, a 12,355-acre (4,999.8 hectare) wilderness area in the northwestern Balagne region, is on foot. The nature preserve's crown jewel—and most accessible area—is its untouched coastline: 25 miles (40.2 km) of wild beaches and rocky coves backed by oak and pine trees, as well as arid scrubland. Hike the lightly traveled Sentier Littoral (coastal path) along the pristine middle ground where the rugged terrain meets the Mediterranean.

Take three days to make the walk, starting at the western end of the path in Ostriconi and ending at the eastern terminus in St. Florent. Stop frequently to lounge on dazzling (and, often, deserted) white-sand and pebble beaches, swim in turquoise waters, and breathe the pleasantly pungent aroma of the wild maquis, the highly scented shrubbery covering the interior of Désert des Agriates and more than half of the island. There's little shade and virtually no drinking water available on the path, so wear a wide-brimmed hat and carry plenty of fluids. You may encounter grazing cattle on the beach near the eastern end, but won't see another soul for long stretches.

Camping isn't permitted on the beach, so make advance reservations for the path's only campgrounds—in Ghingu for the first night and behind Saleccia beach for the second night. Both sites have water sources for refilling bottles. When you reach the end of the path, splurge on a sea-view balcony room at the Hotel Demeure Loredana in St. Florent and rest your weary feet.

HIGHLIGHTS

• Tackle the epic GR20, one of Europe's most challenging long-distance hiking and climbing routes.

• See the inaccessible purple-red rock cliffs of the Scandola Nature Reserve, a UNESCO World Heritage site.

• Visit wild, deserted white-sand beaches on a coastal walk along the barren Désert des Agriates.

WHERE TO GO

Wander the Bewitching Corners of the Quiraing

Scotland's Isle of Skye has a well-deserved reputation as a mystical and otherworldly place. Nowhere is this more evident than the Quiraing. Part of the Trotternish Ridge, the Quiraing is a geologic wonderland where volcanic landslips have formed sharp cliffs and basalt pinnacles on steep slopes above the sea. A circuitous 4.3-mile (7 km) trail winds through the fascinating landscape, passing sites such as the Table, a hidden grassy plateau, and the Prison, a fortress-like rock structure. Don't miss the Fairy Glen outside the village of Uig, a mini-Quiraing with cone-shaped green hills and little lochs.

Step Back in Time at the Callanish Stones

People have inhabited the Isle of Lewis, part of the Outer Hebrides, for some 5,000 years. Those early settlers left an enduring monument: the Callanish Stones, erected roughly 2,000 years before Stonehenge. A gently climbing walk reveals the main site, which is composed of 50 stones—some over 15 feet tall (4.5 m) and weighing five tons (4.5 metric tons)—placed in the shape of a cross. Further trekking along boggy tracks leads to several less visited sites with unique characteristics. Callanish III—Cnoc Fhillibhir Bheag in Gaelic—has 20 stones in a remarkable double circle.

Take In the Beauty of Loch Lomond and Trossachs National Park

A half hour outside Glasgow, Loch Lomond—the "Gateway to the Highlands"—is Great Britain's largest freshwater lake. The lake forms part of Trossachs National Park's 720 square miles (1,865 sq km) of deep forests, shimmering lochs, and looming mountains. Walking paths

crisscross the land and link inviting villages. In Breadalbane, the northeast corner of the park, you can visit Rob Roy's grave and the Falls of Dochart, a rushing white cascade that flows around the island of Inchbuie.

Embrace the Wild in Cairngorms National Park

Covering 1,748 square miles (4,528 sq km) in the heart of the Scottish Highlands between Inverness and Aberdeen, Cairngorms is the United Kingdom's largest national park. Hundreds of trails wind through ancient Caledonian pinewoods, deep valleys, and the highest summits in the British Isles (mountain climbers flock to the park to "bag a Munro"—Scottish mountains more than 3,000 feet/914 m high). Nearly half of the park is considered "wild land," and those with an adventurous spirit can try one of the Cairngorms Hill Tracks, rough walking routes through uninhabited country that require detailed maps and compasses for navigation. Stalwart hikers tackle the Speyside Way, one of Scotland's four official Long-Distance Routes that follows the valley of the River Spey for 65 miles (104 km) from the shore of Moray Firth to the edge of the Grampian Mountains.

Explore the Neolithic Village of Skara Brae

Located in the North Sea, the Orkneys are composed of 70 rocky islands frequently pounded by wind and waves. In 1850, a great storm revealed the ancient stone roofs and ceremonial structures of Skara Brae, Europe's most complete and best preserved prehistoric site. Older even than the Egyptian pyramids, the rocky village dates as far back as 3000 B.C. A scenic coastal walking route along the Bay of Skaill leads to seven dwellings nestled in green turf, still containing original stone furniture. Five miles (8 km) southeast is the Ring of Brodgar, a 5,000-year-old stone circle that was part of a sacred pilgrimage route to a temple complex and the ancestral tomb of Maeshowe, carved with runes from Norse crusaders.

OPPOSITE: Basalt pinnacles loom over the Sound of Raasay in the Isle of Skye. ABOVE: A Eurasian eagle owl sits in heather at Cairngorms National Park.

EPIC SHOT

Showing the epic scale of the Jökulsárlón Glacier Lagoon, a woman paddles among ice floes on an inflatable paddleboard. The lagoon, which forms part of Vatnajökull National Park, is dotted by broken icebergs. As climate change affects the area, more and more icebergs are breaking off and melting into the lagoon, especially in the summer months. Between 1975 and 1998, the lagoon has nearly doubled in size. It now stretches seven square miles (18 sq km).

The shores of Jökulsárlón make this an even more spectacular place to visit. The black-sand beach is dotted with translucent ice sculptures that have been washed ashore. It has been nicknamed "The Diamond Beach."

IMAGE BY **BEN HORTON**

CLOCKWISE FROM TOP LEFT: A Bengal tiger in Ranthambore, India; the Great Arch of Chunzhang Cave; the temples of Bagan in Myanmar; Guangzhou city lit up at night

CHAPTER 4

ASIA

A continent rich in history, majestic landscapes, and bustling cities

JAPAN

PEAK EXPERIENCES

The sacred summits of the Japanese Alps and Mount Fuji in the Land of the Rising Sun

Spiritual experiences abound on a journey to Japan. Visit glittering temples and shrines, take part in tea ceremonies with Buddhist monks, find inner peace in rock gardens, meditate with Zen priests, and unwind with a shiatsu massage.

And then there's the ultimate pilgrimage. Religious followers and adventurers alike choose to follow centuries-old routes and ascend to the country's highest peaks, traditionally believed to be the sacred home of holy spirits, called *kami* in the Shinto religion.

Southwest of Tokyo, the mythological spectacle of Mount Fuji pokes through the clouds. Just beyond are the soaring Japanese Alps, a series of lofty ranges that form the island's spine between Kyoto and Tokyo. Amid these cool forests, dramatic canyons, and tumbling cascades, you can almost hear the whispers of gods.

Consider Mount Fuji in particular. Tackling its summit on the well-beaten Yoshida Trail is a Japanese rite of passage in the truest sense, and the feeling at the top is nothing shy of euphoria. You could even call it a religious experience. In the Shinto faith, salvation could be achieved only by reaching this point. No matter your faith, to stand on its crater is to gaze upon the glory of the Land of the Rising Sun from one of the planet's most poetic vantages.

Travel Tips

WHEN TO GO: Snow blankets the high peaks into summer, with high-altitude areas closed from mid-November to mid-April. Cherry blossoms add pops of pink each spring, and fall foliage lasts from late September to early November. Beware of typhoon season (August and September).

PLANNING: The Japan Rail Pass allows unlimited train travel between destinations for foreign tourists for 7, 14, or 21 days.

WEBSITES: us.jnto.go.jp; japan-guide .com; japan-alps.com/en; env.go.jp/en/ nature/nps/park/index.html

Motsumoto Castle in Nagano

Mount Fuji

Fulfill bucket-list dreams and summit Mount Fuji, Japan's tallest and most iconic peak, which soars 12,389 feet (3,776 m) in the sky with nearly perfect symmetry. UNESCO recognizes Fuji as a time-honored "source of artistic inspiration" and a sacred element of Buddhism and Shintoism. Though the eight-mile-or-so (12.9 km) Yoshida Trail is open only from July to early September, more than 300,000 hikers set their sights on the mountain's most popular hiking trail each year—forming a human train as they stream up the snowcapped stratovolcano, staying in mountain huts, and buying warm ramen and bottled oxygen from shops along the path.

Follow their lead and rise before dawn to join the crowd on the crater rim as the day's light breaks. So revered is the sunrise from Mount Fuji, the Japanese have a special word for it: *goraikou*. For a less trodden experience, take one of the other trails up the mountainside: the forested Subashiri, the more remote Gotemba, or the steep, shorter Fujinomiya. Just remember the old Japanese adage: "A wise man will climb Mt. Fuji once; a fool will climb Mt. Fuji twice."

Hikers can also circumnavigate Fuji on the historic Ochudo Trail, a mostly flat walk among ancient conifers about halfway up the mountain.

Northern Alps

Explore the Hida Mountains of the Northern Alps at Chubu Sangaku National Park, which encompasses many popular outdoor destinations. Soak up the scenery at the beloved highland valley of Kamikochi and set out on foot across the symbolic bridge of Kappabashi and along the forested banks of the Azusa River. Hike past a wind cave and up the slopes to the Dakesawa mountain hut, or climb to the top of the rugged Mount Yakedake ("burning mountain"), an active volcano that last erupted in 1995.

Tackle all or part of the 56-mile (90 km) Tateyama Kurobe Alpine Route (closed in the winter), which links the spectacular scenery between Omachi and Toyama by footpath, cable car, trolley bus, and ropeway. Don't miss the sheer snow walls near Morodo.

Made famous during the 1998 Nagano Winter Olympics, the Hakuba Valley and its nearly 10,000-foot-high (3,048 m) peaks are world-renowned for skiing, hiking, and climbing. Take the chairlift to the top of the sheer jumps at the Hakuba Ski Jumping Stadium.

In Nagano, visit the castle in Matsumoto—a designated National Treasure and Japan's oldest existing fortress—and paddle a canoe or kayak around serene lakes and rivers, such as Lake Aoki. In the Norikura highlands, snowshoe or cross-country ski to frozen Zengora Falls; in the warmer months, hit the trails on foot or two wheels. Rejuvenate weary bodies in the milky hot springs situated halfway up Mount Norikuradake, one of Japan's first places to spot fall colors. Year-round, ski junkies flock to the perpetually powder-blanketed Big Snowy Valley. Peer into the dizzying Kurobe Gorge from an open-sided sightseeing train; from the terminus, head out on hiking trails into the pristine forest inhabited by wild Japanese macaques and sika deer to remote hot springs and steep cliffs. For more snow monkey encounters, head to Jigokudani Yaen Koen (aka "Hell's Valley"), where more than 150 snow monkeys can be observed bathing in natural hot springs.

Take a break from chasing summits to experience authentic Japanese countryside in the rugged Shogawa River Valley. See the UNESCO World Heritage–designated villages of Shirakawa-go and Gokayama, where the steeply slanted thatched roofs of farmhouses mimic the hands of Buddhist monks in prayer and also mirror the mountainous backdrop.

OPPOSITE: **With walking sticks in hand, climbers descend Mount Fuji along the Yoshida trail.** RIGHT: **Macaque monkeys bathe in the natural hot springs at Jigokudani Monkey Park.**

Central Alps

Traverse the lush Kiso Valley of the Central Alps on foot. Follow the ancient Nakasendo Trail, or Sumarai Trail, which connected Kyoto and Tokyo during the Edo era (1603–1867). Spend a leisurely day walking the well-preserved section between the restored feudal post towns of Magome ("horse basket") and Tsumago, just over five miles (8 km) apart, for a glimpse of Old Japan. In the 1860s, Princess Kazunomiya is said to have traveled this path with her 25,000-strong entourage. Step on rough stones placed here in the 17th century as you weave through pine and cedar forests and among terraced rice paddies and bamboo groves. Pause at tumbling waterfalls and serene shrines, and around the halfway point, stop for tea in a traditional-style house. A dozen or so brass bells dot the route; ring them to announce your coming to any foraging black bears.

Southern Alps

Revered as a spiritual place for mountain worship since ancient times, the Minami Alps are a UNESCO Biosphere Reserve. More rain falls here than in many other parts of Japan, and alpine flora, tea fields, and fruit orchards flourish in the fertile soil. Ten peaks surpass 10,000 feet (3,048 m), including Japan's second highest, Mount Kitadake, making the range a playground for adventure-minded hikers and climbers. A popular circuit takes in the triple-crowned cluster of Mount Ainodake, Mount Kitadake, and Mount Notori. Do as the locals do and recover afterward in the area's natural hot springs.

HIGHLIGHTS

• Walk through the lush Kiso Valley on an Edo-era footpath once frequented by samurais and shoguns.

• Watch an unforgettable sunrise from Mount Fuji's sacred summit.

• Take in the spectacular highland scenery of the Kamikochi plateau on winding hiking trails.

9-DAY ITINERARY

Day 1

Starting in Chengdu, follow the G318 National Highway west along the Dadu River. Today's 255-mile (410.3 km) drive leads past 14,101-foot (4,297.9 m) Zheduo Mountain, the first of the trip's parade of towering peaks. Stop for the night in Xinduqiao, a postcard-perfect town known and named for its bridge over the Liqi River.

Day 2

From Xinduqiao, the tour continues west toward the Yalong region, considered the cradle of Tibetan culture. Shortly after the halfway point on today's 240-mile (386.2 km) drive, you'll stop in Litang, one of world's highest elevation (nearly 13,000 feet/ 3,962.4 m above sea level) settlements. Litang has a Wild West vibe (evidenced by the cowboy hats and grazing yaks) and is home to an impressive Tibetan Buddhist monastery, which you can visit. Continue west to Batang, a historic Tea Horse Road stopover.

Day 3

Today's drive is shorter (160 miles/257.4 km), but white-knuckle-rugged on mainly dirt and gravel (and often rock-strewn) roads. Tours go slowly as the highway winds along deep river gorges, clings to sheer cliffs, and crosses up and over snow-covered Dongda La pass, elevation 17,000 feet (5,181.6 m). Snap the requisite selfie at the border sign on the Jinshan River Bridge connecting Sichuan to Tibet.

Day 4

See Tibetan nomads tending grazing yaks, horses, and sheep on the drive across the Bangda Grassland toward Yela Shan, a

mountain pass known less for its elevation and more for its stomach-churning descent through 72 hairpin curves. Today's drive covers about 125 miles (201.1 km), ending at Rakwa Tso, a stunning glacier-fed lake.

Day 5

This day's 85-mile (136.7 km) route passes Midui Glacier, near the headwaters of the world's highest river, Yarlung Tsangpo. A short hike offers views of the bottom of the glacier, showing its alarmingly rapid retreat (it is about 13 percent smaller than it was in the early 2000s).

Day 6

Prepare to be amazed by 143 continuous miles (230.1 km) of breathtaking views, beginning with the ginormous and jagged canyon of Yarlung Tsangpo—called the "Everest of Rivers" for an average route elevation topping 13,000 feet (3,962.4 m)—and ending in Nyingchi, eastern Tibet's largest city, which is blanketed with blooming peach trees in spring.

Day 7

The last long drive (260 miles/418.4 km) of the trip leads to sky-high Lhasa (elevation 11,970 feet/3,648.4 m), a center for Buddhist pilgrimages exuding a mystical atmosphere. From Nyingchi, follow the path of the Nyang River through the verdant valleys and lofty passes of the Hengduan Mountains, considered a global biodiversity hotspot. After crossing over 16,646-foot (5,073.7 m) Mila Pass, the route descends into the Lhasa Valley via the new Lhasa-Nyingchi High Grade Highway opened in late 2018. Approaching Lhasa, catch your first views of the magnificent Potala Palace, a UNESCO World Heritage site and highest palace in the world, perched on Red Mountain at 12,139 feet (3,699.9 m) above sea level.

Days 8 and 9

Spend at least two days exploring Lhasa's Buddhist pilgrimage sites, beginning with 1,300-year-old Potala Palace, the Dalai Lama's winter residence. Tour the gardens of neighboring Norbulingka, the Dalai Lama's summer palace, and adjacent Jokhang, considered Tibet's most sacred temple. Listen for the lilting chanting of monks as you meander the ancient halls of Drepung Monastery. Observe the spirited and theatrical debates held by the resident monks at Sera Monastery. Visit historic Ganden Monastery, considered one of the "Three Great Temples" along with the Sera and the Drepung monasteries, also in Lhasa. Be sure to tour Barkhor Street, site of the city's old market.

OPPOSITE: The Potala Palace sits at 12,139 feet (3,700 m), making it the highest palace in the world. ABOVE: A young Thuma Tibetan nomad

Once Upon a Time in Mongolia

By Erin Craig

THE TSAATAN HAVE HERDED REINDEER through the subarctic taiga forest for centuries—first in their native Tuva and then, when borders were redrawn under Soviet influence in 1944, in Mongolia. They've become a tourist attraction only in the internet age, as the world's hidden corners have been discovered by search engines.

That's not to say it's easy to get there. The taiga is remote, even by Mongolian standards, and overland travel is time-consuming. Mongolia is three times the size of California, but it has fewer miles of paved roads than Rhode Island.

The sky clears to ocean blue as the car lurches up the edge of the taiga. Our Tsaatan host, Delgermagnai Enkhbaatar, is waiting with the horses. Though we see snow on the nearby mountains, our route is mostly swamp. Our mounts stagger through the bog like drunks. We arrive at camp in chilly darkness.

A lake mirrors the rising mood. Reindeer stand spindly legged around the family's conical shelter, or ortz. The sky is streaked with shooting stars. *Rats,* I think. *This might just be a little bit magical.*

"The Tsaatan are not an 'undiscovered tribe,'" admonishes the herding community's website. Yes, they have a website. And *Tsaatan* means "people with reindeer" in Mongolian—not their native language. The herders call themselves Dukha. "You will not be the first or last person they have hosted," the website continues. "They are a modern people who have welcomed visitors from all over the world."

We pass a few of these visitors on our way into the taiga on horseback, their nylon waterproof jackets vivid against

---

BELOW: Tsaatan riders leave winter camp on a caribou caravan through the Hunkher Mountains. OPPOSITE: A Tsaatan elder brews tea over a wood fire.

the darkening forest. Our guides greet each other warmly. The foreigners exchange tight little nods, each regarding the others as inter-lopers. Then we ride on, pretending the encounter hadn't happened.

For all our arrogance, it quickly becomes apparent that the only lost tribe on the taiga is us. We'd armed ourselves against physical remoteness with maps and GPS, but there is no app for cultural dislocation.

This isn't just embarrassing but potentially dangerous. The taiga isn't a forgiving landscape. Enkhbaatar had bear and wolf teeth among the carved trinkets he sold. Hypothermia is a real possibility, even in August. I am an experienced traveler, but I have brought nothing useful to the experience besides a can-do attitude.

Meanwhile, Enkhbaatar's family is clearly at home with both their ways and ours. The kids know how to swipe through smartphone apps. Most of their play, however, mimics the adults' work—making fires, fetching water, tending the animals.

My ineptitude is brought home when Enkhbaatar demonstrates how to steer with the single guide rope. We are interrupted by a strange sound: a "Für Elise" ringtone. Without a word, Enkhbaatar hands the rope to his child and disappears into the ortz. "*Baina uu?*" I hear him answer the phone. My own cell hasn't picked up a signal for days.

I abruptly realize I am sitting on a reindeer with no clue how to ride it. If it bolts, I'll be halfway to Siberia before Enkhbaatar returns. I look at the 18-month-old holding my reins. "You've got this, right?"

Storytelling is reflective. The words we choose to describe the Tsaatan—*mystical, lost, exploited, endangered, noble, wise*—imply our own roles in the story as well. We might cast ourselves as adventurers, self-righteous skeptics, or even the comic relief. None of these versions are really about the herders at all; it's just us wandering around the taiga looking for a mirror.

Such reflections are as problematic as they are compelling. They invariably lead to discussions of "authenticity," which is just the erudite version of talking behind another culture's back. The topic comes up one afternoon as we sit in Enkhbaatar's guest ortz, wearing the carved-antler necklaces his wife sold us as souvenirs. Is tourism undermining the Tsaatan's traditional culture? Does the fact that others have come here before us invalidate our own experience?

Meanwhile, one ortz over, Enkhbaatar's dad has satellite TV. He powers it with solar panels hauled into the wilderness on the backs of reindeer. The family knows all about the outside world, takes what they want, and are content to keep the rest at a distance.

Sitting in camp on our last night, I count shooting stars against the sweep of the Milky Way. The sky shimmers yellow at the edges as a full moon rises behind the mountains. Such sights are indelible, no matter how the story might be told. I am just glad I have a part in it.

• *Erin Craig is a freelance writer based in Asia.*

OPPOSITE: A Tsaatan boy wears a traditional Mongolian nomad outfit as he rides his family's reindeer. ABOVE: A Tsaatan yurt sits below a rainbow in the stunning landscape of Taiga.

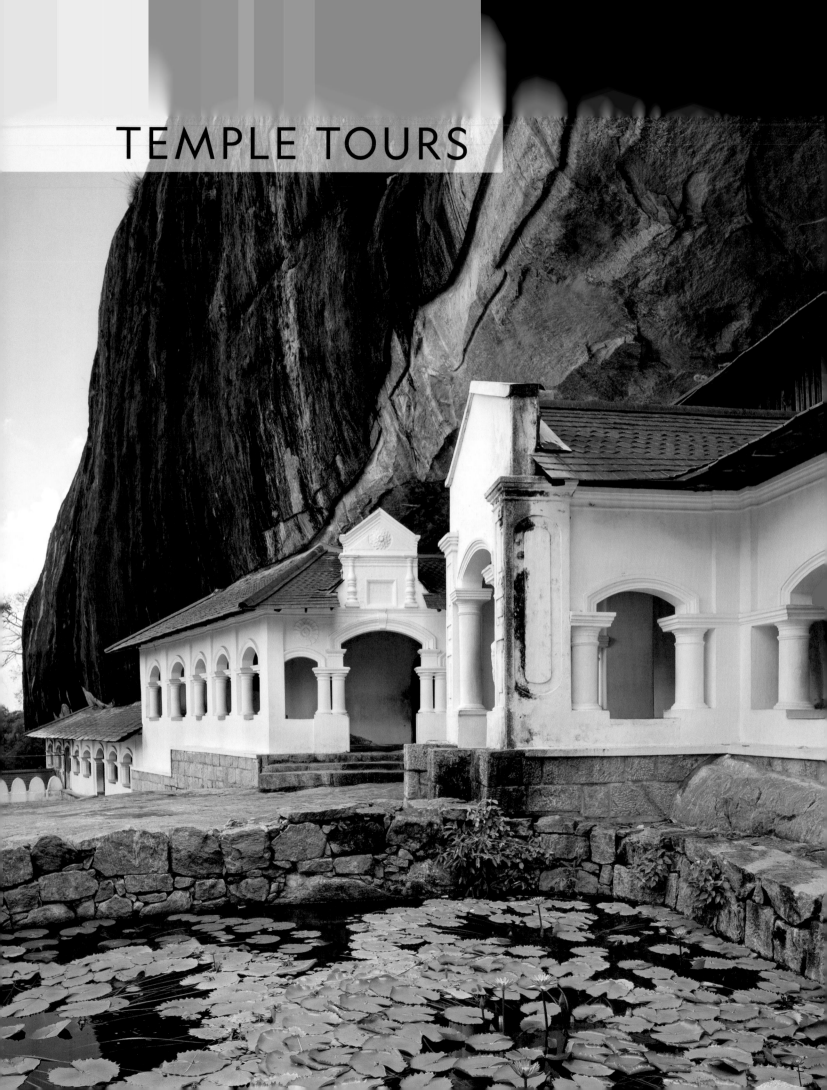

1 WAT PHOU, LAOS

A trip to Laos promises temple tours for every mode of travel—whether that's cycling to golden Pha That Luang in Vientiane or kayaking to Wat Phou's pre-Angkorian Khmer ruins. Dating back to the sixth century, the Wat Phou complex is a series of temples, shrines, and waterworks, ambling through lush river valleys between the Mekong River and Lingaparvata Mountain.

2 TEMPLE TRAILS, JAPAN

One of only two ancient pilgrimage trails recognized by UNESCO, Japan's Kumano Kodo weaves shrine to temple to hot spring through Kii Mountain forests and 800-year-old trees, ending at Kumano Nachi Taisha, a vermillion shrine framed by Japan's tallest single-drop waterfall.

3 DAMBULLA CAVE TEMPLES, SRI LANKA

Dambulla harbors the biggest and best preserved cave temple complex in Sri Lanka. More than 80 cave temples dot the region, many over 2,000 years old. The five Golden Temple caves that are open to the public feature hundreds of statues, a 47-foot-long (14 m) reclining Buddha, and over 22,000 square feet (2,043 sq m) of murals.

4 BEOPJUSA TEMPLE, SOUTH KOREA

Korea's largest statue, the 108-foot-tall (33 m) golden "Future Buddha," sits at the sixth-century Beopjusa Temple in Songnisan National Park. Less than four hours from Seoul, the temple complex includes a 17th-century wooden pagoda, elaborate muraled halls, and three national treasures.

5 LAOJUN MOUNTAIN TEMPLES, CHINA

The golden-roofed temples topping China's Laojun Mountain brush the sky at an overall height of more than 7,000 feet (2,134 m). Join the hundreds of Taoists who climb the temple path's steep stairs on their knees to visit this former refuge of Chinese philosopher Laozi. Afterward visit the ancient stone carvings in Luoyang City's 1,700-year-old Longmen grottoes or tour White Horse Temple, the oldest Buddhist temple in China.

6 TAKTSANG GOEMBA, BHUTAN

Wedged 10,000 feet (3,048 m) above sea level, Bhutan's multilevel Tiger's Nest temple commemorates the granite cliff site where lotus-born Guru Rinpoche came to meditate. The guru may have arrived by flying tiger, but today's travelers hike a steep trail past thundering waterfalls and bird-filled forests. Take your time exploring Taktsang's four glowing temple spaces, eight caves, and colorful balconies.

7 CAVE TEMPLES, INDIA

Ellora's rock-cut caves contain a warren of Hindu, Buddhist, and Jain temples, some dating back to 200 B.C. The Kailasa complex includes a parade of life-size elephant sculptures and depictions of a 10-headed demon king. Check out the waterfall near cave 29 and the dramatic *chaitya*—an arched sanctuary—in cave 10. Travelers should consider trekking to Phugtal, a cliff-clinging monastery and temple in the Lungnak Valley.

8 BADRINATH TEMPLE, INDIA

Located on the cusp of snowy Tibet, Uttarakhand's colorful Badrinath Temple is the most important Vishnu temple and the final holy shrine on India's pilgrimage route in the Garhwal Himalaya. Plan your trip for May, June, September, or October to avoid both blizzards and monsoons.

9 AYUTTHAYA HISTORICAL PARK, THAILAND

After a morning swim under Erawan National Park's seven-tiered waterfall, head three hours east to the ancient temples of historic Ayutthaya, once one of the most powerful cities in the world. Visit Bang Pa-in, the royal palaces, the temple in a tree at Wat Bang Kung, and numerous other Ayutthaya wats on Grasshopper Adventures' bike-and-ferry tour out of Bangkok.

10 KATHMANDU VALLEY, NEPAL

Nicknamed "the City of Temples," Kathmandu is steepled with prayer-flag-fringed UNESCO sites and exquisite Newari architecture. Circle the enormous stupa at Boudhanath. Climb up to the "holy monkey" temple of Swoyambhunath. And visit fifth-century Pashupatinath during *bagmati aarati,* a lamp-lit evening ritual of song and dance along the holy Bagmati River.

OPPOSITE: The Royal Rock Temple is built into cliffs in Ceylon. ABOVE: A performer puts on a spectacular display outside the Beopjusa Buddhist temple.

VIETNAM

PADDLING AND PEDALING VIETNAM

Journey along beguiling bike paths and ancient waterways.

Curving more than 1,000 miles (1,610 km) along the Indochina Peninsula, Vietnam entices rafters and bikers to explore its green mountains, terraced rice paddies, and fascinating sea caves.

The country has a strong cycling culture. In Ho Chi Minh City (Saigon), the largest city, it's been estimated that there are more than two million bicycles, and millions more motorbikes, so active travelers will be in good company as they explore the country on two wheels. Highway 1, the site of many critical battles during the Vietnam War, runs the length of the country from its northern border with China to Nam Can at the southern tip. A favorite route for cyclists, its scenic sections trace the coastline of the South China Sea. A bike is also the best way to roam historic cities, including the ancient capital of Hanoi, founded in the early 11th century and inhabited since prehistoric times, and the coastal retreat of Hoi An, whose Old Town is a time capsule of a seafaring port from centuries past.

Vietnam's endless waterways offer exploration of a different kind. By canoe or kayak, discover the country's more natural wonders, from the immense Mekong Delta to mountain-shadowed Ba Be Lake to the incredible karst formations in Halong Bay and Phong Nha-Ke Bang National Park.

This is the land—and sea—of adventure opportunity.

Travel Tips

WHEN TO GO: The best time for cycling and kayaking trips is October through February, when the rainy season has ended and temperatures are cooler.

PLANNING: Vehicles nominally drive on the right side of the road in Vietnam but can converge in all directions when traffic gets heavy. Right of way is determined by the largest vehicle—meaning it's rarely the biker. Operators that offer active trips include National Geographic Expeditions, G Adventures, and World Expeditions.

WEBSITES: vietnam.travel; nationalgeo graphic.com/expeditions; gadventures .com; worldexpeditions.com

A floating village in Ha Long Bay, Vietnam

WHAT TO DO

Cycle Hanoi

Vietnam's charming capital offers delightful urban bike rides to culture-rich sites, from impressive monuments like the Ho Chi Minh Mausoleum and 11th-century Temple of Literature to the Old Quarter's fascinating den of narrow alleys, filled with silk and lacquerware shops and street food stalls serving steaming bowls of pho. For a less congested ride, head to the cycling route along the Red River (with separate lanes for bicycles and motorcycles) and wheel along three bridges over picturesque West Lake for a view of Tran Quoc Pagoda, the oldest Buddhist temple in Hanoi.

Kayak Halong Bay

Studded with nearly 2,000 karst pinnacles that rise from jade-green sea, Halong Bay is one of Vietnam's most magical places. Take to the water to examine the limestone islets up close, discovering turquoise lagoons, hidden grottoes, and elegant arches that glow purple at sunset.

Bike Sapa

The area around the town of Sapa, located in the towering peaks of Lao Cai Province at an elevation of 4,920 feet (1,500 m), offers dazzling scenery for intrepid mountain bikers: Wisps of clouds cling to forested peaks and terraced rice paddies cascade down the hillsides. A selection of rugged trails pass by welcoming hill tribe villages populated by Hmong, Zay, and Yao peoples. Come in September, harvesttime, when the paddies turn a brilliant yellow.

Canoe Ba Be Lake

Known as the "emerald of northern Viet-nam," Ba Be is the country's largest natural lake. A peaceful canoe trip along the five-mile (8 km) lake, located in Bac Can Province, shows off the limestone mountains, deep valleys, caves, and waterfalls of the surrounding Ba Be National Park. The richly biodiverse park is home to hundreds of unnamed plant species, as well as ethnic minorities such as the Tay people, who build their homes on stilts near the lake.

Cycle Hoi An

The streets of Hoi An's Old Town—named a UNESCO World Heritage site for its exceptional preservation of a 15th to 19th-century Southeast Asian trading port—are closed to motorized traffic most of the day, allowing for a leisurely ride past ancient bridges, bustling markets, and lantern-lit alleys. Pedal out into the countryside to visit artisan villages such as Cam Thanh, Kim Bong, and Thanh Ha, where you can learn about traditional boat building, woodworking, and pottery making.

Kayak the Cham Islands

Located about 11 miles (18 km) offshore from Hoi An, the eight Cham Islands are a UNESCO World Biosphere Reserve. The surrounding waters of Cu Lao Cham Marine Park provide a protected habitat for some 135 species of coral, five species of lobster, and more than 200 types of fish, including the endangered (and enormous) six-foot-long (1.8 m) humphead wrasse. Due to monsoon weather in the winter, the islands are accessible for only seven months of the year, which helps preserve their unspoiled state and variety of wildlife. Paddle or dive the crystal-clear water to uncover its treasures below the surface, pristine beaches, and verdant jungle.

Bike Hai Van Pass

Hai Van, meaning "ocean cloud pass," traverses a spur of the Annamite Range, twisting through 13 miles (21 km) of rugged terrain along the coastal route between Hue and Da Nang. This is for serious bikers only: It's a nearly seven-mile (11 km) climb to the top, much of it at a 7 percent gradient. The breathtaking ascent (literally) will get your blood pumping and thighs burning, but the reward is unparalleled views of misty mountains and azure ocean, followed by an exhilarating descent to the sea.

OPPOSITE: With tree-lined hills for scenery, a boat glides through Ba Be Lake. RIGHT: Cyclists make their way past lush green rice paddies in the outskirts of Vietnam.

Kayak Phong Na Cave

A UNESCO World Heritage site, the extraordinary Phong Nha-Ke Bang National Park contains the oldest karst mountains in Asia, formed about 400 million years ago. Daring kayakers can plunge into a vast underground river network that runs through hundreds of caverns, including Phong Na Cave, one of the largest wet caves in the world. Lit only by headlamps, paddle more than a mile (1.7 km) over bottle-green waters past eerie grottoes and fantastically shaped stalactites.

Cycle and Paddle the Mekong Delta

With its ultraflat landscape engraved with a maze of rivers and streams, the Mekong Delta is a haven for biking and boating. Known as the "rice bowl" of Vietnam, the vast fertile delta supports endless rice paddies and floating gardens that stretch to the horizon. Drift down tree-lined canals spanned by bamboo-pole bridges; then cycle to fruit plantations and riverside communities that make handicrafts out of coconut fibers.

Bike Cat Tien National Park

Covering some 280 square miles (720 sq km) in Dong Nai Province about 93 miles (150 km) north of Ho Chi Minh City, Cat Tien National Park is a wonderland for wildlife. The mountain biking path crunches over volcanic rocks as it winds through the park's lowland tropical rainforest and wetlands past lava tubes and towering teakwood trees. Protected in the dense foliage are wild Asian elephants, sun bears, lumbering gaurs, golden-cheeked gibbons, crested serpent eagles, and possibly some of the last remaining endangered Indochinese tigers.

HIGHLIGHTS

• Kayak subterranean rivers in the caves of Phong Nha-Ke Bang National Park.

• Take a bike ride through Hoi An's historic Old Town and nearby artisan villages.

• Spot Asian elephants and sun bears as you ride in Cat Tien National Park.

Tourists are paddled in bow boats beneath karst caves in Ha Long Bay.

INDIA

SECRETS OF KASHMIR

Experience a Mughal paradise on Earth.

Mughal Emperor Jahangir considered Kashmir—the summer resort of royalty in northernmost India—a paradise on Earth, a place of which "priests had prophesied and poets sung." The Mughals created the Kashmir Valley's enchanting terraced gardens and established the region as a center of arts and crafts. During their rule, Indian Kashmir was confined to the 5,400-square-mile (13,986 sq km) valley, isolated from the rest of the country by snow-covered Himalayan ranges. Today, Kashmir is part of India's Jammu and Kashmir state, which includes Jammu, Kashmir, and Ladakh on the high Tibetan Plateau.

The cool mountain air, crystalline lakes, top-of-the-world views, and sense of being away from it all that once drew Mughal royalty here continues to enthrall travelers today. But anyone venturing to Kashmir has to keep in mind its modern geopolitical realities. India, Pakistan, and China all claim part or all of the wider Kashmir region. India's Jammu and Kashmir state covers the southern and eastern portion of the region and is separated from Pakistan Kashmir by the 435-mile-long (700 km) Line of Control military border. While travel within Jammu and Kashmir generally is safe, the political subtext and geographical barriers have kept Emperor Jahangir's paradise a secret to much of the outside world.

Travel Tips

WHEN TO GO: May to mid-October for most activities, since roads over mountain passes typically close November to April; mid-October to November for Kashmir stag rutting season; December to March for snow leopard tours.

PLANNING: Many tour operators, such as National Geographic Expeditions, Responsible Travel, and Thomas Cook, offer guided expeditions to Jammu and Kashmir. Dress modestly since the region is predominantly Muslim.

WEBSITES: jktourism.org; kashmirtreks .in; nationalgeographic.com/expeditions; responsibletravel.com; thomascook.in

Boats dot the waters of Dal Lake.

WHAT TO DO

Ride a High-Elevation Gondola

Gulmarg, situated on the lower slopes of 14,403-foot (4,390 m) Mount Apharwat, is a small ski area boasting big-thrill free-ride runs and one of the world's highest cable cars. Expert skiers with avalanche equipment can roam the area's ungroomed, off-piste trails, provided they stay clear of the hotly contested Indian and Pakistani Line of Control located just north of the resort. No skiing, however, is required to ride the Gulmarg Gondola to 12,293 feet (3,747 m) above sea level. The up-and-back trip (with time to hike around at the top) provides top-of-the-world views of the Kashmir Valley backed by snowcapped Himalaya peaks.

Pedal Through the Remote Gurez Valley

Be among the handful of visitors to experience Kashmir's green and isolated Gurez region on a guided biking expedition along the Gurez Valley Cycling Trail. Straddling the Kishanganga River near the Indian and Pakistani Line of Control, Gurez is ready-made for adventure with its granite cliffs, dense fir and pine forests, and miles of lightly traveled mountain roads. June to September, mountain biking outfitters lead multiday treks on high-elevation (mainly above 9,800 feet/ 2,987 m) cycling routes. Expect to bike up to four hours a day and camp in tents. Trek highlights include visiting the remote villages of Ganderbal; biking alongside Dal, Manasbal, and Wular lakes; and pumping up and over Razdan Pass, elevation 11,672 feet (3,557.6 m).

Raft the "Grand Canyon of Asia"

Paddle the Class II to IV rapids of the muddy Zanskar River as it roars through its namesake canyon, commonly called the "Grand Canyon of Asia." The stunning, sheer-wall gorge is located in the remote reaches of Ladakh. Sign on with a white-water outfitter to take a multiday expedition on several sections of the Zanskar as the river surges north toward its confluence with the Indus, which begins in Kashmir and flows through Pakistan on its way to the Arabian Sea. The roughly 45-mile (72.4 km) stretch of the Zanskar between the villages of Nyerak and Nimu is a particularly wild romp featuring multiple Class III and IV rapids, towering rock walls, and a tight squeeze through a narrow passage.

Soar Over Srinagar

Paragliding is taking off as an adventure sport in Srinagar, Jammu and Kashmir's largest city. Mid-April to mid-October, tandem paragliding tours launch from an alpine meadow in the Zabarwan Mountains backing Dal Lake. Fly over the water, surrounding green hills, and the cityscape for bird's-eye views of traditional *shikara* (gondola-like boats), the terraced Nishat Bagh Mughal gardens, and Old Town markets below, as well as the Pir Panjal and Zabarwan mountains in the distance.

See the Kashmir Stag

Dachigam National Park is home to the hangul, or Kashmir stag, considered critically endangered and the only surviving subspecies of the European red deer in Asia. The copper-colored male hangul with its multipronged antlers is frequently featured as a symbol of the state of Jammu and Kashmir. The animals retreat to the highest elevations of the park above the snow line in summer, making fall to early spring (generally mid-October to March) the best time for wildlife-watching. Plan to visit during rutting season (mid-October to November), when the roaring mating calls of the males echo through the low-elevation forests.

Explore Mountaintop Buddhist Monasteries

Ladakh, an isolated, high-altitude desert area opened to tourists only since the 1970s, is a treasure trove of Buddhist cultural relics. The Buddhist enclave on the southern rim of the Karakoram Mountains is home to multistoried, whitewashed monasteries adorned with fluttering prayer flags and often protected by massive statues of Buddha. Tour the Hemis Monastery and its impressive museum to see the

OPPOSITE: A skier sprays powder as he makes his way through the trees in Gulmarg. ABOVE: The Leh Manali Highway traverses the high altitudes of the great Himalayan range.

An endangered snow leopard is captured by remote camera climbing a rocky slope.

copper Buddha statue, gold and silver *stupas* (cone-shaped sites used for Buddhist meditation and worship), ancient murals and prayer wheels, and *thangkas* (a traditional painting on cotton or silk, depicting a Buddhist deity).

Ride a Motorcycle Over Some of the World's Highest Mountain Passes

Elevate your ride on a motorcycle adventure of a lifetime. On two wheels, rumble across four mountain passes topping 13,000 feet (3,962.4 m) near Leh, the largest town in Ladakh. The pass with the greatest elevation, 18,379-foot (5,601.9 m) Khardung La, is the second highest—and among the most dangerous—motorable roads on the planet. While inherently risky due to the altitude, road conditions, and staggeringly steep drop-offs, motorcycle rides across Ladakh are a top tourist draw, with numerous outfitters offering day trips and multiday tours.

Search for the Elusive Snow Leopard

Wild snow leopard sightings are rare, even in Hemis National Park, believed to have the world's densest population of the vulnerable big cats. But for animal lovers with patience, keen eyes, and a willingness to trek (a mule carries your gear) in subzero winter temperatures, a guided expedition in the park could result in a glimpse of the elusive "gray ghosts." Sign on for a small group tour in the Rumbak Valley, best known for wildlife sightings. Even if you don't spot one of the snow leopards, other species, such as Eurasian lynx, red fox, and Tibetan wolf, live in the park and are easier to see against the stark, white winter landscape.

HIGHLIGHTS

• Go white-water rafting through the awe-inspiring "Grand Canyon of Asia."

• Take a motorcycle trip over some of the world's highest mountain passes.

• Embark on a winter expedition in search of the elusive snow leopard in Hemis National Park.

On a Horse in Oman

By Peter Gwin

WHEN I TELL THE HORSE BREEDER that I've come to Oman to ride an Arabian horse, his eyes twinkle, and I think he'll offer to let me ride one of his sublime horses, but he doesn't. Instead, his nephew asks for my notebook and writes down a name.

Days later I'm standing in the shade of a date plantation outside the oasis town of Al Hamra, west of Muscat. Thanks to the old Bedouin and a daisy-chain of contacts, I meet Al Sher, who, as it turns out, is a trainer from stables owned by Oman's monarch, Sultan Qaboos bin Said Al Said, a devoted horse lover. He's agreed to take me on a ride while on a visit to his home village.

He arrives on the back of a dark brown mare, riding barefoot and wearing loose cotton trousers, a long white shirt, and an immaculate Omani prayer cap. He leads behind him another brown mare, and I note that both horses fit one description of classic Arabians: not too tall, wide chests, short ears.

Historians believe that horses were first domesticated in Eurasia, but it can be argued that they were perfected in Arabia. Forged in the brutal conditions of the desert, these horses could withstand heat, cold, and thirst and were highly prized. On a raid or in battle, a Bedouin would trust his life only to an Arabian horse.

I also note that each is outfitted with a traditional Omani saddle, which is little more than a blanket and has no stirrups, forcing a rider to maintain perfect balance and grip the horse with his legs.

I have a bad feeling. There are no soft landing spots to

BELOW: An Omani rider and his horse perform at a Bahla horse festival.
OPPOSITE: Ali Salem Mehsin, 74, who owns the Al Hamri stables in Bidiya, continues to ride in horse festivals.

Nam Wah

With some of the wildest white water in Thailand, the gushing green Nam Wah (Wa) curves and branches through a rural and rarely visited region along the Laotian border. Some 50 miles (80 km) of the river's midsection are commercially rafted, and the most exciting sections necessitate three days and two nights on the river. Trips depart from Nan, a Chinese-influenced, temple-filled town and gateway to the far-flung Doi Phu Kha National Park to the north. It's the only real settlement near this part of the river, but it isn't close; the drive to rafting put-in points can be anywhere from one to two hours. The Wah winds south through deciduous and evergreen forests in the low-lying mountains of the Luang Prabang range, and through Mae Charim (Jarim) National Park, home to diverse birdlife including great hornbills, white-rumped falcons, and an important population of endangered green peafowls (the males of relative blue peafowls are instantly recognizable as peacocks). With 80-odd regularly spaced low-grade stretches and 20 noteworthy Class III and IV rapids, the river regularly threatens to buck passengers and moves along at a steady clip. Get out in the sleepier sections to swim and look for giant Asian river frogs. On its lower reaches, it's also possible to ride the river on traditional bamboo rafts.

Pai

Farther west in Thailand's Mae Hong Son Province abutting the border with Myanmar are two jungle-clad intertwined white-water rivers ripe for rafting. Some choose an adventure on the Khong, navigating around 28 miles (45 km) over as many as 15 sets of Class IV rapids as it winds to its confluence with the Pai. On the journey, take a short

trek to swim in the pools below Su Sa waterfall's wide cascade, tackle a 23-foot-high (7 m) cliff jump, and later soak in some hot springs. Though it can be accomplished in one long day, it's worth taking your time in this area. Two-day expeditions along the Middle Pai river starting in Muang Pang traverser 60 or so rapids on a 43.5-mile (70 km) route through rocky gorges and jungles filled with wild mango before ending in the picturesque Thai-Burmese city of Mae Hong Son. It also has more waterfalls, hot springs, and mud baths. Both routes end near the northern boundary of Namtok Mae Surin National Park, home to gibbons, bears, palm civets, and even a few tigers. Some visitors couple regional rafting trips with trekking, caving, and visits to wildlife sanctuaries or Lahu, Lisu, and Shan traditional villages.

Mae Taeng

A 90-minute drive northwest of Chiang Mai, northern Thailand's largest city, the Mae Taeng River awaits. Seven miles (12 km) of frothing rain-swollen brown water—including a rip-roaring stretch of Class III and IV rapids—negotiates the Mae Taeng Valley past rice paddies and small villages. With opportunities to see domesticated elephants and birds like the wire-tailed swallow and chestnut-capped babbler, rafting here makes for a worthy day trip from the bustling ancient city. Even more exciting? From November through January, Siam River Tours offers overnights around the full moon. After dark, rafters venture back onto the water to take on a tamer 2.5-mile (4 km) stretch flashlight free. See the route illuminated by soft moonbeams and listen to the nighttime sounds of the jungle.

Nam Ou

Coursing south toward artsy Luang Prabang, the sleepy Nam Ou, a Mekong tributary, winds through spectacular scenery. It's not exactly white water, but there can be some Class II and III rapids, as well as

exciting whirlpools and eddies, when water levels are low and rocks are exposed. Still, the wide, green thoroughfare is popular with kayakers for good reason: Vine-draped trees blanket pointy karst hills; rural villages line its banks; and water buffalo, elephants, and saffron-clad monks bathe riverside. Don't be surprised if you're not alone. Just off the white-sand beaches, throngs of other watercraft—including bamboo rafts pulled through the water by guides with long poles—gather to visit the thousands of golden Buddha statues tucked inside the sacred Pak Ou Cave.

Nam Tha

Outfitters load rubber rafts and kayaks into the Nam Tha River outside Luang Namtha for day tours that navigate small stretches of Class II and III rapids. While the river isn't a particularly wild ride, this remote waterway in north-central Laos offers incredible culture and wildlife-spotting opportunities. The river meanders along the eastern boundary of Nam Ha National Protected area, an 860-square-mile (2224 sq km) preserve near the Chinese border. Forest-dependent Khamu, Akha, and Lanten tribal villages inside the park welcome visitors, and villagers are often employed by rafting companies to prepare a customary lunch over an open fire. For longer immersion in their traditional way of life, opt for multiday rafting trips or rafting/ trekking combos that include village home-stays. On the river, keep your eyes peeled for other jungle residents: countless color-ful butterflies, silver pheasant, huge guar, barking deer, Asian elephants, and the elusive clouded leopard.

HIGHLIGHTS

• See remote wildlands and visit tribal villages in otherwise hard-to-access reaches of Southeast Asia.

• Experience the thrill of navigating chal-lenging Class III to IV rapids; then camp out under the stars.

• Watch for riverside life including gib-bons, birds, frogs, domesticated buffalo, and elephants.

The river reflects the lights of Wat Johngkham as the sun sets.

SEE PLACES BEFORE
THEY DISAPPEAR

1 THE GREAT WALL OF CHINA

More than 10,000 miles (16,000 km) long and more than 2,000 years old, the Great Wall of China loses bricks to time and tourists every day. Despite recent efforts to survey the damage and reinforce unstable sections, preserving the entire structure seems nearly impossible. Limit your footprint by hiking the less busy Jiankou section or touring via helicopter.

2 HIMALAYAN GLACIERS, NEPAL

Scientists estimate that more than one-third of the glaciers in the Himalaya could disappear by 2100. So even if you don't plan to summit Everest, the 3,000-plus glaciers are worth a visit *now*. An autumn hike across lakes, remote Sherpa villages, ancient stupas, and Ngozumpa—Nepal's longest glacier—promises the most stable and clear weather.

3 STARGAZING HOT SPOTS, CHINA

Stargazing has become difficult in China: Hong Kong's light pollution may be the worst in the world, Chengdu is building an artificial moon, and Beijing's smoggy ceiling has been dubbed an "airpocalypse." Nevertheless, eager adventurers can still find space to look to the skies. The lush gorges of the Yangtze remain one of the world's top night-sky destinations.

4 ITA THAO VILLAGE, SUN MOON LAKE, TAIWAN

Taiwan's largest and only natural lake is a fiercely blue, mountain-ringed paradise. Sun Moon Lake's 19-mile (29 km) cycling loop weaves along verdant hills, Buddhist temples, and car-free suspension bridges. Sun Moon is also home to Taiwan's smallest recognized tribe. Like many other indigenous groups, the Thao lose ties to tradition every year. Visit Ita Thao now to see traditional dancing and bamboo fish trap weaving while it's still being practiced.

OPPOSITE: The entire Great Wall of China spans some 5,500 miles (8,850 km) from the Korean border into the Gobi. ABOVE: A brown bear walks along a river in Kamchatka, Russia.

5 KAMCHATKA, RUSSIA

UNESCO is in love with Kamchatka, designating the peninsula as a "landscape of exceptional natural beauty with its large symmetrical volcanoes, lakes, wild rivers and spectacular coastline." Hikers and fly fishermen are in love with it too, thanks to super-hard-to-get-to fishing holes, pristine scenery, and epic crater hiking. Still, in a land where sometimes four volcanoes erupt at once, it's best to go soon.

6 THE SUNDARBANS, INDIA

At almost 346,000 acres (1 million hectares), the Sundarbans is one of the world's largest mangrove networks—home to more than 260 bird species, estuarine crocodiles, king cobras, dolphins, tree-climbing fish, sea turtles, and endangered royal Bengal tigers. Unfortunately, sea levels are rising faster here than anywhere else in the world, threatening endangered species and millions of residents alike. Boats are the best avenue for exploring this endangered place.

7 BAGAN, MYANMAR

As a result of earthquakes, erosion, and irresponsible tourists, fewer than half of Myanmar's famous Bagan temples are still standing. That said, there are still more than 2,000 temples and pagodas to choose from. Consider exploring the area by electric bike, horse cart, or hot-air balloon. (See page 254.) Due to preservation efforts, temple climbing is discouraged.

8 LAKE POYANG, CHINA

Situated in the middle of the third longest river in the world, you'd assume Lake Poyang had constant replenishment. But with the dry season starting earlier every year, the freshwater lake has receded more than ever before, shrinking the habitat of rare finless porpoises, endangered Siberian cranes, and thousands of migratory birds. Birding excursions paddle out from Nanchang toward the north shore of Lake Poyang to see egrets, spoonbills, storks, swan geese, and more.

9 FLOATING MARKETS, MEKONG RIVER

Already increasingly dependent on the tourism industry, the Mekong River's spectacular floating markets are quickly disappearing as development alters the interest in local commerce. Whether you navigate the Mekong by kayak, rowboat, glider, or onshore by mountain bike, make time for fresh watermelon, local coffee, and Vietnamese noodles served from a local sampan.

10 SHIRETOKO NATIONAL PARK, JAPAN

One of Japan's last remaining stretches of unspoiled wilderness, eastern Hokkaido's Shiretoko National Park is a hiker's paradise. A boardwalk prevents damage to surrounding wetlands, volcanic lakes, and snowy mountains. Seasonal freezing and thawing of drift ice (a delicate process susceptible to climate change) supports the park's unique ecosystem of phytoplankton, salmon, trout, endangered Blakiston's fish owls, and one of the highest populations of brown bears in the world.

SPELUNKING IN TOKYO'S HIDDEN CAVES

Explore the depths of Japan in a way you never thought possible.

Tokyo is an amazing place. The experiences that you can have there are as varied as they are wonderful. Some of them are deep and meaningful. Others are spectacular and full of fantasy. There are towering skyscrapers, neon lights, fantastical eats, and robotic wonders—not to mention modern technology and innovation that will blow your mind. What you don't expect on a trip to Tokyo is a nature retreat.

But for those who like to step outside (nay, underside) the city for a little adventure, one of the best experiences you can have is in Okutama. Located in the western part of Tokyo, about two hours outside the city center, this small town— population about 5,000—plays host to a truly natural experience, often hard to find in the concrete and glass showroom of the city. It comes in the form of 250-million-year-old limestone stone caves. Inside, you'll find hidden wonders and rock formations, often lit in colorful neon lights (you are in Tokyo, after all). Combine your underground adventure with the towering trees, rushing waterfalls, and robust wildlife on offer at Mount Odake and Mount Mitake. These caves are not something you'd typically expect from a metropolis known for electronics, but that's the beautiful thing about Tokyo and the Tama region.

Travel Tips

WHEN TO GO: March to May and September to November are the best times visit, when rainfall is low and temperatures are mild.

PLANNING: To get to the Mount Odake Caves, take the train to the JR Musashi Itsukaichi station and then the Kamiyozawa bus to the Ootake Shonyudo Iriguchi stop. To reach the Nippara Caves, take the train to Okutama station and then the bus to Shonyudo bus stop, which is a five-minute walk from the entrance.

WEBSITES: gotokyo.org/en; japan.travel/en

The entrance to the Ootake Limestone Caves

Ootake Limestone Caves

Okutama opens your world up to two different cave experiences. The first, the Ootake Limestone Caves, were discovered in 1961 and opened to the public in 1962. They offer a great chance to explore the great outdoors and the great beyond that lies beneath.

For anyone who has ever wanted to really experience caving, this is the perfect place to start. The cave gives visitors a chance to step out of their comfort zone and explore an easily accessible adventure. You are handed a helmet on arrival. As you get deeper inside the 98-foot (300 m) cave, you will soon find yourself climbing up and crouching down to squeeze through the narrow openings. The caves have a campground located on-site, so you can take your time while exploring both above- and belowground without having to rush back to your hotel in the bustling center of Tokyo.

Mount Mitake

At Mount Mitake, you have two choices. The first is to hike up from the base, which takes about an hour and is roughly 1.5 miles (2.5 km) to the summit, 3,047 feet (929 m) above sea level. At the top, you are greeted not only by a breathtaking view, but also by the Musashi-Mitake Shrine, believed to be a place of worship for nearly 2,000 years.

The hike itself is a nature lover's paradise: diverse plants like the colorful frost flower and animals like the Japanese giant flying squirrel reside here.

For those who want to experience views without the effort, a cable car takes you to the top. It costs 590 yen (U.S. $5.29) to ride one way and the experience takes about six minutes to reach the top.

OPPOSITE: A spelunker peers through nooks and crannies of the Ootake Limestone Caves. ABOVE: The Nippara Limestone Caves are lit in color.

Mount Odake

You won't want to miss the summit of Mount Odake. The hike to the top takes an hour or so from Mount Mitake, and the views from the 4,156.8 feet (1,267 m) summit are well worth the effort. The panoramic vista of the surrounding countryside is breathtaking and brings with it the renewed and fresh feeling of hiking pride only a summit can.

Nippara Limestone Caves

The Nippara Limestone Caves—a plethora of natural geological formations—are another way to explore the depths of Japan. You'll see stalactites and stalagmites, as well as get a fascinating glimpse into some of the underground shrines and holy places of Japan. Like the Ootake Limestone Caves, the Nippara Limestone Caves are located near Okutama, in the Tama region of Tokyo.

The first thing you'll notice when you're inside the cave area is the temperature, where it remains a constant 52°F (11°C) all year. The next thing you'll notice is the surreal beauty of the rock formations that both hang down from the ceiling (stalactites) and reach toward the sky from the ground (stalagmites). To add to the experience, the caves have been lit up by typical-of-Tokyo LED lights that showcase the spectacular patterns in the rocks.

There's a sense of calm within the caves, which has drawn people to them for centuries. The Nippara Limestone Caves were a holy place for Buddhist monks of the Shugendo sect and, as a result, shrines, statues and other holy relics that date back to at least A.D. 774 can be found inside. Be sure to check out the Suikinkutsu site, where a pot buried in the ground catches droplets of water and resonates with a soft hum. It's a transcendent experience.

Tama River

There is no better way to end your day of hikes and underground exploration than with a cool soak in the calm Tama River. Located near the Mitake train station, it's the perfect spot to wind down and relax before heading back to bustling Tokyo. At the river, you can swim, rent fishing rods (and cook what you catch), or just soak everything in from the shore.

HIGHLIGHTS

• Escape the bustling city to explore two underground limestone caves.

• Hike the summit of two mountains for breathtaking views and holy sites.

• Cool off in a river less than two hours outside Tokyo's city center.

Walkers make the easy climb to the summit of Mount Mitake.

JAPAN

OFF THE BEATEN PATH

From picturesque ski slopes to mineral hot springs, there's more to Japan than Tokyo.

Travelers find plenty of excuses to visit Tokyo, but there's another reason to make the trip: Japan's capital is an ideal jumping-off point for adventure. There are surprising excursions all within a few hours' radius of the city where you can ski, soak, or savor and be back to Tokyo in a flash. Ski on the island of Hokkaido, soak in the hot springs below the mountains of Hakone, and dine on Japanese delicacies in Japan's third largest city, Osaka.

And then there is Kyoto, another hot spot just starting to attract tourists. The high-speed *skinkansen* ("bullet train") gets you to this former imperial capital 281 miles (452 km) from Tokyo in just two and a quarter hours. What awaits in Japan's seventh largest city is truly phenomenal: UNESCO World Heritage sites, beautiful shrines, wild places, and wildlife. Kyoto is a true embodiment of Old Japan, awash with beautiful vestiges of its past glory. Beyond the futuristic train station lies a city with centuries-old wonders, breathtaking temples, serene Zen gardens, narrow cobbled alleyways, bustling markets, and a vibrant nightlife. By effortlessly blending the past and present, Koyto is an alluring destination for history buffs, art lovers, gourmands, and outdoor enthusiasts—and will make you forget all about the Tokyo you left behind.

Travel Tips

WHEN TO GO: Tokyo and Kyoto are hot and humid in the summer and cold in the winter, so visit on the shoulder seasons: September to November and March through April.

PLANNING: If you're planning on taking any trips from Tokyo's city center, it's worth buying the 7-Day Japan Rail Pass, which costs about the same as a round-trip ticket to one destination on the bullet train.

WEBSITES: niseko.ne.jp/en/; moku nosho.com/en/; gorakadan.com; hajime-artistes.com

Kyoto's Golden Pavilion, a Zen Buddhist temple

WHAT TO DO

Hit the Ski Slopes of Hokkaido

Nearly a quarter of Japan's landmass, this island to the north contains less than 5 percent of the country's population. Characterized by soaring mountains, picturesque farms, and wide-open spaces, the region is closer in temperament to Utah than Tokyo. Take a 90-minute flight north to Sapporo's New Chitose Airport, then drive two hours west to the storied Niseko United ski area. After exploring the resort's massive snowfall by ski or snowboard, turn toward Japan's legendary hospitality at Niseko's Moku No Sho, a 25-room *ryokan* (traditional inn). Warm up by the fireplace with a Hokkaido single malt whiskey, the perfect antidote for tired legs.

Soak in the Hot Springs in Hakone

Since Japan is volcanically active, thousands of *onsen* (hot springs) dot the country. A top place to experience onsen culture is at Gora Kadan, a rejuvenating ryokan in the small mountainous town of Hakone. From Tokyo Station, take a 40-minute bullet train ride to Odawara Statino; Gora Kadan is a 40-minute drive from there. The inn, housed in the Kan'in-nomiya imperial family's former summer retreat, features two open-air baths (one for women, one for men) fed by mineral-rich waters. For first-timers, Gora Kada makes bathing etiquette less intimidating with English signs and everything guests need, from towels to bath soaps.

Eat Local Specialties in Osaka

Japan's third largest city is a revered destination for foodies—so much so that the Japanese word *kuidaore,* which means to eat yourself bankrupt, is synonymous with the town. After a bullet train ride southwest to Osaka, head to the neon-lit Dotonbori district, home to hundreds of street food vendors and eateries packed in alleyways. Try the two most famous dishes: *takoyaki* (octopus fritters) and *okonomiyaki* (a savory pancake). The city also has four Michelin three-star restaurants, one being Hajime, where the signature dish, *chikyu* ("planet Earth"), features 110 herbs and vegetables. Before leaving town, don't miss the Momofuku Ando Instant Ramen Museum.

Spot Wildlife in Arashiyama

Once you've made it to Kyoto, head to the Arashiyama Mountains where a leisurely 40-minute hike brings you to Iwatayama Monkey Park, inhabited by a troop of more than 170 Japanese macaque monkeys that roam free in their natural habitat. It's a perfect place to watch these playful creatures frolic while enjoying panoramic views of the city.

Visit a Temple Turned Natural Wonder in Kyoto

Saiho-ji, commonly referred to as Kokedera, is an eighth-century Zen Buddhist temple and UNESCO World Heritage site that attracts visitors to its untapped moss garden. The two-tiered garden is a serendipitous consequence of a flooding that took place during the Edo period (1603–1867). Today, this verdant natural wonder is meticulously manicured and preserved by the monks with more than 120 different varieties of moss carpeting the grounds in various shades of green.

Find Serenity in Sagano Bamboo Forest

The rolling foothills of Kyoto's Arashiyama National Park are home to the iconic Sagano Bamboo Forest. The verdant grove is accessed via a 14th-century Buddhist

OPPOSITE: **Flourishing cherry blossoms line the local Kyoto railway.** RIGHT: **A woman kneels on a tatami mat for a traditional tea ceremony.**

A chef prepares local delicacies at a night market in Osaka.

たこせん

たこ焼
5個入 350円
10個入 650円

temple, Tenryu-ji. Experience a unique serenity from the wind rustling through the soaring trees making a "zawa zawa" sound and the filtered sunlight filling the space with a tranquil green glow.

Sip Tea in Gion and Higashiyama

As a birthplace of Sado, the Japanese tea ceremony, the historic neighborhoods of Gion and Higashiyama are perfect places to visit *machiyas* (traditional Japanese wooden townhouses) and learn about the ancient art of tea-making in Kyoto. During the ritual performed on a tatami floor by a professional tea master, you'll have a chance to learn about the philosophy and etiquette of drinking tea, as well as master the basics of making matcha.

Visit Ancient Monuments in Kyoto

In the City of Thousand Shrines, Kiknkaku-ji Temple, commonly known as the Golden Pavilion, sits in the middle of a large pond, the crown jewel of its surroundings. The temple gets its name from the gold leaf that covers the entire exterior of the top two floors and was deservedly named one of 17 locations making up the Historic Monuments of Ancient Kyoto.

Walk the Halls of a Feudal Castle

Nijo Castle, the residence of Tokugawa shoguns, stands in the heart of Kyoto as a testimony of the power that the shoguns wielded over the emperors throughout the Edo period. The castle impresses with its moat and exterior stone walls, as well as the elaborately painted screens that decorate the interior. Its palace buildings are arguably the best surviving examples of Japan's feudal era architecture.

HIGHLIGHTS

• Bite into local delicacies while wandering the street markets of Osaka.

• Walk through a rustling bamboo forest and 14th-century Buddhist temple.

• Ski remarkable mountains; then rest weary bones at mineral hot springs.

THE TRANS-SIBERIAN RAIL

This legendary railway takes you across Russia—from the Kremlin to quaint interior villages.

Set out on an epic train journey across one-third of the world, traveling from Vladivostok, Russia, to the heart of Moscow along the legendary Trans-Siberian Railway. From the Mongolian steppe to Lake Baikal's remote shores to the snowcapped Ural Mountains, trace the history of tsars, exiles, and Mongols. Encounter remote cultures and the unique architecture of Siberia's wooden cottages and Moscow's onion domes.

Traveling by train evokes a sense of nostalgia and adventure as you cover vast distances with speed and ease, visit remote towns and villages, and observe everyday life against an ever changing and beautiful backdrop. There's no better way to experience an encompassing look at Russia—the world's largest country—and explore all of its rich culture and national treasures.

National Geographic Expeditions offers a tour of this spectacular country from the comfort of the *Golden Eagle Trans-Siberian Express*. Off the train, adventure awaits. Stopping in 11 locations across Russia and Mongolia, there is plenty to do and see—from an insider's tour of the Kremlin at your last stop in Moscow to exploring Mongolia's Gorkhi-Terlj National Park. Along the way, epic scenery right outside your window offers stunning views of the Selenge River and sweeping countryside.

Travel Tips

WHEN TO GO: The best time to plan your trip is in the late spring, from the end of April to early June. The weather is milder and the sun is out longer—making for longer available hours for sightseeing both on foot and from your passenger window.

PLANNING: The weather can change from one place to another as you travel across Russia; come prepared and pack light layers.

WEBSITES: nationalgeographic.com/expeditions/; kosmo-museum.ru; lakebaikal.org; nationalmuseum.mn/

Luxe cabins aboard the *Golden Eagle*

14-DAY ITINERARY

Day 1

The trip begins in Vladivostok, a strategic naval outpost that was closed to most of the world from World War II until the end of the Cold War. Get acquainted with this modern city on a tour that includes the brightly painted railway station and Our Lady Grieving Orthodox Church. See the Pacific Navy War Memorial and the steamboat *Krasny Vympel,* take in the views of its city and its bay from the Eagle's Nest observation platform, and stroll through the historic Vladivostok Naval Cemetery. Then, climb aboard the *Golden Eagle* and set off on the journey across Russia.

Day 2

The first stop is in Khabarovsk. Debark to explore the city's lively squares and visit the Natural History Museum by the Amur River. Learn about the flora and fauna of the region and see artifacts from the indigenous tribes of the Goldi and the Gilyak.

Days 3 to 5

As the train slips past rolling hills and Siberian villages of log houses, watch the remote and ever changing countryside pass by as you enter the sweeping Mongolian steppe. It takes two days on the train to reach Mongolia's capital city, Ulaanbaatar, but it's worth the wait. On the morning of your arrival, visit the National Museum to trace the history of Genghis Khan and explore the culture of the steppe nomads. Then head to nearby Gorkhi-Terelj National Park to enjoy the alpine scenery as you hike its trails, watch a Mongolian horseback riding demonstration, and visit a tradition *ger* (felt tent). In Ulaanbaatar, you can also watch a traditional performance of Mongolian throat singing—where one vocalist creates multiple pitches at once—and dance.

Day 6

The train rolls through the valley of the Selenge River, which flows into Lake Baikal. Stop in Ulan Ude, the capital of the Buryat Republic and once a major trading post between China and Irkutsk. Pay a visit to a village of Old Believers, descendants of 17th-century exiles whose fascinating culture has changed little over millennia. Watch them perform their unique choral music.

Day 7

Arrive at beautiful Lake Baikal, a UNESCO World Heritage site that locals call "the sacred sea." The lake basin holds nearly 20 percent of the world's unfrozen freshwater. A sacred site for Buryat shamans, Lake Baikal's Shaman Rock is steeped in legend. As the train route hugs the rocky shores and passes through 33 tunnels, take in the spectacular views before stopping for a stroll around the shore. Later, explore the village of Listvyanka where local families often host you for tea in their homes.

Day 8

Irkutsk is an important Siberian outpost established by the Cossacks in 1652. In the early 19th century, many Russian artists, officers, and nobles were exiled here for their involvement in the Decembrist revolt. Visit the city's historic sights and wander through a delightful collection of classic Russian and Siberian cottages at the Museum of Wooden Architecture. Then,

OPPOSITE: The *Golden Eagle* skirts the rocky coastline of Lake Baikal. RIGHT: Shamanka Rock sits in Baikal, the largest freshwater lake in the world.

watch a bell-ringing performance at the Decembrist House Museum.

Days 9 to 11

Take in the stunning scenery as the vast Siberian taiga unfurls on the daylong journey to the next stop. In Novosibirsk, Siberia's largest city, stop for a few hours to see the opera house and Lenin Square. Then it's on to Yekaterinburg, where Russia's last tsar, Nicholas II, and his family were executed by the Bolsheviks in 1918. Visit the Romanovs' execution site, now a church dedicated to their memory, and view the city's ornately decorated wooden houses.

Day 12

Explore Kazan, the capital of Tatarstan, perched on the banks of the Volga River. Tour the city's Kremlin, the turquoise-topped Qol Sharif Mosque, and the Peter and Paul Cathedral. Pay a visit to the Kazan Conservatory and watch a concert performed by its students. Then set off on a cruise around the walls of the city's Kremlin before departing for Moscow.

Days 13 and 14

Take an afternoon city tour of Moscow and a guided stroll through the famous Red Square at night. In the morning, it's time to explore the legendary Kremlin. Next, visit St. Basil's Cathedral and view court regalia from the Romanov dynasty at the Armory Museum. Then it's off to the Monument to the Conquerors of Space, which sweeps some 360 feet (109.7 m) into the sky.

HIGHLIGHTS

• Climb aboard the *Golden Eagle Trans-Siberian Express* and travel along one of the world's most legendary railways.

• Take an insightful insider's tour of the Kremlin.

• Sip tea in the village of Listvyanka, perched along the shores of beautiful Lake Baikal.

The Kazan Kremlin has structures that date back to the 10th century and the Muslim period of the Golden Horde.

A snow-dusted hiking trail follows a frozen stream in the Stok Valley.

BORNEO

INTO THE HEART OF BORNEO

Southeast Asia's wild and wonderful treasure island

xploring the Southeast Asian island of Borneo can feel like one endless pinch-me moment. There are alluring, steamy jungles filled with a tangle of secrets ready to explore while hiking muddy trails or drifting down snaking rivers on a traditional longboat. Offshore, dazzling coral reefs await; inland are the majestic misty mountains. And then there are the spectacular karst caves and jungle lodges tucked away in pristine nature reserves.

In this real-world Zootopia, home to 44 endemic mammals and an astonishing array of birds, you can come face-to-face with the proboscis monkey, with its impossibly long nose, or the Bornean orangutan, bearded since long before facial hair was in fashion. The tarsier, looking like something out of *Star Wars*, lurks here too, as does the diminutive Bornean sun bear and the pygmy elephant. And at every turn, there's a flying frog or eye-catching lizard.

Unforgettable encounters are de rigueur on the world's third largest island. In the north, Malaysian Borneo makes a relatively accessible microcosm of the island, from the rugged interior to dazzling Gaya Island, while Indonesia's southern portion and independent Brunei offer their own unique experiences. Political borders aside, the entire landmass sets the scene for one boundless wildlife safari that won't soon be forgotten.

Travel Tips

WHEN TO GO: High season is June to September; make arrangements months in advance. Monsoon season (November to February) floods the forests of the Kinabatangan River Basin and allows access to oxbow lakes that attract wildlife.

PLANNING: Most international travelers fly into the airport in Kota Kinabalu, in Malaysian Borneo. Use mosquito nets and repellent to protect against malaria and dengue fever.

WEBSITES: bruneitourism.com; sabah tourism.com; sarawaktourism.com; sabahparks.org.my

An orangutan in Tanjung Puting National Park

WHAT TO DO

Walk on the Wild Side in Sabah

Adrenaline seekers typically direct their attention to the Malaysian state of Sabah, on the northern end of the island, and for good reason: hiking through the jungle, spotting rare creatures on wildlife safaris, diving among coral reefs, spelunking through caves, and climbing the island's tallest mountain, just to skim the surface.

Crisscross the jungle canopy on the aerial walkways of Kabili-Sepilok Forest Reserve, on the eastern coast. From bridges 50-plus feet (15 m) in the air, you can scan the trees for tropical birds like trogons and black hornbills. Return at dusk to glimpse nocturnal wildlife such as tree frogs and alien-like tarsiers. The next day, observe a feeding session at the Sepilok Orangutan Rehabilitation Centre, where rescued orangutans are reintroduced to the wild. At the adjacent Bornean Sun Bear Conservation Center, you can come face-to-face with the world's smallest bear. Or board a safari cruise and float down Kinabatangan River through a flooded wonderland teeming with biodiversity, including several primate species and a colorful array of birds. Explore the nearby Gomantong Caves, home to thousands of bats and swiftlets, as well as scorpions and cockroaches.

For a chance to see a who's who of unusual animal species, head to Tabin Wildlife Reserve. Its residents include pygmy elephants, banteng, leopard and marbled cats, flying squirrels, and binturongs (bearcats). Hike to one of the reserve's seven gurgling mud volcanoes, which serve as mineral-enriched salt licks for the area wildlife, and climb the observation tower for sweeping views of the surrounding landscape. Another reserve, the pristine Danum Valley Conservation Area, offers guided hikes where you can search the jungle for rare species such as the Bornean gibbon and maroon langur.

During the dry season (March to August), trek up the steep slopes of Mount Kinabalu, crowned by dramatic granite spires. It's the highest point between the Himalaya and New Guinea and earned Malaysia its first UNESCO World Heritage site. From the summit, your gaze can reach as far as the Philippines on a clear day.

From Sabah's capital of Kota Kinabalu, take the ferry to Gaya Island, where coral gardens provide a haven for endangered green sea turtles, clownfish, and seahorses—and exceptional snorkeling and scuba diving opportunities.

Trek Through Sarawak

Along the northwest coast of Malaysian Borneo, Sarawak offers easy access to equatorial rainforest, highlands, and legendary bat caves, as well as the cultural riches of Kuching, the bustling capital of Sarawak.

Discover the sheer cliffs and sandy bays of Bako National Park, traveling from Kuching by vehicle and longboat. Well-marked trails lead the way to its iconic sea stack, remote beaches, and forested hilltops. Along the way, encounter the resident proboscis

monkeys and long-tailed macaque monkeys, as well as hundreds of bird species.

Next, trek between longhouses on old forest trails in the remote Kelabit Highlands. Glide down the Santubong River, keeping watch for crocodiles and the rare Irrawaddy dolphin as you pass through mangrove forests. Board a traditional longboat for a river cruise in Batang Ai National Park, home to infamous bearded pigs and elusive wild orangutans that you can spot while walking the jungle trails.

Go spelunking in the intricate cave system of Gunung Mulu National Park, a UNESCO World Heritage site. In Deer Cave, the world's largest cave passage, a colony of more than three million bats has taken up residence. Join a local guide for a night walk among the park's twinkling fireflies and luminescent fungi.

A Rare Experience in Brunei

The independent sultanate of Brunei bisects Malaysian Borneo. Though international travelers often pass it over, the tiny nation is rich in protected rainforests begging to be visited. Intrepid travelers are

---

OPPOSITE: **A river cuts through the verdant Danum Valley.** ABOVE: **Muller's Bornean gibbons leap across the canopy of Tabin Wildlife Reserve.**

Gunung Mulu National Park's
Clearwater River Cave is the
eighth longest cave in the world.

rewarded with world-class diving in coral reefs and among World War II shipwrecks. In the gilded capital city of Bandar Seri Begawan, a 23-mile (37 km) boardwalk connects an expansive settlement on stilts. Called Kampong Ayer, the 600-some-year-old community is considered the world's largest water village.

For a true wilderness experience, embark on a thrilling longboat ride along twisting waterways to Ulu Temburong National Park, accessible only by guided tour (and to scientists who flock here for research). Climb steps to a canopy tower and walkway, chase butterflies into the jungle on short hikes, and swim in waterfalls and mountain streams.

Wilderness at Its Best in Kalimantan

Indonesia claims a vast tract of the southern portion of the island of Borneo called Kalimantan. Venture into this jungle-shrouded territory for pure wilderness experiences. Explore the snaking Sekonyer River on a traditional boat, or *klotok*, and keep an eye out for wild orangutans and proboscis monkeys swinging between trees. With a local guide, visit the Camp Leakey orangutan research outpost, founded in 1971 by Birutė Galdikas, a student of the famed anthropologist Louis Leakey, in the remote Tanjung Puting National Park.

The most intrepid of hikers can cross all of Borneo on an epic trek through more than 550 miles (885 km) of rugged interior—a 16-day journey from east to west. Or tackle shorter hikes through the misty Meratus Mountains.

Divers head to the Derawan Archipelago in the Celebes Sea to come face-to-fin with manta rays and see nesting green turtles in the cerulean waters.

HIGHLIGHTS

• Explore Tabin Wildlife Reserve, home to nine primate species, three cat species, and some 220 species of birds.

• Descend into the intricate cave system of Gunung Mulu National Park, a UNESCO World Heritage site.

• Board a traditional longboat and glide along jungle waterways.

Culture in a Meal in Afghanistan

By Paul Kvinta

I CAN'T SEE THE WOMAN'S FACE—but it's not because she wears a burka, as many women in Kabul do. It's because she won't open the front door more than two inches. She stares at me from behind a chain lock and mumbles into a cell phone. After what seems an eternity, she hangs up and says something in Dari to my driver, who is standing next to me.

"Faheem is stuck in traffic," he tells me. "He will be here in 30 minutes. She says you can go inside and wait."

Faheem is a well-known Kabul newspaper editor, and he has invited me to his apartment for dinner. His wife opens the door all the way and motions for me to enter. She wears a blue head covering and a half-smile. She is shy and welcoming. I remove my shoes, as is the custom, and she shows me silently to a room off the main hall. Then she leaves, closing the door behind her.

I never see her again.

There is no furniture in the room, just a traditional Afghan carpet and a television set with three children flopped before it playing video games. They glance at me with indifference and continue playing. I seat myself on the carpet. After a few minutes, I hear the woman's voice from the other room, and the oldest of the children, a boy of about eight, puts down his video controller and leaves the room. When he returns, he's carrying a tray with a pot of steaming green tea and porcelain cup and saucer. He pours me a cup, then resumes playing his video game. Almost immediately, his mother calls him again. This time he returns to me with a bowl of pistachios. He tries

---

BELOW: A pomegranate is sliced in half to display its ruby seeds.
OPPOSITE: A man sells naan from his stall in Kabul.

reaching for the controller again, but his mother's firm voice intervenes once more. He brings me a bowl of dates, then one of pine nuts, then the teapot again. For the rest of the evening, he remains on point and vigilant. My teacup is never empty.

As I nosh on these snacks and wait for his father, I contemplate this exceedingly gracious and generous hospitality, which I experience everywhere in Afghanistan. Providing guests with your very best is a celebrated value in the culture. No one knows this more than the woman behind that door, even though she is circumscribed from hosting me herself. So she does so through her child, anticipating my every need.

Faheem arrives, greets me warmly, and hugs his children. The young ones scamper off, but the eight-year-old keeps hustling. As his father and I fall into deep discussion, the boy unfolds a *dastarkhan,* the traditional dining cloth, on the carpet before us. He then presents us with a copper basin and pot, pouring water over our hands and offering us soap and a towel.

Soon, various food-laden dishes appear: first, oval-shaped pieces of warm naan bread topped with sesame seeds, followed by *dolmas* (grape leaves stuffed with rice), mincemeat, and spices. Then comes *palao,* a pilaf with raisins, carrots, and nuts; and *qorma,* a lamb stew with onions and cilantro. We eat traditionally, with our right hands, using the naan to scoop up each item. The food just keeps coming: yogurt, oranges, pomegranates, honey-sweet baklava. Not only does the final result approach gustatory nirvana—the savory contrasting exquisitely with the sweet, the spices dancing lightly across my tongue—but the *dastarkhan* on which the plates are set suggests a richly colored work of art.

For two hours, Faheem regales me with stories: about how he lost an eye during the post-Soviet mujahideen wars, about how he was in the same room with Ahmad Shah Massoud when the legendary Northern Alliance leader was assassinated by al Qaeda fighters. But as compelling as all of this is, my thoughts meander repeatedly to the woman in the next room.

I imagine her tirelessly slicing, dicing, boiling, and frying in a kitchen that is no doubt sweltering. Does she even like to cook, I wonder? Does she have any hobbies? Does she share her husband's political views—and voice them?

It's late when Faheem finally walks me to the door. I put on my shoes and thank him for the wonderful meal and engaging conversation. It's his pleasure, he assures me, and he promises that we'll talk again.

As I head into the frosty winter evening, my stomach feels warm, full, and satisfied. As for Faheem's wife, the fabulous cook, I never even learned her name.

OPPOSITE: Traditional Afghan dishes are served family style. ABOVE: Afghan cakes and biscuits are shared with guests.

• *Paul Kvinta is a writer based in Atlanta, Georgia.*

INDIA

ROYAL RAJASTHAN SAFARI AND PUSHKAR FAIR

Revel in the regal splendor of an Indian safari and traditional celebration.

Rising from copper-colored sands in India's regal northwest state of Rajasthan is an architectural treasure trove—medieval stone forts, sixth-century Maru-Gurjara temples, ornate palaces, elaborately carved ancient ruins, the legendary Blue and Pink Cities of Jodhpur and Jaipur, and royal Udaipur with its sumptuous white marble palaces and majestic gardens. Royal Rajasthan also boasts Ranthambore National Park, one of India's top spots to see and photograph Bengal tigers, and it hosts the annual Pushkar Fair, or Pushkar Mela, one of the world's oldest camel-trading markets and one of India's signature cultural and religious festivals.

To make the adventure here more meaningful and memorable, resist the temptation to hit all the highlights across Rajasthan—which is more than twice the size of Florida—in one trip. Instead, take a deep dive into Jaipur, Rajasthan's capital and largest city, and allot ample time to explore Ranthambore and experience the sights, sounds, and pungent aromas (to be expected when thousands of camels gather) of the Pushkar Fair.

This epic trip is a six-day loop, beginning and ending in Jaipur. There are wildlife-viewing opportunities throughout, and the grand finale is two frenetic days among the throng of camel traders, tourists, and pilgrims gathered in Pushkar.

Travel Tips

WHEN TO GO: The annual Pushkar Fair takes place in October or November and lasts two weeks. Visit during the first week to see camel trading and fairground competitions. The second week is devoted to religious activities.

PLANNING: The easiest way to travel around Rajasthan and to the fair is by private car and driver, or on a small group or custom trip like those offered by G Adventures or Kensington Tours.

WEBSITES: tourism.rajasthan.gov.in; gadventures.com; kensingtontours.com; deraamer.com; khemvillas.com; sewara .com/property/history-pushkar-resort

Flowers are gathered for puja offerings.

6-DAY ITINERARY

Day 1

Take a morning tuk-tuk (motorized rickshaw) tour of Jaipur. Known as the Pink City for the preponderance of buildings painted terra-cotta pink (the color was chosen to set a warm, welcoming tone for the 1853 royal visit of Prince Albert, Queen Victoria's husband), Jaipur is a mesmerizing maze of bazaars, gardens, and palaces. Go inside the Chandra Mahal City Palace, or "Palace of the Moon," a seven-story home of the maharajahs (the first floor is open to the public). Tour the city's pink-and-red-sandstone jewel, "Palace of the Winds." Tell time using the world's largest stone sundial at the 18th-century Jantar Mantar Observatory, a UNESCO World Heritage site. Then experience the wild side of the city by staying in rustic or luxury tents at Dera Amer, a wilderness camp and wildlife sanctuary north of the city.

Day 2

Start the day with a strenuous cardio workout: the 10-minute climb up the "Hill of Eagles" to Amber Fort. The steep incline makes the route challenging (an ambulance is stationed at the top), but it's more than worth it for the Pink City views below and the elaborate courtyards, intricate mosaics, and grand halls inside the magnificent fort complex. Make the day a Jaipur fort trifecta with stops at the city's Nahargarh and Jaigarh forts.

Day 3

Head south to Ranthambore National Park, located about three and a half hours away by car. Formerly the private hunting grounds of the Maharajas of Jaipur, the

park's 151 square miles (391 sq km) of dense forests and open plains are home to an assortment of exotic wildlife, including tigers, leopards, sloth bears, and snub-nosed marsh crocodiles. Take an early evening jeep safari to catch a glimpse of Ranthambore's regal Bengal tigers, which regularly roam around the crumbling ruins of the ancient Ranthambore fort complex. Spend the night just outside the park in a luxury tent at Khem Villas.

Day 4

Wake up before dawn for a sunrise safari drive through the park or a Chambal River Safari (offered by Khem Villas) to see the critically endangered gharial crocodile. Wildlife-watching in both early evening and early morning boosts the number of animals you'll see. After the land or water safari, head east (about six hours) to Pushkar. In early evening, visit Pushkar Lake,

one of India's holiest sites (due to the belief that dipping in the waters can wash away sins), to see Hindu pilgrims bathing at the 52 *ghats* (waterside staircases) ringing the lake. Overnight at the Green House Resort, an eco-friendly boutique hotel, or in a cottage at serene Pushkar Resorts to rest up for tomorrow's hectic first day at the Pushkar Fair.

Day 5

Dive into the sea of humanity to fully experience the whirlwind of dust, animals, and nonstop activities that is the Pushkar Fair. Timing your visit to coincide with the fair's early, festival-focused days affords the opportunity to watch competitions, such as "longest moustache," cricket matches, camel races, and beauty contests. Spend a full day absorbing the spectacle—spirited livestock trading, camels adorned with elaborate bejeweled accessories and colorful saddles, and music and dance performances.

Day 6

Arrive early at the fair to take a morning camel safari into the Thar Desert and see the camels and traders before the crowds arrive. Before leaving Jaipur, sample some of the fair's Rajasthani street food like indulgent *rabdi malpuas* (sweet and slightly crunchy fried pancakes), *idli* (steamed rice cakes), and *dal vada* (deep fried lentils).

OPPOSITE: **A juvenile Bengal tiger rests on a tree. There are fewer than 2,500 Bengals left in the world.** ABOVE: **The Hawa Mahal (Palace of the Winds) looks onto the Sireh Deori Bazaar.**

HIGHLIGHTS

- See magnificent palaces and forts on a tuk-tuk tour of the Pink City of Jaipur.

- Take jeep and boat safaris to look for tigers and endangered crocodiles.

- Experience the colossal Pushkar Fair, one of the oldest camel-trading markets.

THE HILLS OF SRI LANKA

Lush green landscapes and laid-back tea escapes

Away from the chaos of Sri Lanka's population-dense coastal cities, the frenzied pace and temperatures cool down as the elevation climbs. Palm trees give way to fragrant spice plantations with rows of native cinnamon trees whose bark has been traded since the time of the ancient Egyptians. Beyond the rolling hills and valley lakes, the highest peaks are capped in evergreen forest. Here, wild jungles and misty manicured tea terraces undulate through Sri Lanka's interior. A huge swath of the Central Highlands earned UNESCO status in 2010—this is Sri Lanka at its wildest and most charming.

National parks and forest reserves protect grassland and cloud forests that house endemic plants and rare and unusual wildlife, including grizzled giant squirrels, purple-faced langurs, slender lorises, and Sri Lankan leopards. Treetops ring with the chatter of thrushes, flycatchers, bulbuls, and warblers. Tucked in amid the wavy terrain are sacred religious sites and British hill station holdovers from the country's 152 years as a colony. Rows and rows of tea in neat hedges blanket the land, making Sri Lanka the world's fourth largest producer of the beverage. Crowded railcars built to transport tea to the coast now take visitors on the journey between Ella and Kandy, said to be among the world's most scenic train rides. Hop aboard and see what the hills of Sri Lanka have to offer.

Travel Tips

WHEN TO GO: Sri Lanka's dueling monsoon seasons mean timing is key. Stick to the Central Highlands (and southern beaches) between December and March, when they are driest and busiest, or in the shoulder seasons in April and September to beat most rains and crowds.

PLANNING: Consider reading John Gimlette's *Elephant Complex* before you go. The detailed travelogue explores Sri Lanka's unique history and complexities following its recent civil war.

WEBSITES: srilanka.travel; national geographic.com/expeditions

Temple of the Tooth in Kandy

7-DAY ITINERARY

Day 1

Bustling capital Colombo (a significant port since the fifth century) blends the new with the historic. Peruse colorful textiles, demon masks, and colonial weaponry in the two-story National Museum; then follow the seaside promenade at Galle Face Green, an urban park, to watch perched pelicans and flying kites on the beach beyond. Take a tuk-tuk to the 17th-century fort, where the Dutch East India Company's former hospital now houses a handful of upscale boutiques and restaurants. Dine at Ministry of Crab for succulent, local lagoon crab served baked, buttered, curried, or garlic chili style.

Day 2

Head for the hills via Hatton and Dalhousie, small towns to the northeast of Adam's Peak. Rising 7,359 feet (2,243 m), Adam's Peak is revered by several major religions. Also called Sri Pada, or "sacred footprint," the flat temple-topped peak bears a large footprint housed in a small building, bejeweled and lined with brass. Buddhists believe it was made by Buddha himself, Hindus say it belongs to Lord Shiva, and Christians say it's the mark of St. Thomas. During pilgrimage season between December and May, the devout line up in the dark to navigate more than 5,000 crumbling steps to reach the summit by dawn (visitors can trek the four hours to the summit almost any time of day). At the top, enjoy a bird's-eye vantage of the rivers and forests in the Peak Wilderness Protected Area that wraps 86.5 square miles (224 sq km) around the site.

Days 3 and 4

Continue east to Nuwara Eliya, a former British hill station that retains much of its

OPPOSITE: Dancers perform in the Kandy Esala Procession in Kandy, a UNESCO World Heritage site. ABOVE: The beautifully green landscape of the hill country of Sri Lanka

colonial charm. On the scenic drive, pull over to see two Kotmale Oya River waterfalls in short succession. Well-established Ceylon tea estates, grown here since the 1860s, sprawl into the hills beyond town. Take a tour to navigate the rows of hip-high plants and learn to identify the choicest leaves as you help the traditionally female pickers pluck.

In nearby Horton Plains National Park, highland plateaus connect Kirigalpotta (7,858 feet/2,395 m) and Totapola (7,734feet/ 2,357 m), some of the country's highest mountains. The varied topography—from rivers and lakes to grasslands and cloud forests—ensures a huge plant diversity, including fragrant wild rhododendrons and nelu flowers that bloom just once every 12 years. A 5.6-mile (9 km) circular hike from the visitor center offers the chance to spot some local wildlife: sambar deer, native squirrels, river otters, and colorful forest birds. An endemic species of slender loris, a tiny nocturnal primate, hides in the park, but don't expect to spot one—decades can pass between sightings.

Day 5

Horton Plains' wild elephant herds were hunted to extinction more than a century ago. It's worthwhile, then, to take the four-hour detour south to Udawalawe National Park, home to several hundred of the behemoths and one of the easiest places in the country to spot them. Game drives bump through grass, shrubland, and riverine forest in search of bathing and feeding groups. On the way you'll likely spot other Udawalawe inhabitants, including

A train makes its way across the Nine Arches Bridge.

crocodiles, monkeys, and some of the 210 species of migratory and resident birds.

Day 6

Bustling Ella is Hill Country's visitor hub, and more tea estates hedge its periphery. In 1890, Scottish businessman Thomas Lipton bought 5,500 acres (2,225 hectares) of the surrounding hills and began to build his tea empire. At Lipton's Seat, a lookout outside town, survey the endless rows and spirals of tea bushes, neatly striating the landscape in green. It's said that the viewpoint's strange name is a nod to when Sir Thomas himself used to sit there and take it all in. Then head to the large and popular Uva Halpewatte Tea Factory, which was built in 1940 and still processes single estate teas. Learn about the processing, production, and history of the area's famous Ceylon tea.

Day 7

Make your way back to the edge of the highlands via the scenic railway to Kandy. The blue train chugs over Ella's gorge-spanning Nine Arch Bridge as it sets off past waterfalls, small villages, and forest on the rickety seven-hour journey north. (For the best photos, opt for second-class seats; windows don't open in the air-conditioned first class.) Kandy was the capital of Sri Lanka's last independent Sinhalese holdout, and came under colonial rule only in 1815. Explore the city's traditional architecture. Don't miss the lakeside Temple of the Tooth. The revered complex houses a sacred relic, a canine said to be Buddha's, tucked away in a tiny golden casket visible only during *pujas* (prayers).

HIGHLIGHTS

• Pick and sip Ceylon tea in gorgeous terraced plantations.

• Take a winding scenic train ride through hills blanketed in jungle and waterfalls.

• Experience Sinhalese culture and religion with traditional dance performances and a visit to the Temple of the Tooth in Kandy.

MYANMAR

MYANMAR BY LAND, AIR, AND SEA

Discover alluring Buddhist temples and pristine landscapes in a long-forbidden country.

After being closed to most travelers for nearly 50 years while it was ruled by a military junta, Myanmar has begun to open up. Decades of seclusion mean the country still retains extraordinary, virtually untouched sites that are little known to the outside world. That isolation also means roads can be undeveloped and rough, and it can take many hours to reach far-flung landmarks, but hardy adventurers up for the challenge can be some of the first visitors to the country's many marvels.

Ninety percent of Myanmar's population practices Buddhism, a rich heritage reflected in the countless sacred Burmese sites, from glittering Shwedagon Pagoda and the Golden Rock to the thousands of temples scattered around the ancient city of Bagan. Of the 10,000 built on the Bagan plain between the ninth and 13th centuries, some 2,200 remain, including gilded Shwezigon Pagoda and Ananda Temple with its four 31-foot-high (9.5 m) Buddha statues facing the cardinal directions.

There's more to Myanmar than temples, of course. You can sample sizzling Burmese street food after dark at Yangon's riverside night market; visit enchanting floating villages on Inle Lake; escape to the uninhabited tropical islands of the Mergui Archipelago in the Andaman Sea; and cruise the famed Irrawaddy River— the legendary waterway that Rudyard Kipling called the "road to Mandalay."

Travel Tips

WHEN TO GO: November to February, with warm, dry days, has the best weather. Accommodations can fill up quickly, so book well in advance; October is a good alternative. November to May offers the best diving and sailing, with calm seas and reliable wind.

PLANNING: Sites sacred to the Burmese require covered knees and shoulders for both men and women, and shoes must be removed before going inside.

WEBSITES: myanmar.travel; burma boating.com; intrepidtravel.com; balloon soverbagan.com; nationalgeographic .com/expeditions

Mergui Archipelago in Myanmar

WHAT TO DO

Take a Hot-Air Balloon Ride Over Bagan

It's an iconic sight: gently floating hot-air balloons drifting above the thousands of temples on the Bagan plain. Three companies currently offer flights; the first established, Balloons Over Bagan, has been in operation for 20 years. During ballooning season (October to March), riders gather in the predawn darkness to watch the balloons being filled and take off at first light to watch the sunrise bathe the centuries-old temples in a rosy glow. For 45 minutes, you float where the wind chooses to take you, over an ancient landscape dotted with temples, pagodas, and stupas—the oldest dating to the 11th century.

Explore the Floating Villages of Inle Lake

A ribbon of blue in a valley between two mountain ranges in Shan State, Inle Lake is famed for its floating villages and gardens, as well as fishermen who use conical nets and a distinctive traditional rowing style, with one leg wrapped around an oar. Hop into a slender wooden long-tail boat to access the hidden reaches of the nearly 14-mile-long (22.5 km) lake, from the floating market of Ywama (host of handicraft workshops for silk weavers and woodcarvers) to the hundreds of small crumbling stupas of Shwe Inn Thein Paya, a complex of pagodas reached by a long, covered walkway from the village of Inn Thein.

Gaze in Awe at Shwedagon Pagoda

Perched on a hill overlooking Yangon (formerly Rangoon, the largest city in Myanmar), the dazzling Shwedagon Pagoda is the most sacred site for Burmese Buddhists. The 2,500-year-old temple, plated in gold and encrusted with more than

OPPOSITE: **The best way to see the 2,000-plus Bagan temples is from the sky by hot-air balloon.** ABOVE: **A fisherman casts his net in Inle Lake.**

4,500 diamonds, is believed to contain strands of the Buddha's hair. The temple complex is a major gathering place for locals in the evenings: monks meditate, friends greet each other, and devotees light candles, offer flowers, and purchase small squares of gilt to press on Buddha statues. Join the crowds circling the immense, 360-foot-high (110 m) stupa to find your birthday corner. Were you born on Tuesday night, Sunday morning, Friday afternoon, or anytime in between? There's a shrine for each one, where you can dip water to pour over a Buddha statue and bring yourself good luck.

Climb to the Golden Rock

One of the holiest sites in Myanmar, the Golden Rock rests at the summit of 3,600-foot-high (1,100 m) Mount Kyaiktiyo in Mon State. The gilded boulder, covered in gold leaves pasted on by male devotees, with a small pagoda atop, appears to defy gravity as it delicately balances on the edge of a cliff. Most visitors stay in the town of Kinpun at the base of the mountain. You can take a bus or a cable car (Myanmar's first) to the summit. For the truly energetic, a five-hour hike from Kinpun up a paved trail passes stupas and overlooks with views of the surrounding hills. In November, the Kyaiktiyo Pagoda Festival sees devotees light 9,000 candles and present offerings of food and flowers to the Buddha.

Sail the Mergui Archipelago

In the Andaman Sea off the southern coast of Myanmar lie isles of enchantment: the Mergui Archipelago, made up of some 800 islands, only 50 of them inhabited. Little known or visited due to Myanmar's long seclusion, the islands haven't been altered by development or pollution. They offer lush jungle, deserted white beaches, turquoise

waters that shimmer after dark with bioluminescent plankton, and vibrant coral reefs
that invite diving and snorkeling. Sailing
journeys aboard catamarans equipped with
kayaks and stand-up paddleboards are the
best way to explore this paradise. You'll
also likely catch a glimpse of the Moken—
the indigenous people of the archipelago
who live aboard dugout boats and free-dive
for fish and mollusks.

Cruise the Irrawaddy River

The Irrawaddy River, the lifeblood of Myanmar, is navigable for nearly 990 miles
(1,600 km) year-round, from Bhamo, near
the border with China, all the way to the
Andaman Sea. It curves through the heart
of the country, from its source high in the
Himalaya past rice fields, steep cliffs, thick
greenery, and the historic cities of Mandalay, Bagan, and Yangon. Several operators,
including National Geographic Expeditions,
offer trips on luxe riverboats.

Delve Into the Pindaya Caves

The Pindaya Caves in central Myanmar
hold an astonishing surprise among their
stalactites: a treasure trove of Buddha
images. The 500-foot-deep (152 m) main
cave, the only one open to the public, is
filled with some 8,000 Buddha statues that
date back to the 18th century. The statues
are made from a variety of materials, including marble and teakwood, and feature
unique depictions seen nowhere else—for
example, the Buddha holding a single seed
in his upturned palm. The best time to visit
is March, when the Pindaya Cave Festival
celebrates the end of the harvest season
and traditional dance troupes perform
under centuries-old banyan trees.

HIGHLIGHTS

• Float over Bagan's thousands of
centuries-old temples in a hot-air balloon.

• Sail on a catamaran among the pristine
islands of the Mergui Archipelago.

• Take a boat trip to visit silk weavers at
Inle Lake's floating markets.

Locals stroll past the
Shwedagon Pagoda at sunrise.

HONG KONG

VISIT HONG KONG LIKE AN EXPLORER

From pristine islands to stunning skyline views, explore this captivating city like a local.

A t first Hong Kong doesn't seem to make sense. It is simultaneously Western and Asian, both a concrete jungle and an actual jungle, and equally glitzy and gritty. But somehow, the city balances it all beautifully, and this unique DNA courses through the veins of every resident and every neighborhood. Life here is fast-paced because Hong Kong makes it easy to do it all. Called Manhattan on Steroids, The City That Doesn't Sleep in the East, and Asia's World City, no moniker can do justice to the altitude, pace, and sheer scale of daily life in Hong Kong. The former British colony—officially handed over to China in 1997—showcases how deep tradition runs in a neon city. You can take a hike before work, have dirt-cheap dim sum for lunch, then later indulge at a Michelin-starred restaurant. There is a lot going on in this modern city, so don't forget to pause and take it all in.

Amid the skyscrapers and busy streets, visitors and locals alike don't realize that Hong Kong has only a few dozen pink dolphins left, that it is home to more coral species than the Caribbean, or that there are more endemic species found here than anywhere else in the world. The Hong Kong Explorers Initiative aims to encourage people to explore and appreciate the city's wild side. Here are a few ways you can do that in a city of plenty.

Travel Tip

WHEN TO GO: Find sun and pleasant temperatures from October to early December. Winters are dry and summer is hot, humid, and wet. Avoid spring, the cloudy season in Hong Kong.

PLANNING: Martin Booth's memoir *Gweilo* describes colonial Hong Kong in the 1950s. It's a great read for understanding the history of the modern city you are visiting.

WEBSITES: http://hkmaritimemuseum .org/eng; henest.com.hk; pmq.org.hk; hk.history.museum/en_US; hkdolphin watch.com/

A traditional dim sum lunch

WHAT TO DO

Travel for Good
Check out Café 8, at Central Pier No. 8 in the Hong Kong Maritime Museum, or the Nest near St. John's Cathedral in Central. They're run by the Nesbitt Centre, which gives job skills training and opportunities to people with learning disabilities.

Seek Out Traditional Crafts
Head to PMQ in Central, where the government converted old police living quarters into a hub for local designers and creatives. You'll find everything from traditional crafts to modern housewares. And there's the food: a bakery and confectionary shop with wild sweet treats, Taiwanese cuisine at Garden Meow, premium teas at Gong Fu Teahouse, and Sake Central, an osumami bar.

Take a Class
Take a tai chi class, and you might start to understand why Hong Kong has one of the highest life expectancies in the world. The Chinese martial art is practiced for both defense training and myriad health benefits. Its philosophy is modeled after the yin and yang—forces of balance that inspire the practice's moves.

Travel Back in Time
The Hong Kong Museum of History offers an incredibly well-executed overview of the city's history, from the big bang (seriously) to Hong Kong's handover from the United Kingdom back to China in July 1997. Expect life-size re-creations of Hong Kong icons, like sampans, double-decker trams, and long-gone traditional stores.

OPPOSITE: **Clear Water Bay offers white-sand beaches perfect for camping and picnics.** ABOVE: **A tai chi master and students practice the martial art at the Peak Tower.**

Go Island-Hopping
Take a hike on one of Hong Kong's less visited islands, like Tung Ping Chau or Peng Chau. Tung Ping Chau, part of the Hong Kong UNESCO Global Geopark, sits on the Mirs Bay, and is Hong Kong's easternmost island. The crescent-shaped landmass is famous for its odd rock formations made of siltstone, mudstone, and chert. Peng Chau is often called Hong Kong's hidden gem. Here, modest tourism has left the wilderness largely unspoiled and lifestyle very laid back. There are no cars on the island, so get your hiking boots ready. The Peng Chau Heritage Trail is a leisurely ramble past historical sights, or take in 360-views of Hong Kong from the top of Finger Hill, a 45-minute hike.

See the Last Pink Dolphins
If you want to see Hong Kong's few remaining pink dolphins, book one of the tours that Hong Kong Dolphinwatch runs a few times a week. Though practices are improving, the smaller tour operators in Tai O on Lantau Island rarely travel far enough for guests to actually be able to see the dolphins, and when they do encounter dolphins, they often get too close or chase them. Dolphinwatch follows ethical practices and allows more opportunity to see these rare mammals.

Savor the Flavors
Head to Temple Street in Jordan and sample food from any of the street-side restaurants and stalls offering a variety of Cantonese cuisine, like clay pot rice.

Explore the Outdoors
A visit to Hong Kong would be incomplete without time spent in the city's great outdoors. Take a hike to get incredible views of its famous skyline, and you may encounter wild monkeys, boars, or porcupines. Or head to Sai Kung, where you'll find pristine beaches and blue waters fit for kayaking and snorkeling. Hong Kong has more reef fish species than Hawaii.

HIGHLIGHTS
• See some of the last remaining pink dolphins off the shores of the island.

• Taste popular dishes from street stalls and the city's top restaurants.

• Hike rocky beach shores and an unspoiled island.

THE CAUCASUS MOUNTAINS

Take a trip to one of the resorts used in the 2014 Winter Olympic Games.

Krasnaya Polyana is Russia's answer to Vail or Aspen. It's the country's preeminent ski town with three ski complexes, plenty of hotels, and a preponderance of snow. It also happened to be the site of many of the events of the Sochi Winter Olympic Games.

Much of the intrigue of the alpine events of the 2014 Games' surrounded their venue, Rosa Khutor, a mega-resort in the Caucasus Mountains, 25 miles (40.2 km) from Sochi proper. The town below, Krasnaya Polyana, was little more than a 300-person village, known for its honey and wildflowers and without reliable road access through 2006. In 2007, the skiing was served by a single lift.

In 2014 that all changed. The mountain's spectator area alone hosted about 10 times what that single lift once carried in a year. Rosa Khutor is now one of Europe's largest luxury resorts, with supposedly ubiquitous Wi-Fi and gondolas gliding up the slopes like airborne ant trains.

Visitors negotiate vast off-piste snowfields, groomed runs, and steep gorges flanked by waterfalls. If skiing at the resort appeals, the bounty of what lies beyond might appeal even more. Backcountry guides and helicopter services based in Sochi ferry the adventurous into the wilds of the Caucasus, a blank canvas of untracked snowfields and opportunities in warmer weather.

Travel Tips

WHEN TO GO: If you're looking to ski, plan your trip from December to April, the peak time for fresh powder. For warmer travel, early May to late September offers what you're looking for. Summer travel offers hiking and boating opportunities.

PLANNING: Check ski resorts' websites to find out when artificial snow is guaranteed. You can reach the premier ski resorts from Sochi by high-speed train. Rosa Khutor and Krasnaya Polyana are a 30- to 40-minute ride from the city's center.

WEBSITE: rosaski.com/en/

The medieval fortress of Keselo in upper Omala

WHAT TO DO

Take to the Slopes

Thanks to the 2014 Winter Olympics, several of the area's ski resorts have been rebuilt to world-class stature. Krasnaya Polyana, for example, was expanded to 10 times its previous size, and Rosa Khutor was equipped with an artificial snow system that allows skiing four months a year. At Rosa Khutor, 47.8 miles (77 km) of downhill trails await skiers and snowboarders with altitudes as high as 7,611 feet (2,320 m). Three other resorts in the Krasnaya Polyana area offer impeccable skiing and snowboarding: Aplika Service (10 lifts, 15.5 miles/25 km of trails), Gazprom Mountain Resort (16 lifts, 12.6 miles/20.2 km of trails), and Gorky Gorod (11 lifts, 18.6 miles/30 km of trails).

Climb Mount Elbrus

The mountains, of course, are good for far more than winter sports. In the off-season, hikes, such as up Mount Akhun, which offers a viewing tower, are a great option. In the distance, Mount Elbrus, technically an inactive volcano, rises 18,510 feet (5,642 m) into the air, making it the highest mountain in Russia. Dynamic in both region and terrain, Mount Elbrus stands as a watchtower in the Caucasus Mountains between Europe and Asia. Elbrus is a large, double-coned volcano, whose summits vary by about 65 feet (20 m). For climbers with moderate skills, Mount Elbrus presents a strenuous yet rewarding climb. The mountain's location

affords visitors excellent opportunities to see the region's large melting pot of ethnic groups, such as Turkish, Georgian, Azeri, and Russian.

Cross the Tusheti Nature Reserve

The Tusheti Nature Reserve sits on the northern slopes of the Greater Caucasus Mountains. The peaks and valleys of the Tusheti region offer a rewarding, if tiring, trek. Starting at the village of Omalo, you'll make your way through stunning landscape to the beautiful hillside village of Dartlo, one of the most attractive in the Tusheti region, followed by Chesho and Parsma. You'll be able to stay in guesthouses along the way, and can easily spend a couple of days in this area alone. If you

go farther, you'll come across the abandoned village of Dadikurta and connect with another trail going through the river valley, dotted with more abandoned villages, and returning eventually to Omalo. Another popular option is to continue the journey from the village of Parma toward the Atsunta pass. Once you've crossed this you'll find yourself in Khevsureti, a remote, high mountain region in the northeast.

Sip Tea in Sochi

Located at the foot of the towering Caucasus Mountains and stretching for 90 miles (145 km) along the beckoning Black Sea, Sochi is a subtropical resort town with a twist: The mountains block the cold air rushing from the north, so the city is bathed in the warm, moist air from the south. This subtropical city, whose climate resembles that of Portland, Oregon, has beaches, and easy access to the ski slopes. Sochi is the only place in Russia where tea is produced, and it's home to one of the world's most northern tea plantations. Learn the science and history of growing tea at the Dagomys Tea Plantation, where you can also enjoy a traditional tea ceremony, with tea poured from a samovar, and a folk performance in full costume.

OPPOSITE: Skiers and snowboarders take to the trails at one of Sochi's winter sport resorts.
ABOVE: A traditional feast of tea and bread is served at a Sochi area tea house.

Yachts and boats anchor at port in Sochi—the small town was revived by the 2014 Winter Olympics.

EPIC SHOT

Emily Harrington navigates her way through complicated climbing moves on the limestone karst formation Moon Hill in Yangshou, China. The 200-foot (61 m) arch is the heart of the local Chinese climbing community and was created when the Moon Cave collapsed. The arch features bolt-protected climbing for "sport climbing." Making your way along—or under—the arch isn't just about thrills; it's pure difficulty and requires concentration and strength, not to mention the gymnastic climbing its shape demands. Should dangling from the rock not prove to be your cup of tea, visitors can also climb the 800 or so marble stairs, called "Appreciated Moon Path," that lead to the top of the Moon Hill.

IMAGE BY **KEITH LADZINSKI**

CLOCKWISE FROM TOP LEFT: A blue stripe clownfish peering out of its host anemone; a diver exploring reefs in Tubbataha National Park; a view of Lake Toba in North Sumatra, Indonesia; a surfer riding the legendary wave at Teahupoo in Tahiti

CHAPTER 5

OCEANIA

Verdant islands, crystal-blue waters, and abundant coral reefs
await in this oceanic paradise.

A SOUTH ISLAND ADVENTURE

Explore wild beaches, stunning fjords, and glaciers by land, sea, and air.

Seventy percent of New Zealanders (aka Kiwis) live on the more urban North Island. But the South Island, about an hour's drive from Queenstown, is full of places to explore. New Zealand's South Island is split by the snowcapped spine of the Southern Alps, fringed with wild beaches and lush forests, laced with gorgeous fjords, and iced with glaciers. Every season brings its own beauty, from spring's bright green carpet on the mountain slopes to fall's moody morning mists and golden foliage. No matter the time of year, residents and travelers find plenty of heart-pumping ways to take in the scenery, whether on foot, by boat, atop skis, or in a vintage biplane.

Set off on an unforgettable multisport adventure through this enchanting land, paddling along the pristine northern coast in a sea kayak, trekking across national parks dotted with sparkling lakes, and soaring by helicopter to a remote wilderness trail. Get to know the charm and personality of lesser known towns like Nelson and Wanaka and gaze at majestic Mount Cook—the sacred Aoraki in Maori culture and New Zealand's highest peak. Cap off your adventure with a cruise on the breathtaking Milford Sound. On this 11-day adventure, inspired by National Geographic Expeditions' South Island Tour, you'll find wild spaces and plenty of wildlife to explore.

Travel Tips

WHEN TO GO: New Zealand's summers are December to February, the months with the best overall weather. Fall (March to May) and spring (September to November) also see moderate temperatures.

PLANNING: Travelers should be physically fit and prepared for moderate levels of activity. Local guides offer insight into the natural history of South Island.

WEBSITES: nationalgeographic.com/expeditions; lakewanaka.co.nz; doc.govt.nz/parks-and-recreation

Alpine parrots nuzzle in Arthur's Pass National Park.

11-DAY ITINERARY

Days 1 and 2

Start in Nelson, a sunny hub of artists and craftspeople on the northern shores of South Island facing Tasman Bay. Then it's on to Kaiteriteri to catch a water taxi to Abel Tasman National Park, established in 1942. Set out on the Abel Tasman Coast Track, declared one of New Zealand's Great Walks by the Department of Conservation. Hike through lush native forests along granite and limestone cliffs and pristine gold-sand beaches.

Day 3

Spend the day sea-kayaking Tonga Island Marine Reserve. Established in 1993, the sanctuary protects 4,534 acres (1,835 hectares) of island and ocean landscape next to Abel Tasman National Park. Paddle into inlets and intimate coves, keeping an eye out for dolphins, fur seals, and blue penguins. From the beach at Onetahuti, a take-out point, hike the Coast Track, about five miles (8 km) back to Awaroa Bay.

Day 4

Leave the park by water taxi; then drive through Motueka Valley, dotted with orchards, hop plantations, and sheep and cattle farms. Arrive at the town of Murchison and take a walk through a privately owned deer farm to Murchison's "eternal flames"— an endlessly blazing fire in the middle of the forest floor, fed by methane gas from deep underground. According to local lore, the fire was ignited in the 1920s by the match of a careless hunter and hasn't stopped burning since. Then follow the Buller River toward the West Coast. The coastline stretches for 500 miles (804.6 km), but you'll never have to worry about crowds—only 40,000 people live in the entire region.

OPPOSITE: **Glassy Hooker Lake reflects the snowy peaks of Mount Cook.** RIGHT: **A family-friendly trail in Abel Tasman National Park**

Day 5

Set off on a hike that follows the Pororari River upstream into the diverse landscapes of Paparoa National Park. Pass through the Pororari River Gorge, a valley lined on both sides by dramatic limestone cliffs and bluffs, and visit the famous Pancake Rocks of Punakaiki—bizarre geological formations created 30 million years ago from the remains of marine flora and fauna.

Day 6

Drive south along the dramatic Great Coast Road before heading inland to Canterbury. Keep an eye out for the endemic kea parrots as you enjoy a short hike in Arthur's Pass National Park, located in the heart of the Southern Alps. Wander among the enchanting limestone outcrops of Castle Hill, where early Maori people hunted and grew kumara, a sweet potato. Continue to Methven, a ski town in winter and a popular base for outdoor adventures throughout the year.

Day 7

Drive to Aoraki/Mount Cook National Park, winding your way among picturesque hills, rolling farmlands, and turquoise-hued glacial lakes. Ascend the Sealy Tarns Track, and enjoy stunning views of the majestic Southern Alps, including Mount Cook, New Zealand's highest peak.

Day 8

Set out on the spectacular Hooker Valley Track, following the Hooker River below snowcapped peaks and ascending to a glacial lake. Along the way, take in the epic views of this dynamic, ice-carved landscape. Then head to the charming lakeside town of Wanaka, an ideal launching pad for exploring Mount Aspiring National Park.

Day 9

Spend the day on an unforgettable adventure in Mount Aspiring National Park. Drive

north, passing Hawea and Wanaka lakes en route to Makarora, a tiny settlement on the Haast Pass road. Then board a helicopter for an extraordinary flight among the ice-carved peaks of Mount Aspiring National Park—the southern extension of the South Westland UNESCO World Heritage area. Land in the remote Siberia Valley and embark on a hike along an old pack trail down through beech forest to the Wilkin River. Then the adventure continues with a thrilling jet boat ride, skimming along the river's calm waters below snow-dusted peaks and emerald valleys.

_____

Day 10

Drive down the sweeping Crown Range Road to Te Anau, a mountain-framed town known as the "gateway to fjords." Set out on the Kepler Track—another Great Walk—hiking along the shores of Lake Te Anau and traversing red beech forests edged by limestone cliffs. Opt to continue on the track as it climbs through forest up to a tussock-covered meadow and take in exhilarating views of the lakes and peaks of the Fiordland wilderness.

_____

Day 11

Venture into Fiordland National Park, home to nearly three million acres (1.2 million hectares) of verdant, glacially carved wilderness. Embark on a cruise through Milford Sound, one of New Zealand's most breathtaking natural wonders. Glide past cascading waterfalls and sharply hewn cliffs, and watch for bottlenose dolphins, fur seals, and, during the breeding season, rare Fiordland crested penguins. Then hike part of the Routeburn Track—yet another Great Walk.

HIGHLIGHTS

• Take on three Great Walks of New Zealand in one epic trip.

• View all of Mount Aspiring National Park by helicopter and jet boat.

• Travel across the dramatic Great Coast Road for stunning views.

Kayakers beach their vessels to explore
Abel Tasman's landscape.

AN ADVENTUROUS DAY IN QUEENSTOWN

The best experiences for 24 hours in the "adventure capital of the world"

Queenstown. It really is a place that needs no introduction. It's a guaranteed good time year-round. The city is constantly humming, occupied by an endless stream of travelers eager to taste the Adventure Capital of the World. With a lucrative tourism industry and high number of visitors, Queenstown is often referred to as "the bubble."

Arguably the most popular tourist destination in New Zealand, Queenstown is a small town with a massive itinerant population who typically spend only a few days in the resort. Because visitors want to cram a lot of living into a short time frame, the vibe is one of frenetic energy. To escape the hyped-up atmosphere, head for the mountains or the lake, and you will find peace and tranquility.

The question is not why should you go to Queenstown, but why not? Encircled by a necklace of majestic mountains on the shores of Lake Wakatipu, this jewel at the bottom of the globe exerts a magnetic force. Explore the little alpine town for adventurous activities like hiking, luging, and biking, and seek out the plethora of relaxing activities, particularly the fine wining and dining. Without exception, visitors to Queenstown—no matter their pleasure—fall under the spell of the city's mesmerizing beauty.

Travel Tips

WHEN TO GO: Avoid New Zealand school vacations, Chinese New Year, and the high-season midsummer and mid-winter months. Opt for spring and autumn, when the region is less crowded. Skiers should visit July through September, New Zealand's winter, for the best snow.

PLANNING: Queenstown may be sassy, sophisticated, and cosmopolitan, but the dress code is casual outdoor attire, even in the evenings

WEBSITES: arrowtown.com; skyline.co.nz; queenstowntrail.co.nz

The city of Queenstown lights up at night.

WHAT TO DO

Get Up Early

If you're up for a bit of early morning exercise, you'll be rewarded with panoramic views from the top of Queenstown Hill. If you prefer to ease into the day, take a drive to Lake Hayes for mirrorlike reflections, or stroll along the Queenstown waterfront to the One Mile carpark for views of the Remarkables mountain range.

Eat at the Chop Shop

Located down a little alleyway and up a flight of stairs, the Chop Shop Food Merchants used to be Arrowtown's best kept secret. With its cozy setting, unique furniture (think lamps constructed out of bike chains, plants in bags), and reputation for being consistently outstanding, the cat is out of the bag. The Asian fusion menu blends flavors creatively, and the coffee is some of the best in Central Otago.

Explore Arrowtown's History

A visit to Arrowtown, with its quaint buildings steeped in history, feels as if you've stepped back in time. A gold rush in the 1860s brought 1,500 miners who camped along the river, which eventually led to the establishment of a permanent town. Today a procession of small heritage buildings stretches toward a tree-lined avenue of tiny miners' cottages. Take a stroll through the historic Chinese Village; the people who lived there were the definition of resilient.

Skyline Gondola

The most iconic view of Queenstown is from the top of Bob's Peak. This view is undeniably breathtaking and never gets old,

no matter how many times you've seen it. The easy way up is to take the Skyline Gondola, a scenic cable car ride that gains 1,476 feet (450 m) in altitude. (If you're going to stay in Queenstown longer, you can buy a gondola annual, which also entitles you to exclusive discounts.) The harder, or more active, way is to hike up the Tiki Trail. You'll reach the top in about an hour, which emphasizes how steep the track is.

Luge

A trip up the gondola combined with a few spins on the luge track is a must-do when visiting Queenstown. It's competitively priced, super-scenic, and undeniably fun. The luge slogan, "Once is never enough," is apt; make sure you go for the five-ride option. And while you're not allowed to race on the track, it's hard not to get a little bit competitive.

Hit the Trails

The primo way to explore the region and witness jaw-dropping scenery not visible from the road is by foot or cycle. Rent bikes (or electric bikes) and spend a day or weeks cycling the outstanding Queenstown Trail, a 74.5-mile (120 km) network of tracks beside

crystal-clear lakes and rivers, through deep gorges, over high suspension bridges, past historic ruins, and amid *Lord of the Rings* landscapes.

Queenstown's Nightlife

Within the space of 1,640 feet (500 m), you're spoiled for choice when it comes to bars. Whether it's craft beer, boutique rum, wine, cocktails, an ice bar, or cheap drinks you're after, there's something for everyone. For live music, try Little Blackwood; for cocktails served in a teapot, head to World Bar; for the cheapest drinks in town, it has to be 1876; and for a good time, simply go anywhere. Be sure to walk through the alleyways that link up between Beach Street and Church Street, where there are lots of hidden gems to be discovered.

HIGHLIGHTS

• See the sun rise over the city from Queenstown Hill.

• Explore a gold rush town with heritage buildings and miners' cottages.

• Take a spin on the luge track—a one-of-a-kind adrenaline thrill ride.

Face-to-Face With the Great White Shark

By Carrie Miller

"SHARK!" I DROP MY FORKFUL of eggs and bolt out of the lounge, pinballing off the carved wooden pillars of the boat as it rolls gently in the open swells of the southern Indian Ocean. On this research ship, the shout ignites thrill, not panic. A female known as Jumbo, more than 17 feet (5.2 m) in length, is circling our vessel. From where I stand on the upper deck, she looks like a bronze airplane, her pectoral fins the wings.

The great white was my favorite animal when I was growing up in landlocked Minnesota. *Carcharodon carcharias,* "the ragged-tooth one," is the world's largest predatory fish. To me, sharks are everything that is wild, untamed, and unpredictable about the world. When I was 12, my father bought me a small shark tooth sharp enough to prick a finger, and put it on a necklace. "If you wear this in the ocean," he told me, "the sharks will recognize you as one of their own and won't harm you."

Now, as I sit on the back platform, my legs dangling into the open hatch of the surface cage, I think about the tooth, which I'm wearing under my wet suit. I'm impatient to get in the cage, but I also feel the edginess that keeps all of us, especially the crew, ultra-alert when the sharks are around.

BELOW: Sharks use their teeth, which have up to 15 degrees of flexibility, to explore the way fingers do. OPPOSITE: A multiday expedition on the *Princess II* immerses guests in the world of great white sharks.

Jumbo's large dorsal fin slices through the water a few feet from the cage as the back of the ship heaves in the swells. "Don't look at the cage," the divemaster advises me, tightening the straps on my weight belt. "Keep your eyes on the horizon; it will help you keep your balance."

He hands me one of four regulators that connect to a central air hose, and I descend the short ladder to the bottom of the cage. My breath quickens as I feel the cold water press against my thick wet suit. It takes me a moment to acclimatize to breathing through a regulator.

Pivoting in the cage seven feet (2.1 m) underwater (I'm not yet a scuba diver), I scan the blue for any flash of white, any movement, but Jumbo is gone. The only sound is my breathing. Then the back of my neck begins to prickle. I slowly turn.

Jumbo's pointed nose is six inches (15 cm) from my stomach, as close to the lower viewing window of the cage as she can get. I could touch her if l dared. She seems to consider squeezing her whalelike girth through the small window opening before dropping one of her fins and banking away. I shoot backward to the center of the cage, shaking with the shock of having a 1.5-ton (1.4 metric ton) shark successfully sneak up on me.

Jumbo doubles back and glides past the cage again, within arm's length of that lower window. Her eye is not the dead matte black from the movies but brown, with a lively blue ring around the outside. She turns and passes me again, rolling onto her side to get a better look. I'm the only one in the cage, the sole focus of her attention. I drop to my knees, lean forward. Our eyes meet, and I feel a thrill of awe and terror.

Globally, some critics say that shark diving and the practice of baiting sharks with food accustom them to boats. Teasing the sharks with bait too close to the cage puts them at risk of damaging themselves so tourists can get those iconic wide-jawed photographs. Scientific research on this issue has been inconclusive. In Australia, shark cage diving is highly regulated. The truth is, sharks have more to fear from us than we do from them. Few of us grasp sharks' critically important role as apex predators in

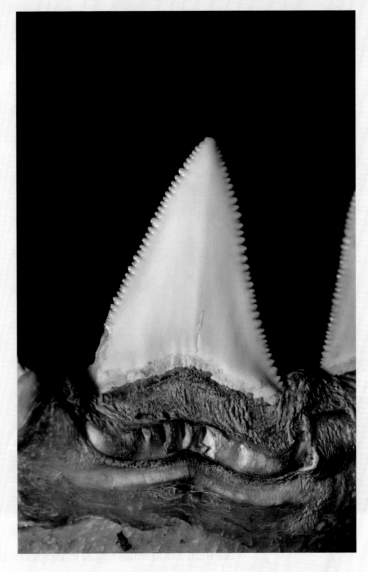

the marine environment. We don't know how many swim the oceans, but scientists are sure that even a slight shift in that delicate ecosystem will have calamitous results for marine life and the industries dependent on it.

On our last evening, I join others for a round of shark dice, a baffling game with rules we passengers suspect the crew make up as they go. I reflect on what shark diver Rodney Fox tells me: "Sharks are our monsters—ours to protect and ours to love. Mornings and nights out here, you realize you're alone in a wilderness, on the edge of a huge ocean, but you've been allowed a glimpse of something otherworldly."

I've had that glimpse, and my hand strays to the talisman tooth hanging around my neck.

OPPOSITE: A cage diver snaps a picture of Jumbo, a female great white shark. ABOVE: Sharks lose teeth frequently, but they can be replaced within a day.

Carrie Miller is a writer based in New Zealand and the author of 100 Dives of a Lifetime.

it the alluring sobriquet the "Forbidden Isle." With its remote location, restricted access, and more arid climate than its island neighbors, Niihau's waters are among the clearest and its coral ecosystems some of the most pristine in the state. Charters make the two-and-a-half-hour journey across the often choppy Kaulakahi Channel, the domain of whales, dolphins, tuna, and even whale sharks, to explore them. At the sites, including tiny rocky outcrop Lehua Rock, drift in open ocean currents past near-shore spires, gorges, arches, and vertical walls that drop hundreds of feet. Some creatures—like the Hawaiian grouper and schooling hammerhead sharks—are rarely seen elsewhere in Hawaii. But the real highlight is the regular presence of curious and endangered Hawaiian monk seals, whose population has dwindled to just 1,400 individuals, making them among the world's rarest marine mammals.

Corsair, Oahu

On a sandy seafloor populated by spindly, shy garden eels lies "The Corsair," one of Hawaii's only accessible true wrecks. The Vought F4U Corsair fighter plane crashed into the sea about three miles (5 km) off Hawaii Kai in Oahu's Maunaloa Bay during a training exercise in World War II. The pilot escaped unharmed, but the plane sank, landing upright, in more than 100 feet (30 m) of water. Divers can hover above the cockpit, glance at its gauges, and even see the intact rudder pedals. Green moray eels and the occasional sea turtle poke in and out of the downed plane. Because of its depth, time spent at the wreck is brief, but the surreal experience of watching Galápagos sharks swim past a plane is worth every second.

HIGHLIGHTS

• Swim through underwater lava tubes and inside sunken volcanic craters.

• Witness the world's largest daily migration in the deep water off Kailua-Kona.

• Explore pristine Polynesian reefs and meet endangered monk seals.

Divers descend an opening to First Cathedral off Lanai.

FIJI

BEYOND THE BEACH IN FIJI

Take in the island chain's gorgeous interior.

Fiji is so synonymous with an aquatic lifestyle that its name graces the label of a brand of bottled water. Made up of more than 300 islands, the South Pacific republic is a snorkeling and scuba diving sanctuary thanks to its surplus of kaleidoscopic reefs. But there are also plenty of memorable onshore activities for those feeling waterlogged. The islands are known as well for lush green mountain peaks, warm tropical waters, and some of the most hospitable people on Earth.

The 333 islands that make up Fiji in the South Pacific comprise beaches, coral gardens, and rainforests. Most people live on the largest island, Viti Levu, which is also a popular tourist destination. The former British colony gained independence in 1970, but it wasn't until the island nation turned back to democracy in 2001 that it became a travel hot spot again.

There's plenty of adventure to be had here—from seeking out famous Fijian pearls, hiking "the roof of Fiji," and white-water rafting the "Grand Canyon" of the islands. Of course, come with your scuba or snorkeling gear in tow; there's lots to see under the aquamarine waters, from stunning reefs to endemic fish species. This itinerary is for off-the-beaten-path adventures in a place barely touched by Western influences, where life remains pure and simple.

Travel Tips

WHEN TO GO: Fiji is hot and humid from November to April, so aim for the dry and milder season from May to October to get the most from the outdoors.

PLANNING: Pack a few conservative clothing items if you plan to visit local villages; women should have shoulders covered, and men should pack longer shorts. Most travelers fly in to Nadi International Airport and island-hop by boat or domestic flights.

WEBSITES: fijipearls.com; talanoa-treks-fiji.com; matangiisland.com/; fijiresort.com

Horseshoe Bay protects a lively coral reef.

WHAT TO DO

Put Your Head in the Clouds

Take adventure way above sea level on Tomanivi, "the roof of Fiji," located on the main island of Viti Levu. Often surrounded by cloud cover that gives hikers a reprieve from the sun's strong rays, the more than 4,000-feet-high (1,219.2 m) peak offers a rainforest landscape with citrus trees, purple wildflowers, and a playlist of parrot calls. This is no casual nature walk. Half of the three-hour ascent slopes so steeply that summit seekers occasionally have to pull themselves up using tree trunks and moss-covered rocks. Few tourists venture into Viti Levu's interior, so it's likely that you'll share the route with local villagers from Navai, who scramble up the narrow path to catch wild pigs.

The very bold can attempt to trek Fiji's highest mountain alone, but tour operator Talanoa Treks works with guides who've spent their life on Tomanivi and can help visitors avoid repeatedly falling in the mud on the way down.

Walk for a Cure

The 240-acre (97 hectare) hideaway of Matangi, a former coconut plantation that's now a luxury resort complete with tree houses, is a 20-minute boat ride from Taveuni, Fiji's garden island.

The hotel's most valuable amenity is Horseshoe Bay, a neon turquoise inlet boasting an untouched coral reef. Resort staff offer walks highlighting the healing properties of local flora. Cropping up along the path are *noni* trees for treating ulcers, *tarawaikaka* plants to fight infection, and *uthi* trees that soothe sore throats.

There's fauna along the hike too. In addition to coming across a few stray cows and goats noshing, trekkers are likely to encounter native birds like orange

doves, which feast on the abundant soursop, a green thorny fruit with a pulpy, creamy center.

But the pièce de résistance of the walk is the bird's-eye view of the electric blue bay from the top of the island's ridge, which seems to have restorative properties all its own.

Float a Gorge-ous River

Like a tropical Grand Canyon, the Navua Gorge slices through the volcanic heart of Viti Levu, the largest island of the Fijian archipelago, and redefines island paradise. The Upper Navua represents one of the most unique conservation cooperatives in the world, and one of the only protected rivers in the South Pacific. In 2000, an alliance of nine local leaders, two villages, a logging company, and a government entity placed a ban on logging, mining, and road construction within 656 feet (200 m) of either side of the river's lapping waters. Take a trip on one of the longest navigable slot canyons in the world, at roughly 18 miles (30 km) long. Sheer walls rocket 150 feet (45.7 m) skyward as Class II and III rapids rush through 20-foot-wide (6.1 m) channels. Waterfalls and constant spray pour from the jungle above, keeping this oasis teeming with life.

Try Garden-to-Table

Jean-Michel Cousteau Resort doesn't take its sustainable association lightly. Many of the fruits and vegetables used at Matangi's restaurant are sourced on resort grounds.

Stroll around the property's organic garden and greenhouse, brimming with basil, coriander, eggplant, rosemary, ginger, and more. Overhead, vines of passion fruit provide shade from the sun, along with outstretched mango trees. Besides plants of the edible variety, there's also a nursery nurturing native flowers and trees that will eventually be introduced into the wild landscape.

The waters surrounding the resort are protected as a marine reserve, so you can't collect fresh catch from the reef. But if you pick out local lobsters or crabs from the nearby Savusavu market, executive chef Raymond Lee will cook them for you, along with special treats from the garden.

HIGHLIGHTS

- Stay at a former coconut plantation with views of Horseshoe Bay.

- Soar above the clouds on a hike along Tomanivi, "the roof of Fiji."

- Paddle Class II and III rapids in the heart of Viti Levu.

OPPOSITE: **Beyond the beach, rafters explore the Upper Navua River gorge in Fiji.** ABOVE: **Verdant hills and lakes make up Fiji's interior, a worthy expedition away from the beach.**

The Navua River is one of the longest navigable slot canyons in the world.

1 TUBBATAHA REEF, PHILIPPINES

Thanks to Tubbataha's 600-plus fish species, 11 shark species, and 13 cetacean species, the biggest problem you'll have diving here is deciding where to look. This liveaboard-only UNESCO site, located in the Coral Triangle, can be reached only from March to early June. More than 300 coral species paint the ocean floor between dramatic cliff faces and swim-throughs.

2 PORT LINCOLN, AUSTRALIA

Coastal Port Lincoln has hosted Australia's largest commercial fishing fleet, surfers, sailors, and, in 1975, the entire cast of *Jaws*. Today, Port Lincoln's Dangerous Reef and Neptune Islands are more involved in shark education than shark attacks. These reefs are the only place in the world where divers can go cage diving on the ocean floor with great whites.

3 BEQA LAGOON, FIJI

Known as the "Soft Coral Capital of the World," the Fijian archipelago is a nonstop sensory extravaganza. Beqa Lagoon, located just south of Viti Levu, is a 150-square-mile (388 sq km) site where divers can sometimes see more than eight shark species on a single tank. The newly protected Fiji Shark Corridor leads the way to even more exhilarating encounters.

4 THE SOLOMON ISLANDS

Almost 1,000 volcanic islands span across 1,000 miles (1,609 km) of clear blue water in the Solomon Islands, all of it hiding 1,000 wrecks begging to be explored. Pelagic shoals race around steep blue walls. Swim-through lava tubes house seahorses, octopus, whip coral, and eels. Underwater volcano eruptions shake giant schools of barracuda and shark. There are also sunken World War II vessels, neon nudibranchs, underwater mountains, and jungle caves for diving.

5 RAJA AMPAT, INDONESIA

Indonesia's Raja Ampat Islands nurture more than 500 coral species and 1,074-plus fish species—possibly the ocean's most diverse coral reef. Choose between endless dive sites like Cape Kri (record holder for the most species seen in a single dive), Fabiacet (to see hammerheads and green turtles), and Mioskun (home of Wobbegong carpet sharks).

6 KONA, HAWAII

Drifting 50 feet (15 m) deep in the open water off of Kona, Hawaii, divers on Jack's Diving Locker's "Pelagic Magic" tour get to see streaming net-caster jellyfish, bioluminescent zooplankton, fireworms, squid, eels, and tiny glowing marine snails, as the extraordinary creatures ascend on their nightly vertical migration.

7 OLWOLGIN CAVE, AUSTRALIA

Situated in Australia's Roe Plains, the Olwolgin Cave offers more than six miles (9.7 km) of flooded navigable tunnels, some so narrow you have to carry one tank ahead of you. Let a flipper sweep the floor, and sediment will cloud your view for the rest of the dive; don't, and you'll have a look at dangling tree roots called the "Hanging Gardens of Babylon."

8 SIPADAN, MALAYSIA

Watch sharks spear through thousand-strong shoals of chevron barracudas and jack fish vortexes at Barracuda Point off Malaysia's Sipadan Island. Vertical walls anchor sea fans, sponges, and black coral. Other critters caught in the sway include bumphead parrotfish, crocodilefish, and delicate Moorish idols. Many see more than 20 green and hawksbill turtles per dive.

9 AMERICAN SAMOA

American Samoa harbors some of the largest and oldest coral in the world, including 26-foot-wide (7.9 m) boulder coral and Fagatele Bay's 42-foot-wide (12.8 m) "Big Momma" brain coral. The South Pacific archipelago is so remote and difficult to get to that the surrounding reefs have remained in pristine condition, a haven for sharks, eagle rays, humpback whales, and more than 950 fish species.

10 S.S. *COOLIDGE*, VANUATU

The S.S. *Coolidge* hit two mines and sank off the coast of Espiritu Santo in 1945 fighting in WWII. Now, the 656-foot-long (200 m) vessel is surrounded by lionfish, barracudas, rifles, disco scallops, moray eels, and porcelain icons. Dive the wreck at night to see schools of bioluminescent flashlight fish and glittering plankton.

OPPOSITE: A diver hovers above shockingly bright coral in Tubbataha, Philippines. ABOVE: Tim Muscat negotiates his way through scalloped walls in Olwolgin Cave.

TAHITI MOMENTS OF MANA

Finding the fifth element in French Polynesia

The first ocean voyagers to the Polynesian islands likely originated from Southeast Asia more than a thousand years ago. Island riches lured Europeans and Americans to Polynesian shores. The legendary mutiny on the H.M.S. *Bounty* took place after a layover in Tahiti. A deserter named Herman Melville jumped ship in the Marquesas, an experience that inspired his first book. The long colonial struggle for control was finalized in 1880, when the king of Tahiti ceded the scattered islands to France.

French Polynesia isn't a singular sensation but a mosaic of moods spread across 118 small island and atolls—only 67 inhabited. It's not a place of museums or hot spots, but rather an elemental destination of earth, water, air, fire, and something else even more elusive. Jagged mountains, dark volcanic soil, and steep rainforests exert their own power. Land may be the forgotten element in the South Pacific, where neon blue lagoons dominate. But there is so much more to explore.

Every island in French Polynesia is unique, each with its own personality and affiliation to one of five island groups. Tahiti and the other Society Islands are the most visited, the Marquesas the most northerly, the Tuamotus the flattest, while the more southern Austral and Gambier archipelagos remain virtually unvisited. The Polynesian spirit compels travelers to explore beyond each new horizon.

Travel Tips

WHEN TO GO: Temperatures in Tahiti are balmy year-round, but you'll have less humidity and rain in the Southern Hemisphere's winter, which is from June to September.

PLANNING: Flights fly direct from the United States to Papeete, Tahiti, the capital of French Polynesia. Air Tahiti operates inter-island flights, or opt for cruise ships for a more leisurely way to get to far-flung islands.

WEBSITES: nationalgeographic.com/expeditions; topdive.com; kamoka.com

A vanilla orchid flower, manually fertilized

WHAT TO DO

Hike the Highlands

Hike up into the tropical highlands of Moorea—a trek that will involve your hands as much as your feet—for a view of sister island Tahiti, just a short ferry ride away. Pulling on smooth vines and hopping mountain brooks, tromp upward through a rainforest of cool shadows and diaphanous orange and red flowers—plants that are so outlandish they nearly seem fake. The hollow trees surrounding your path are *mape,* or Tahitian chestnut, which were carried to the island by the first Polynesians. The hike takes more than an hour to reach the knife's edge of Moorea's volcanic ridge, a steep black basalt wall. From the narrow lookout at Trois Cocotiers (Three Coconuts), you can see the whole of Moorea: the heart-shaped island, the gleaming turquoise of Opunohu Bay, and the unbroken green carpet that sweeps from the shoreline up to the peak of Mount Rotui.

Peer Below the Surface

Seventy feet (21.3 m) below the ocean surface, suspended in the clear void outside Moorea's reef, come face-to-face with a lemon shark, striped pilot fish, and a parade of blacktip reef sharks. Coral meadows glow with all the colors of cotton candy. Silvery fish, purple-tipped sea anemones, and giant clams fill the frame of your mask, an epic reminder that life is pulsing below the waterline. The abundance, accessibility, and scale of sea life make these islands an underwater paradise.

For rare and natural encounters, in-the-know divers turn to the Tuamotu Archipelago where Rangiroa and Tikehau islands offer amazing biodiversity, even for casual snorkelers. Inside the Fakarava Lagoon, the dark blue world transforms into a swirl of schooling sharks—tiger, hammerhead, tawny nurse, and blacktips. The lagoon is also home to the highest concentration of gray reef sharks in the world.

Enjoy the Riches

Taha'a is a round island blanketed by vanilla farms. Here, the scent is homegrown. Vanilla is part of the landscape and the air. It's also scented by jasmine and the tantalizing and unique scent of the national tiare flower, a calming, sunny, lemony perfume. Explore the island gardens and take a tour of an authentic vanilla farm to experience the local flavor. Or visit Kamoka Pearl, a sustainable family-run pearl farm on Ahe Atoll in the Tuamotu Archipelago that welcomes visitors.

Get a Tattoo

The traditional Marquesan *patutiki* tattoo inspires contemporary versions of the art form, and travelers can receive a permanent souvenir, custom-designed by artists who know how to trap the secret language of symbols into the skin.

Explore Polynesia's History

At Hiva Oa, travel into the mountains above Puamau village to see Ma'ae Lipona, home to one of the largest ancient tiki statues in Polynesia. Then, visit Calvary Cemetery, the final resting place of French artist Paul Gauguin and Belgian singer Jacques Brel.

OPPOSITE: Moorea's Opunohu Bay is a popular anchorage spot for yachts, sailboats, and cruise ships. RIGHT: Tahitian pearls, harvested from a sustainable farm in Ahe Atoll, sit in a clamshell.

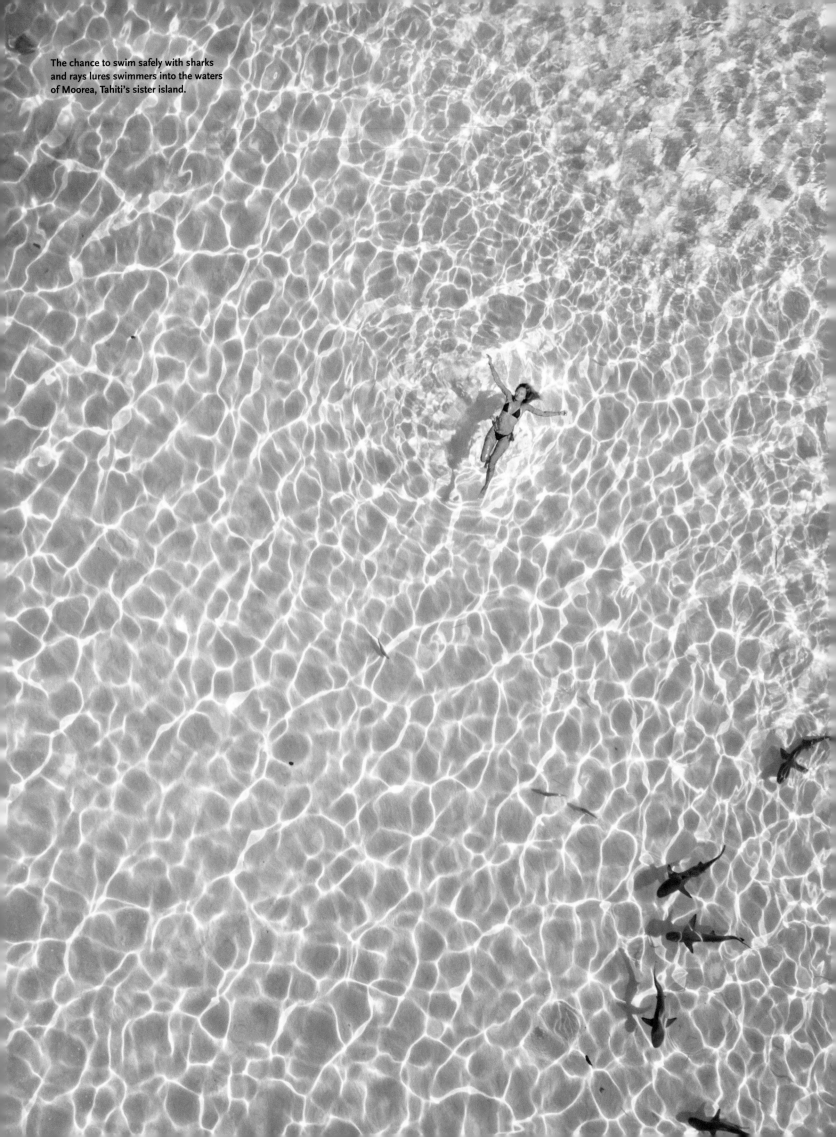

The chance to swim safely with sharks and rays lures swimmers into the waters of Moorea, Tahiti's sister island.

SNORKEL AND KAYAK PRISTINE SEAS

Discover the extraordinary undersea wonders of Palau's sparkling reefs.

dentified by National Geographic and Enric Sala's Pristine Seas project as one of the richest marine ecosystems on the planet, the Pacific archipelago of Palau is home to an aquatic wonderland of more than 1,300 species of fish and some 700 species of corals.

This beautiful island nation is a world leader in marine conservation, with an ancestral tradition of environmental protection that dates back thousands of years, and an ambitious modern conservation program that includes the creation of a historic 193,000-square-mile (nearly 500,000 sq km) marine reserve—one of the largest of its kind in the world.

Set out on an unforgettable adventure, inspired by National Geographic Expeditions, to experience Palau's treasures firsthand. Snorkel and kayak among emerald islets in the UNESCO World Heritage–listed Rock Islands; experience the "underwater Serengeti" of Ngemelis Island; hike to dazzling waterfalls; encounter fish, turtles, and reef sharks underwater; kayak to stalactite-adorned caves and hidden lagoons; and swim among nonstinging jellyfish. Then meet Palauan people who strive to honor and protect their natural heritage that dates back 3,000 years. Whatever you're seeking, this magical island nation has something to offer everyone, by land, by air, and, most extraordinarily, by water.

Travel Tips

WHEN TO GO: Diving is at its best in Palau between November and April when the greatest number of pelagics visit and water visibility is high.

PLANNING: Palau is a marine life sanctuary, so follow guide instructions and regulations for interacting with sea life. Palau has only one airport—the Roman Tmetuchl International Airport—outside Airai on the southern coast of Babeldaob island. Flights are direct from Guam, Manila, Taiwan, and Seoul.

WEBSITE: nationalgeographic.com/expeditions

A jellyfish surfaces at Risong Bay.

8-DAY ITINERARY

Day 1

Take a short speedboat ride to a stunning lagoon where the adventure kicks off with a warm-up snorkel in calm waters alive with vibrant corals and tropical fish. Keep an eye out for blue sea stars, blue-green chromis, and butterflyfish. Later, cruise to Risong Bay, nestled among the mushroom-shaped limestone islets of Chelbacheb, also known as the Rock Islands—a UNESCO World Heritage site renowned for its natural beauty and its extraordinary marine life. Swim through narrow shallow passages lined with pink sea fans to the oasis known as Mandarin Fish Lake, named for the eponymous and elusive fish species that live here. In the shelter of rocky outcrops, snorkel among reefs swirling with diverse fish, including crocodilefish, pajama cardinalfish, and gobies.

Day 2

Travel by speedboat to the Palau International Coral Reef Center (PICRC), which collaborated with National Geographic on the 2014 Pristine Seas expedition to Palau to document the biodiversity of the archipelago's marine ecosystem. As you explore the center, learn about the PICRC's involvement with the Pristine Seas project, launched by marine ecologist and National Geographic Explorer-in-Residence Enric Sala to explore and help save the last wild places in the ocean. Visit the center's aquarium for an introduction to Palau's marine habitats, conservation efforts, and geologic history. Afterward, continue by boat to Nikko Bay, where you'll learn about a coral-spawning study that was completed here and enjoy a private snorkeling excursion in Rembrandt's Cove. Keep an eye out for tropicbirds and terns soaring above, and view World War II artifacts at a former

Japanese bunker. Later, launch kayaks to explore a stunning, stalactite-adorned cave, and paddle through a tunnel to a lake filled with delicate corals.

Day 3

Snorkel in the sheltered lagoons of Ulong, one of the largest of the Rock Islands. Here, an astonishing aggregation of hundreds of bumphead parrotfish gather to spawn in the early morning. Snorkel among fields of branch corals and shimmering fish. Then venture ashore to hike to an ancient village and learn how Palauans once lived in this remote paradise. Pitch in with a local conservation project by planting a giant clam in a marine sanctuary, and witness the fruits of over a decade of planting efforts. In the afternoon, explore the labyrinth of islands comprising Ngeruktabel. Snorkel among myriad colorful soft corals, and swim through a spacious tunnel leading to a hidden lagoon.

Day 4

Set off early to the island of Mecherchar, home to one of Palau's most famous natural wonders: Jellyfish Lake. This saltwater lake has been known to contain up to 20

million nonstinging golden jellyfish, whose ability to sting was lost when the basin was cut off from the ocean hundreds of years ago and they were no longer at risk of being eaten. Later, boat along the coast to discover a treasure of Micronesian history: a two-ton (1.8 metric ton) relic of the world's largest—and heaviest—currency. Examine enormous stone money that was created by the ancient people of neighboring Yap, who traveled by canoe to quarry the stone from the limestone-rich Rock Islands. Next, head to the quiet waters of Ngchus Cove and snorkel over a sunken Japanese fighter aircraft that was shot down in 1944.

Day 5

As the morning tide rises, paddle a kayak beneath a canopy of mangroves into a saltwater lake home to ancient Micronesian cyad plants and rare white-breasted woodswallows. Search for juvenile eagle rays and endemic plants found nowhere else on Earth. Later, explore the opaque waters of the Milky Way Lagoon, where you can enjoy a white mud bath from the lagoon's limestone and calcium clay, believed to have healing powers. Finish the day snorkeling among the multicolored brain corals of the Rock Islands.

The Rock Islands of the
Republic of Palau

Day 6

The first snorkeling site of the day is home to dozens of "super mollusks," including giant clams. Next, it's on to Rainbow Reef to snorkel among shoals where fish drift on gentle currents while feasting on plankton. Visit Ngeanges island, which, after a successful initiative to clear invasive rodents, bustles with native bird species. Enjoy a walk in the forest, searching for chicken-like megapode birds and their enormous nests. Cool off with a refreshing snorkel, watching dazzling damselfish dart in and out of a colossal turbinaria coral formation. Snorkel at a cave where local conservation efforts have helped protect corals from the predatory crown-of-thorns sea star.

Day 7

Experience an "underwater Serengeti" at one of the world's greatest snorkeling sites at the outer reef of Ngemelis, which the Pristine Seas team identified as one of the most vibrant marine-protected areas in Palau. Here, untouched reefs teem with fish, turtles, white-tipped reef sharks, garden eels, and much more. After nearly 20 years as a "no-fishing zone," the Ngemelis Conservation Area allows for close encounters with Napoleon wrasse, bumphead parrotfish, and clown triggerfish.

Day 8

Begin the morning with a gentle hike on Babeldaob, Palau's largest island, known for its botanical treasures. Hike to a pair of remote and rarely visited waterfalls and relax by tranquil pools. Later, drive to an ancient *bai*, or meeting house, where community elders once gathered. View ancient pictographs carved and painted on the trusses, depicting ancient Palauan legends.

HIGHLIGHTS

• Take daily snorkeling excursions in pristine reefs teeming with coral and fish.

• Take a swim among thousands of non-stinging jellyfish unique to the region.

• Kayak through mangroves and into hidden lagoons.

winding roads, and dramatic views of sheer sea cliffs, black-sand beaches, and lush valleys make Molokai ideal for serious road cycling. Rent a ride from Molokai Bicycle to make the 27-mile (43.4 km) trek (one way) from Kaunakakai east to the ancient Halawa Valley on the island's East End. There is a 900-foot (274.3 m) challenging climb up to Puʻu O Hoku Ranch at the 25-mile (40.2 km) mark, but you will have a tailwind on the ride back to Kaunakakai since the prevailing trade breezes blow out of the east.

Hawaiʻi (The Big Island)

Choose from hundreds of miles of hiking trails in Hawaiʻi Volcanoes National Park. The UNESCO International Biosphere Reserve and UNESCO World Heritage site covers 520 square miles (1,346.7 sq km) and protects two volcanoes: the world's largest, 19,999-cubic-mile (83,359 cubic km) Mauna Loa, which last erupted in 1984, and Kilauea, which continuously erupted from 1983 to 2018. Kilauea's lava flows ceased in May 2018 (meaning molten lava and lava glow are no longer visible), and the most recent eruption cycle closed some park trails, including major sections of Crater Rim, which formerly ringed the Kilauea caldera.

For a wilderness adventure in the park—away from areas damaged by volcanic activity—hike the coastal Hilina Pali Trail from the Hilina Pali Overlook down the mountainside to Kaʻaha. The 3.8-mile (6 km) trail follows a switchback stone walkway and offers broad views of a pristine coastal area dotted with sea arches. From Kaʻaha, the trail continues a rugged six miles (9.6 km) to a palm tree–lined beach at Halape, where you can backcountry camp by the ocean.

HIGHLIGHTS

• Cruise down the slopes of Maui's dormant Haleakala volcano.

• Hike the Alakai Swamp Trail through a rainforest in Kauai's Kokeʻe State Park.

•See all six major Hawaiian Islands from the summit of Lanaʻihale.

Tourists watch the sunset behind Lanai
from the top of Haleakala.

FRENCH POLYNESIA

BEYOND THE POSTCARD

Island-hop to less visited places in the French Polynesia island chain.

Experience the heart and soul of French Polynesia while exploring island cultures as well as natural wonders above and beneath the sea. From the pristine reefs of the Tuamotus to the towering peaks of the Marquesas, immerse yourself in a tropical paradise amid some of the most beautiful and isolated islands on Earth. Swim in turquoise lagoons, snorkel over vast coral gardens, and venture ashore to encounter fascinating island cultures.

Take to the waters by kayak or paddleboard, bike to local villages, and connect with the people and traditions of the islands. On Raiatea, discover the historic ceremonial site, called a marae, where Polynesian seafarers began their bold sailing expeditions into the unknown—voyages that would eventually lead to populating Hawaii and New Zealand. Sail among some of the 80 or so atolls of the Tuamotu Archipelago, and dive or snorkel the thriving reefs along this string of tiny islands. Go ashore the seldom visited Huahine, the former residence of Tahitian royalty, and visit ancient sites. Take in spectacular views over Bora-Bora from emerald crags and dive from a private motu—an islet on the outer reef. All of this can be done on one remarkable eight-day island-hopping adventure aboard a National Geographic–Lindblad ship that takes you beyond the typical honeymoon spots and really shows off what French Polynesia has to offer its visitors.

Travel Tips

WHEN TO GO: The island chain is at its best from June to August, when it's dry and the temperatures are comfortable.

PLANNING: Even in the drier seasons, you're in the tropics and will have rainfall nearly every day. With the tropical weather comes a lot of bugs, especially mosquitoes. Pack bug spray and use mosquito nets when available. Knowing a little French can help with getting around on land.

WEBSITE: nationalgeographic.com/ expeditions

Taputapuatea Marae on Raiatea, a UNESCO site

7-DAY ITINERARY

Days 1 and 2

Arrive in Papeete, Tahiti, and take a brief tour of the island before departing on an overnight sail to Bora-Bora in the Society Islands. Jutting out from an aquamarine lagoon ringed with tiny islets, Bora-Bora's angular volcanic crags are a spectacular sight. Explore the island's slopes and shores by 4x4 and enjoy unparalleled views of the island's turquoise lagoon. Then snorkel, dive, kayak, and paddleboard from one of the motus on the outer reef.

Day 3

Encircled by a single fringing reef and sharing a common lagoon, Raiatea and Taha'a offer plenty to explore. One of the most important cultural sites in the Polynesian world, Marae Taputapuatea served as the starting point for Polynesian seafarers heading to Rapa Nui (Easter Island, Chile), Hawaii, and New Zealand. Spend the morning exploring this site on Raiatea; then swim in the warm turquoise seas. Your boat navigates lagoon channels en route to Taha'a, where you can go ashore for a visit to a small family-run vanilla plantation.

Day 4

One of Polynesia's best kept secrets and the former home of Tahitian royalty, Huahine maintains the highest density of ancient marae (sacred sites and temples) in French Polynesia. Visit these sites with cultural experts or archaeologists who will bring them to life. Trace the perimeter of the island on a bicycle; then explore the verdant shoreline by kayak or paddleboard. Finish the day with a swim in the island's crystal-clear lagoon.

Days 5 and 6

Spend two days exploring some of the nearly 80 islands and atolls in the "Dangerous Archipelago." Fakarava is one of the largest atolls in French Polynesia and part of a UNESCO Biosphere Reserve. Snorkel the protected reefs or ride the current into the lagoon on a world-famous drift dive. An uplifted coral atoll, the island of Makatea is one of the most unusual landforms in the Pacific. Navigate limestone caves and grottoes or search for fruit doves and myriad seabirds. Then snorkel and dive among colorful fish on the nearby reef.

While you may not witness it, divers will delight to know that at the south end of Fakarava Atoll, thousands of camouflage grouper arrive in June to breed. In turn, hundreds of gray reef sharks gather to hunt. In 2014, the first time scientists were able to get an accurate count, marine biologists estimated around 17,000 grouper and 700 sharks flooded the channel during the breeding and feeding season.

Day 7

The atoll of Rangiroa is a ring of slender islands known for some of the best diving and snorkeling in French Polynesia. The turquoise lagoon at its center is the second largest in the world. Pass between the palm-fringed islets to anchor inside the lagoon near the village of Tiputa. Visit the tranquil village and spend time with its friendly residents. Kayak, snorkel, and scuba dive in the waters here, home to large schools of pelagic fish, manta rays, dolphins, sea turtles, and hammerheads.

HIGHLIGHTS

• Explore underwater havens of pelagic fish, sea turtles, manta rays, and sharks.

• Kayak or paddleboard along verdant shorelines.

• Dive into history from lands of Tahitian royalty to significant Polynesian sites.

OPPOSITE: Palm trees on Motu Piti A'au frame the lagoon facing the main island of Bora-Bora. RIGHT: A white tern roosts on a limb at the Belvedere on Makatea.

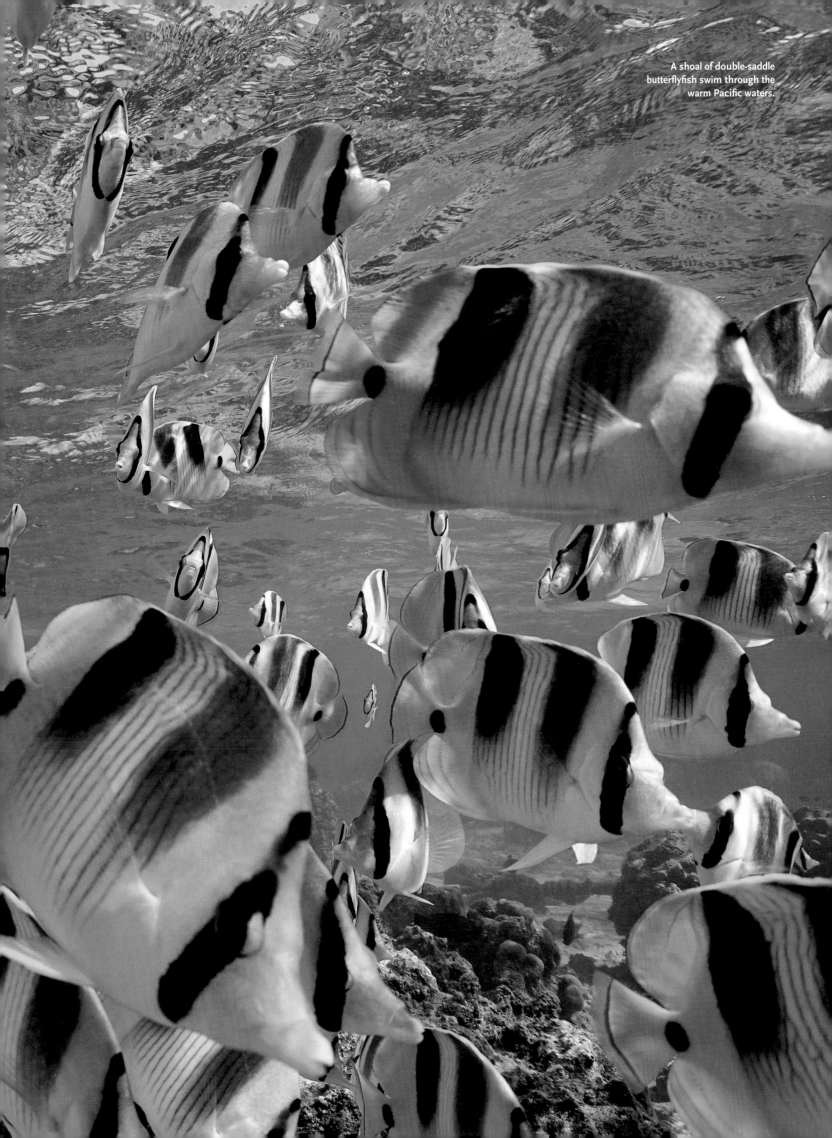

A shoal of double-saddle butterflyfish swim through the warm Pacific waters.

SEA KAYAKING

1 KOMODO ISLANDS, INDONESIA

Kayak the Komodo Islands in May for green landscapes, dry weather, and a chance to see the world's largest "dragons" battle for mating rights. Kayak glassy seas and whirlpool swells with sea turtles, manta rays, and dancing spinner dolphins. There is nothing like snorkeling at sunrise, seeing thousands of fruit bats in flight from Kaaba Island, and at the end of the day, watching the sun set behind a steaming volcano.

2 FIORDLAND NATIONAL PARK, NEW ZEALAND

New Zealand's Fiordland National Park offers a range of kayaking opportunities from white-water excursions on the Hollyford River to paddling the shores of Lake Te Anau, where pristine glowworm caves make for a magical place to stop and stretch your legs. In the remote Doubtful Sound, a mountainous glacier-carved playground offers secret beaches and waterfalls.

3 NITMILUK NATIONAL PARK, AUSTRALIA

Located on sacred Jawoyn land, Nitmiluk National Park is a refreshing, tree-lined sanctuary within Australia's semi-arid Northern Territory. Paddle and portage Nitmiluk's Katherine River gorge-to-gorge to see 40,000-year-old aboriginal "Dreamtime" rock art, cockatoo and crocodile habitats, dramatic waterfalls, and swimming holes.

4 HAWAIKI NUI VA'A, FRENCH POLYNESIA

Polynesians have traveled the Pacific via *va'a* (traditional outrigger canoes) for more than 4,000 years. *Hawaiki nui va'a,* Tahiti's annual va'a race, is known as the most difficult V6 (outrigger) canoe race in the world, covering 80 miles (129 km) of heartbreakingly blue water in three days with no crew change. Visit in autumn to watch teams take off; then rent your own va'a to paddle about in Teahupoo.

5 NAN MADOL RUINS, MICRONESIA

Constructed from basalt and coral boulders between A.D. 1200 and 1500, southern Micronesia's Nan Madol ruins are from the only ancient city built on a coral reef. Kayak the UNESCO site's 90-plus islets at high tide to explore stone palaces, temples, tombs, and ancient homes overgrown with mangroves.

6 LAKE TOBA, SUMATRA

Sumatra's Lake Toba is the biggest crater lake in the world, home to the indigenous Batak people, many of whom still live in intricately carved *jabu* stilt houses. Paddle between Sipiso-Piso waterfall and Pusuk Buhit's natural hot springs.

7 NEW IRELAND, PAPUA NEW GUINEA

Beloved by surfers and divers, New Ireland Province's remote Tigak area is an idyllic place for paddling and snorkeling with dolphins, angelfish, reef sharks, and coral trout. Float past untouched white-sand beaches and turtle nesting sites on Nago Island as you travel between friendly fishing villages where locals still practice the art of carving and painting *malagan* — intricate wooden funerary masks.

8 NAVUA RIVER, FIJI

Head to Fiji's Navua River for white-water expeditions through mossy rainforests, glorious waterfalls, and narrow black volcanic walls feathered with ferns. Upper Navua's native flora and fauna have been protected from habitat loss for over 15 years by the Upper Navua Conservation Area, now managed by local communities in collaboration with Rivers Fiji.

9 NA PALI COAST, KAUAI

Kauai boasts 50 miles (80.5 km) of secluded white-sand beaches and a coastline so beautiful that it has been featured in more than 70 films. Napali Kayak offers 12-mile (19.3 km) round-trip sea kayaking tours that begin in Polihale State Park and trace the Na Pali Coast along sea caves, waterfalls, leaping dolphin pods, and 2,500-foot-tall (762 m) rippled green cliffs.

10 ROTTNEST ISLAND, WESTERN AUSTRALIA

It takes a plane, a train, a bike, and a ferry to make your way to Rottnest—a salt lake and sand dune island off the western coast of Australia. But it's worth the effort for a one-of-a-kind glass-bottom sea kayak tour above 100,000-year-old coral reefs crowded with parrotfish, lobsters, hermit crabs, and nudibranchs.

OPPOSITE: Gigantic falls are put into perspective by kayakers in the Milford Sound. ABOVE: Paddlers make their way beneath a sea arch on the Na Pali Coast.

OUTBACK ADVENTURES ON THE MURRAY RIVER

Uncover hidden gems along Australia's longest river.

The peaceful Murray River in South Australia meanders through a photo-worthy land of ancient red gum forests, spectacular ocher-colored cliffs, tranquil creeks, oxbow lagoons, wildlife, waterbirds, and old communities with stories to tell. It's the kind of region that invites deep exploration—you're just dying to see what's up the next creek, or around the next bend.

A couple of hours' drive from Adelaide, the Murray River has been a vacation destination since 1961, when a local man built 20 houseboats and leased them out. Some of the originals are still in use, but others are brand new high-tech affairs with hot tubs and big-screen TVs. Rent them for your family and friends, and cruise at your own pace.

The Murray River Walk, a unique way to experience South Australia's abundant wildlife, offers an exploration by day on foot and watch the river go by at night while you sleep on board a small ship. The Murray River Walk houseboat is a modern 10-berth, double-decker vessel with a hot shower and a top-deck spa overlooking the river. During the day, walkers cover an easy-to-moderate route that totals 26 miles (41.8 km) in three days; the boat journeys 43 miles (69.2 km). At night guests savor three-course dinners prepared from local food and wines.

Travel Tips

WHEN TO GO: The best time to visit is in the summer, especially in January, when temperatures are high in the day and mild at night. It also stays light until 8:30 p.m., giving you more time to explore.

PLANNING: Include a few days in Adelaide before or after your cruise, or tack on a visit to Kangaroo Island, a short ferry ride away.

WEBSITES: murrayriverwalk.com.au; murrayriver.com.au; visitthemurray.com.au; visitnsw.com; visitmelbourne.com

A pelican lands on the river at sunset.

WHAT TO DO

Hike Along the Riverbanks

A hike to nearby Headings Cliffs reveals breathtaking sandstone columns and buttresses taking on the colors of sunrise. On other days you can explore various creeks and backwaters. Your journey may take you across a billabong—a seasonally dry streambed and its ever spreading mosaic of cracked mud. See anhingas perch on snags to dry their wings and black pelicans skim along the riverbanks. The meandering Chowilla Creek makes for a stunning walk. As you traverse Buyip Reach to the Queens Bend Cliffs, take in the restored wetlands and waterbirds living in the area. Back on the houseboat, watch the sunset illuminate the cliffs where you just walked.

Spot the Wildlife

Venerable old river red gum (eucalyptus) trees dot the landscape. One of them, a massive survivor known as Mother Teresa, is likely more than 1,000 years old. Others show where bark was removed centuries ago by aboriginal people for the construction of bark canoes. In a harvested wheat field nearby, you could spot a mob of emus and their young.

Visit Renmark

A lot of the Murray River action happens around the town of Renmark, population 7,500. Renmark has become a popular spot for such water sports as waterskiing and wakeboarding, as well as for golf and the arts; it's also the home of Australia's largest rose garden. The town's newest attraction, the *Murray River Queen* paddle steamer, formerly a youth hostel, is now a floating restaurant.

Explore Nearby Waterways and Dunes

Beyond the Murray lie other snaking rivers and lakes. The Edward River, in the town of Deniliquin, is worth a side trip for excellent water sports and the town's annual ute muster, a full-day event of music, carnival rides, driving competitions, and bull riding that's held every September. For drier land trips, head to Perry Sandhills to take in the shifting sand dunes.

Sip and See

The Murray River sits in Australia's second largest wine region. The Murray-Darling Basin is home to a number of vineyards in and around Mildura, Victoria. Sip rich reds in the Rutherglen, Victoria area's boutique wineries. Breweries with riverside views are also in abundance here, including Mildura Brewery, one of Australia's best microbreweries.

Understand Murray's Culture

Visit local museums to gain insight into ancient Aboriginal life in the early days of the Murray, as well as the use of paddle steamers plying the waters. In Echuca, find Australia's museum dedicated to beer cans and brewer-related memorabilia. And in Swan Hill, find impressive regional galleries showcasing work by local artists.

Visit National Parks

The river is part of the Murray Valley National Park, but neighboring protected wetlands and nature reserves are worthy adventures while you're in the area. Head to Barmah National Park, which, together with Millewa Forest in New South Wales, forms the largest river red gum forest in the world. It's a great spot for camping and spotting diverse wildlife, as well as horseback riding, fishing, bushwalking, swimming, and canoeing. Another worthwhile stop: the UNESCO World Heritage–listed Mungo National Park, home to the famous Mungo Lady and Mungo Man—evidence of ritual burials that are nearly 42,000 years old. Mungo Lady is thought to be the oldest known cremation in the world.

OPPOSITE: **The Murray River glows in orange and amber hues as the sun sets. ABOVE: A fisherman looks for his next catch near Big Bend Cliff.**

Tales, Totems, and Magic in the Outback

By Cathy Newman

THE GEOGRAPHY OF THE HUMAN heart is formed from places we have traveled and people we have known. Cape York Peninsula, that green spike of land at the northern tip of Queensland, Australia, is a sacred corner of my interior landscape. And not just because of its sometimes dark beauty, but because of people like Arthur and Gladys.

My first night on Cape York Peninsula is marked by strange dreams and fitful sleep. When I mention my insomnia to Gladys Tybingoompa, an elder in the Aboriginal community of Aurukun where I had been invited to dinner, she turns to her brother-in-law, Arthur Pambegan, and tells him to conjure a spell that would keep me safe and allow me to rest.

Arthur's charm, an incantation and the touch of a spear-throwing device called a *woomera* on my shoulder,

worked—for a few nights anyway. And perhaps I shouldn't have been surprised at its impermanence. There is a subtext of sadness here—a common enough tale to be heard in many parts of the world, a story of struggle for landownership between those who lived there first and those who came later. In Australia, that history begins with Captain James Cook, European settlement in the 18th century, and the displaced native Aboriginal people.

Arthur is introduced to me as a famous sculptor of bonefish. I nod when Gladys tells me this. "I know what they are. We have them in South Florida where I grew up, and on the day my brother was born, my father went fishing and caught one." Gladys stares at me with her black

---

BELOW: Dancers perform a traditional Aboriginal dance during a festival in Laura, Australia. OPPOSITE: Paperback trees line a creek near the mining town of Weipa in the outback.

Sixth-century Vigan is the best preserved example of a planned Spanish colonial town in Asia.

DRIVING WESTERN AUSTRALIA'S CORAL COAST

Take a road trip through the uncrowded side of Oz.

Western Australia (WA) is the wild, wide-open, and less traveled side of Oz. Of the more than nine million people who visit Australia each year, only about a tenth go to WA, which covers the western third of the continent and is the country's biggest state. WA is so far off the beaten path that its capital, Perth (population 1.98 million), is considered the world's most remote major city. Its closest neighbor with a population of 100,000 or more is Adelaide, a 1,672-mile (2,690.8 km) drive east.

Fewer people, more room to roam, and breathtaking vistas—endless blue skies, cerulean Indian Ocean waters, red outback soil, and otherworldly rock formations more suited to Mars—make WA a dream road trip destination. The views are particularly stunning along the area's colossal mainland shore, extending 8,000 miles (13,000 km) from the remote, northwestern Kimberley coast to the Great Australian Bight, the open bay indenting Australia's southern coast.

Driving the entire WA coastline (more than twice the distance of a coast-to-coast trip across the United States) likely would take a couple of months or more. A more manageable approach is to choose a section to explore over a week or an extended weekend. A favorite itinerary is a four-day ramble north of Perth, a scenic-vista trifecta: whale-watching, wildflower carpets, and beach-to-outback landscapes.

Travel Tips

WHEN TO GO: June to November for whale-watching, September to October for blooming wildflowers

PLANNING: Rent a four-wheel-drive vehicle at the Perth airport so you can drive the Lancelin dunes and any off-road beach or outback routes. Use the free Experience Western Australia app to plot your route and find the nearest roadside services in remote locations. Several operators offer side tours such as helicopter rides and diving excursions.

WEBSITES: westernaustralia.com; australiascoralcoast.com; ultimate watersports.com.au

Rock formations in the Pinnacle Desert

4-DAY ITINERARY

Day 1

From Perth, drive about 90 minutes north to the beachside town of Lancelin, starting point of the Indian Ocean Drive scenic coastal route. Take a slight detour inland to walk, drive, or, preferably, rent a board to surf the sandy slopes of the Lancelin sand dunes. Covering about 500 acres (202.3 hectares), the powder-white dunes are the largest in Western Australia. If you choose to rumble over the ginormous sandbox in a four-wheel-drive vehicle, stay clear of the knife-edge dune crests, which could have dangerously sheer drops on the back sides.

After playing in the sand, drive an hour north to Pinnacles Desert in Nambung National Park. See thousands of the desert's eponymous limestone rock pillars, some standing up to 11 feet (3.3 m) tall, on the one-way Pinnacles Desert drive. Climbing on the pinnacles isn't permitted, but you can walk (and snap selfies) among them. Spend the night in the nearby town (and rock lobster capital) of Cervantes.

spot. In addition to the typical wakeboarding, tubing, and stand-up paddleboarding, available rentals include flyboards and water-powered jet packs. After a quick lesson, zoom over the surface of the water, spinning in corkscrews and circles until splashdown. Overnight nearby at a marina or oceanfront hotel.

Day 2

Continue along Indian Ocean Drive toward the port city of Geraldton, 140 miles (225 km) north of Cervantes. South of the city, the route curves inland past Greenough, a well-preserved 19th-century colonial hamlet and home of the Instagram-famous "leaning trees." The bending and twisting river red gums, a species of eucalyptus, grow wild along the inland Brand Highway. Widespread across Australia, the leaning variety is unique to the windswept Greenough Flats, where southerly breezes bend, but don't break, their trunks. Park at the designated photo stop for the best views.

Spend the afternoon playing at the Geraldton foreshore, a water sports hot

Day 3

Drive an hour north of Geraldton to Horrocks, where the Bowes River meets the Indian Ocean at Bowes River Mouth. The rock-reef intertidal platform creates consistent waves at the mouth and attracts fearless surfers. Watch the action out of the reef and beach breaks before continuing north another hour to Kalbarri National Park. From July to October, areas throughout it are blanketed with blooming wildflowers in stunning shades of yellow, orange, red, pink, and purple, and migrating humpback whales are visible offshore.

Year-round, Kalbarri dazzles with its stunning sandstone cliffs, gorges, and other wind-and-wave-sculpted rock stars. Along the coast, hike the 1.9-mile (3 km) Rainbow Valley loop trail down a gorge to the ocean for views of crashing waves and the aptly named Mushroom Rock formation. Make the hike at dawn or dusk, and you might

encounter a grazing kangaroo as well. Drive inland to see one of the park's signature geologic sights: Nature's Window. The red-and-white–banded sandstone arch creates a natural frame for photos of the Murchison River gorge below. Spend the night in the coastal town of Kalbarri.

Day 4

Retrace your route back to Perth, taking a break about halfway at Jurien Bay. Stretch your legs by walking out to the end of the new 531-foot (161.8 m) Jurien Bay jetty. Jump into the water to explore the Jurien Bay Underwater Interpretive Snorkel and Dive Trail, where more than 70 reef balls attract a vibrant array of aquatic life including venomous lionfish, crayfish, and octopus. If time allows, soar over the bay on a tandem skydive.

OPPOSITE: A young sandboarder makes his way down the white-sand dunes in Lancelin, Western Australia. ABOVE: A sandstone arch in Kalbarri National Park

EPIC SHOT

The Milky Way arches over the coastal cliffs on the Great Ocean Road. The scenic highway follows the coastline of west Melbourne for 151 miles (243 km) through Victoria. It's legendary—the Australian equivalent of California State Route 1. Like its American counterpart, the drive offers rugged scenery, some of the world's tallest trees, and sea stacks of towering rocks. At each scenic pull-off, interpretive plaques share insights into the area's history and nature. And there's lots of nature to be had: 50-plus species of local orchids along the Erskine River, southern brown bandicoots, short-beaked echidnas, swamp wallabies, fairy wrens, and, of course, kangaroos. One of the road's most awe-inspiring stops is the Great Otway National Park, one of Australia's 16 "national landscapes."

Construction of the Great Ocean Road began in 1919 as a project for soldiers returning from World War I. It took 13 years to complete and is said to be the longest war memorial in the world. Today, the route is one of the finest ways to explore Australia's stunning scenery.

IMAGE BY **BABAK TAFRESHI**

CLOCKWISE FROM TOP LEFT: A humpback whale breaching the waters of Cabo Pulmo, Mexico; Isle Royale National Park in Michigan; a mountain biker taking on the Grand Canyon; hikers taking to trails in Olympic National Park

CHAPTER 6

NORTH AMERICA

Explore national parks, dive in Mexico's cenotes, and hike among some of the world's best nature trails.

RAFTING THE MIDDLE FORK OF THE SALMON RIVER

Experience a world's best white-water trip in one of the world's last wild places.

Tumbling wild and free for 100 miles (161 km), the Middle Fork of the Salmon River is nature-made for one of the world's best white-water adventures. The crystal-clear river begins near the southern boundary of Idaho's 2.3-million-acre (930,776 hectare) Frank Church–River of No Return Wilderness, the nation's largest continuous wilderness area south of Alaska. Running north to the confluence with the main Salmon River, the Middle Fork twists and turns through its glacier-carved canyon, passing along fields of wildflowers and lush meadows, and beneath towering granite crags.

No roads and little development make rafting through the pristine backcountry a true wilderness experience. Few permits are issued to private floaters, and outfitters follow strict "leave no trace" regulations, helping preserve the untamed landscape and middle-of-nowhere vibe. Waterfalls cascade from jagged cliffs. Hot springs bubble up along the riverbank. Bighorn sheep graze on the shoreline. The soothing hum of the river is broken only by the occasional howls of jubilant rafters.

The typical Middle Fork expedition is a six-day crescendo of white-water intensity, with each passing day surpassing the ridiculously high adrenaline-pumping action of the one before. Rafters conquer multiple Class III and IV rapids and as the week unfolds, the river widens, deepens, and swells—pumping up the thrills.

Travel Tips

WHEN TO GO: Trips run June to August. Water levels can be dangerously high in the upper section in early June.

PLANNING: A Forest Service permit is required to float the Middle Fork. The best way to make the trip is on a guided expedition (including meals, camping, and transportation to and from the river) with an experienced adventure outfitter such as Mount Travel Sobek, Northwest Rafting Co., or Western River Expeditions.

WEBSITES: mtsobek.com; nwrafting.com; westernriver.com

Campers set up at Middle Fork on the Salmon River

6-DAY ITINERARY

Day 1

As with most of the journey, nature dictates the starting point of the trip. The two main launch sites are Boundary Creek at the base of Dagger Falls and Indian Creek, a fly-in wilderness site. When water levels are too high or low or snow blocks the road to Boundary Creek, trips typically launch 26 miles (41.8 km) down-river at Indian Creek. Wherever your adventure begins, camp near the launch site the first night so you can hit the river early in the morning.

Day 2

You'll likely get to choose your ride: paddleboat or oar boat. Either way, you'll be paddling, but the second option offers a power boost—a guide pulling two large oars at the back of the raft. If you launch from Boundary Creek, the adrenaline-pumping white-water action begins early in the trip. In the first 21 miles (33.7 km) alone, you'll paddle through a parade of Class III and IV rapids, including Sulphur Side (III), Velvet Falls (IV), the Chutes (III), Powerhouse (IV), and Pistol Creek (IV). Take breaks to soothe sore muscles at Trail Flat Hot Spring (mile 7.3) and Sheepeater Hot Springs (mile 13.1), two of the Middle Fork's many geothermal features. Camp close to the river at Indian Creek (mile 26.2) or Pungo Creek (mile 27.4).

Day 3

After an early breakfast, climb back on the raft and rumble through more white water

OPPOSITE: **A raft turns sideways as it makes its way through white water in the Salmon River.** ABOVE: **A fly fisherman takes hold of his catch.**

at Marble Creek Rapids (III) at mile marker 31.7. From here, the Middle Fork mellows out for several miles. So rest your arms, or depending on the outfitter, you may have the option to swim or fly-fish for native cutthroat and rainbow trout in the calm waters. Get your paddling game back in gear before you hit Jackass Rapids (III) at mile 37.2. Spend the night at Big Loon Camp (mile 49.3) so you can soak in the nearby Loon Creek hot springs.

Day 4

Today's route is a roller coaster of rapids. Packed within a roughly mile-long (1.6 km) stretch of Tappan Canyon are Tappan I (III), Tappan Falls (IV), Cove Creek (II/III), and Tappan (III/IV). At the end of the rapid rush, scan the skies for bald eagles, the river for otters, and the tree-lined shoreline for big-

horn sheep and black bears. Paddle though Aparejo Point Rapids (II) at mile 62.8 before setting up camp at Sheep Creek (mile 65.3). The small Flying B Ranch store (mile 66.7) is within short hiking distance for a well-deserved ice cream or beer.

Day 5

The last full day of rafting arguably is the most scenic. Imposing granite cliffs rise from rocky river-banks as you paddle through narrow Impassable Canyon. Hold on tight for a roaring romp through challenging rapids like Haystack (III), Jack Creek (III), and Waterfall Creek (III). At mile 80.7, stop to make the hike up to iconic Veil Falls. Cool off at the base of the misty cascade, which tumbles over the opening of a grotto tucked in the cliff. Overnight on the sandy beach at Parrot Placer Camp (mile 86.2).

Day 6

Middle Fork saves its best for last. Paddle strong through the half-day home stretch: a big-thrill lineup of Class IV rapids like Rubber (mile 91.1), Hancock (mile 92.2), and Cramer Creek (mile 99). From the last big rapid, it's less than a mile (1.6 km) to the end—the take-out at Cache Bar on the Main Salmon River.

HIGHLIGHTS

- Explore the nation's largest wilderness area south of Alaska.

- Navigate nonstop Class III to IV rapids.

- Angle for cutthroat and rainbow trout when you find yourself in calmer waters.

UNITED STATES

THE GRAND CANYON

An American icon and legendary world wonder, explored from rim to rim

You have to see it to believe it." Few places live up to that billing quite as spectacularly as the Grand Canyon does. Its sheer immensity—at around 6,000 feet (1,829 m) deep, 18 miles (29 km) wide, and 277 miles (446 km) long, it's not the planet's deepest, narrowest, or longest chasm but arguably is its most breathtaking—has earned the geological phenomenon world fame as one of the seven wonders of the natural world. Some five million visitors head to Arizona every year to lay their eyes on this remarkable vista turned national park.

To call the Grand Canyon a layer cake, as its colorful stacks of rock are often referred, belies its fascinating history. For starters, those stratigraphic layers span more than a billion years of geology, from the 258-million-year-young limestone crown on the rim to the primordial Vishnu schist a mile (1.6 km) below. The visual effect is utterly captivating on an all-immersive descent to the canyon floor.

Only 10 percent of all park visitors venture to the remote North Rim—a 21-mile (34 km) hike across the canyon or 220-mile (354 km) drive from the South Rim. And only around one percent make it to the base of the canyon, affording intrepid adventurers ample opportunity to experience at least one land-before-time moment as they hike far from crowds—or any indication of what millennium it is.

Travel Tips

WHEN TO GO: The national park stays open year-round, but the North Rim closes in winter. U.S. school vacation times bring the biggest crowds. Mid- to late September and May provide the most moderate temperatures for hiking rim to rim.

PLANNING: Book early for backcountry permits and reservations—13 months in advance for mule rides and to stay at Phantom Ranch. Check visitor centers for ranger-led programs.

WEBSITES: nps.gov/grca; visitarizona .com; grandcanyon.com

Mules make their way along the South Kaibab.

WHAT TO DO

Hike Rim to Rim

From the South Rim, hop on a shuttle bus to the trailhead of the well-maintained South Kaibab Trail. Set off on foot and view 2,000-year-old rock art and 250-million-year-old fossils as the 6.3-mile (10.1 km) trail plunges deeper into the canyon (be sure to step aside for mule trains to pass). At the base of the canyon, cross the iconic black suspension bridge spanning the muddy Colorado River, about 65 feet (20 m) below. Plan ahead for a permit to overnight at the Bright Angel campground on the riverbanks.

The next day, continue your rim-to-rim voyage via the 14.2-mile (22.9 km) North Kaibab Trail, with the rustic Cottonwood campground around halfway up. Or do the whole thing in reverse, beginning from the North Rim and taking the popular 7.8-mile (12.6 km) Bright Angel Trail back up to the canyon rim, passing the shaded Indian Garden campground.

Grand Canyon hikers looking to bag top bragging rights tackle the park's most difficult named route—the backcountry Nankoweap Trail—to the canyon floor. The trail drops 14 exposed miles (22.5 km) and 6,000 vertical feet (1,829 m) from the North Rim's West Nankoweap trailhead without a single water source or trail blaze along the way. No matter which path you choose, be prepared for a wide temperature range from top to bottom.

Raft the Colorado River

Navigate the murky waters of the Colorado River the way scientist and explorer John Wesley Powell did in 1869 when he encountered the uncharted Grand Canyon. Join a multiday rafting trip on Class IV white-water rapids along a 280-mile (451 km) stretch of the river, split into the 192-mile (309 km) Lower Canyon and 88-mile (142 km) Upper Canyon. Explore side canyons and discover stunners such as the natural amphitheater of Red Wall Cavern and Vasey's Paradise, a tumbling waterfall that pours out of the side of red-stained cliffs. As you float down serene stretches of the river, watch for blue herons and bighorn sheep. Camp along the riverbed and fall asleep under the stars. Permits for self-guided raft trips are doled out by the park via weighted lottery.

Cycle the Rim

One of the most relaxing ways to enjoy the scenery from the rim of the canyon is undoubtedly on two wheels. Rent a bike (or bring your own) and cycle along the South Rim's Hermit Road, punctuated with nine designated viewpoints along a seven-mile (11.3 km) stretch between Grand Canyon Village and historic Hermit's Rest. Between the Abyss and Hermit's Rest viewpoints, a 2.8-mile (4.5 km) greenway offers closer access to the edge of the rim—and a reprieve from motorized traffic. Begin before dawn at Hopi Point, where wide vistas set the stage for epic sunrises; then loop the route before the heat of the day sets in. Meanwhile, mountain bikers can hit the smooth single track of the North Rim's 18-mile (29 km) Rainbow Rim Trail for stunning panoramas into the canyon.

Ride to the Grand Canyon's Floor on a Mule's Back

Since the 19th century, sure-footed mules have served as the Grand Canyon's preferred beasts of burden, navigating the switchback trails from the top of the South Rim to the canyon floor—transporting provisions, mail, and tourists. Take part in the time-honored tradition and experience this bumpy rite of passage. Ride 10 miles (16 km) down the canyon on the Bright Angel Trail, stopping for a picnic lunch and other short breaks along the way. Arrive at the legendary Phantom Ranch cabins and hikers' dormitories for an overnight stay at the bottom; then saddle back up for the return trip the next morning. Shorter single-day mule rides along the South or North Rim are also offered at the national park.

Go on a Trail Ride Through the Forest

Saddle up, this time on a horse, and enjoy a leisurely trail ride among the ponderosa pine trees of the surrounding Kaibab National Forest, near the South Rim. Discover petroglyphs carved a thousand years

OPPOSITE: The sunset creates a warm glow and highlights the unique texture of the Grand Canyon's river-carved walls. RIGHT: Visitors take in the views from the glass-bottomed sky bridge.

ago, and encounter elk, deer, eagles, and other wildlife in this sprawling wilderness.

Snowshoe the North Rim

From December through mid-May, the North Rim roads are closed to vehicles but allow access to snow sports enthusiasts. Strap on a pair of snowshoes or cross-country skis for an enchanting walk through this unique winter wonderland. Apply for a backcountry permit in advance.

Venture to Havasu Falls

Beyond the boundaries of the national park beckons the desert oasis of Havasu Falls, on the Havasupai Indian Reservation. Hike to this famed paradise, where a rushing waterfall spills over travertine cliffs into an aquamarine pool below—among the planet's most picturesque swimming holes. Descend 10 miles (16 km) and a 3,500-foot (1,067 m) drop of vertical terrain to reach the campground and falls. Fall asleep to the sound of the rushing water along Havasu Creek. Hike back out once you've had your fill of the canyon—or catch a helicopter ride to the top from Supai Village, two miles (3.2 km) from the waterfall. (Helicopter rides can also be arranged for the way in.) Plan ahead: Advance reservations are required for hikers and campers, with multiple ranger checkpoints along the route.

Walk Over the Abyss

Peer a dizzying 4,000 feet (1,219 m) down to the canyon floor as you step onto the horseshoe-shaped Skywalk at Eagle Point, a glass-bottomed, vertigo-inducing platform that debuted in 2007 on the west side of the Grand Canyon.

HIGHLIGHTS

• Set off on a thrilling rafting trip down the churning Colorado River.

• Head into the canyon on backpacking treks down to the river.

• Enjoy stunning vistas on two wheels or from a mule's back.

One of the Grand Canyon's many gems:
Havasu Falls in hidden Havasupai

UNITED STATES & MEXICO

BAJA CALIFORNIA SUR

A weekend of flavorful tacos, fresh ceviche, and local wine

On a coastal excursion from San Diego to Mexico, explore relaxed border cities with world-renowned food and wine, quaint towns, and a wide-open road that sweeps past surfers and whales dotting the ocean. Venture through wildlife-rich waters, coastal cliffs and coves, and desert isles on hikes.

Come the right season, you can witness the magnificent gray whale migration from your car's window and venture ashore remote islands to explore pristine beaches dotted with seabirds and cacti. Visit diverse nature reserves, including the rocky windswept shores of Channel Islands National Park, the UNESCO-listed Whale Sanctuary of El Vizcaíno, and the marine-protected area of Cabo Pulmo National Park; and hear from conservationists and community members working to protect these pristine ecosystems. Glimpse Baja culture in sleepy and secluded coastal towns, and encounter the incredible wildlife for which the peninsula is so well known.

Opt to experience the sea during the springtime, the best season to spot pods of humpback, sperm, and blue whales, or take a wellness cruise any time of the year to the remote Isla Espíritu Santo. Weeks could be spent exploring the region of Baja California Sur, but here's how to get started.

Travel Tips

WHEN TO GO: For whale-watching, February through April brings gray, sperm, blue, and humpback whales to the Baja California coast.

PLANNING: You can make the trip from Southern California by car or boat. It's easy to make the journey on a self-guided tour, or book through an outfitter. National Geographic Expeditions offers a multiday cruise from Los Angeles.

WEBSITES: nationalgeographic.com/expeditions; nps.gov/chis/index.htm; baronbalche.com; cantinahussongs.com; laguerrerense.com

A vendor serves up fresh shrimp tostadas.

WHAT TO DO

Visit the Channel Islands

The Channel Islands, a rugged archipelago off the coast of Southern California, has a distinct ecosystem that supports a unique array of flora and fauna. Traverse some of the many hiking trails in this national park, which run along coastal cliffs and into the islands' wild interiors. Keep an eye out for some of the 145 endemic species that inhabit the archipelago.

Dine on World-Class Ceviche

Make your way down the coast to Ensenada for world-class ceviche and tostadas at La Guerrense. After running the stand for three decades, owner Sabina Bandera opened a restaurant down the block. Be sure to stop in if the cart runs out of food, or simply to see her portrait with an octopus wig.

Rumor has it that the margarita was invented at either Bar Andaluz or Hussong's Cantina, just a short walk from each other among Ensanada's lively nightlife scene. Try both, and decide the better one for yourself. Bar Andaluz sits on a beautiful square with historic hidden alleyways. After your margarita there, stroll to Hussong's Cantina to close out the night with live mariachi music and a floor full of peanut shells. The high energy is infectious.

Float on the Bay and Sip on Wine

Wake up as early as possible to enjoy a quiet morning on a boat in All Saints Bay. During the right season (February through April), spot gray and humpback whales on the move. The Baja coast is a great place to whale-watch without being flooded by an excess of tour boats, many of them run by local fishermen. Then fuel up for the winding drive to wine country at Taquería

El Trailero just off of Highway 3 in El Sauzal, with the best *al pastor* tacos and *tacos de cabeza*, which are freshly carved from the skull of a cow. Valle de Guadalupe is Mexico's thriving wine country. Some wineries are well known, while others do not export outside the country and deserve a visit. Tour Baron Balche winery to soak up the process and purchase a few bottles to take home.

Explore a Whale Sanctuary

Board a small *panga* boat to explore the Laguna Ojo de Liebre, or Scammon's Lagoon, situated within the Whale Sanctuary of El Vizcaíno—a World Heritage site. Gray whales migrate here each December, and with luck, you may spot some of the first arrivals. Over 200 bird species have also been identified in the lagoon, including white pelicans, whimbrels, and osprey. Later, visit Guerrero Negro, home to the world's largest saltworks, producing around seven million tons (6.4 million metric tons) of salt each year. See the otherworldly salt flats and learn about the

community's efforts to further its booming industry while respecting the fragility of the surrounding landscapes.

Visit Tecate

Driving back to California can be more direct if you are in a hurry to return, but better to enjoy the relaxed route through Tecate just before you cross the border. Stop for a refreshing fresh-fruit popsicle break, or if time allows, take a tour of Tecate's namesake brewery. Crossing the border requires patience, but locals selling beautiful Mexican tapestries and hats will keep you entertained.

OPPOSITE: Whale-watchers snap photos as a humpback surfaces. ABOVE: A vineyard in the Valle de Guadalupe is bathed in a golden sunset.

EXPLORING NATIONAL PARKS

1 DENALI NATIONAL PARK, ALASKA

Denali is the tallest mountain in North America. The national park surrounding the peak protects six million acres (roughly 2.4 million hectares) of Alaskan outback, home to grizzlies, moose, black bears, and wolves. Go flightseeing, or zip-line through the canopy in Talkeetna.

2 SUMIDERO CANYON NATIONAL PARK, MEXICO

The moss-heavy walls of Sumidero Canyon rise almost 3,000 feet (914 m) above the rainforest. Caves, crocodiles, waterfalls, spider monkeys, and endangered curassow steal the attention of those traveling by boat, while jaguarundi, ocelots, agouti, and anteaters dart across hiking trails on land.

3 EVERGLADES NATIONAL PARK, FLORIDA

Florida panthers, alligators, crocodiles, manatees, black bears, armadillos, and 300-plus species of birds can be found in the marshy mangroves and cypress of Florida's Everglades, a unique ecosystem rapidly disappearing as sea levels rise. Bike the Snake Bight Trail, spend an afternoon "slough slogging" (a walk through the wetlands), or watch for bioluminescent algae on a nighttime airboat tour.

4 ZION NATIONAL PARK, UTAH

From wriggling through fiery slot canyons to multiday Class V white-water kayaking, it seems there's no wrong move in Zion National Park—that is, unless you're hiking Angels Landing. The Angels Landing Trail ascends over 21 steep switchbacks, then narrows to a barely two-foot-wide (0.6 m), 1,000-foot-high (305 m) ridge where bolted chains are the only thing keeping you from soaring off the side. The panoramic view from the top is worth every breathtaking step.

5 MAMMOTH CAVE NATIONAL PARK, KENTUCKY

The world's longest known cave system, Mammoth Cave's limestone tunnels include a bottomless pit, endangered bat colonies, over 1,000 archaeological sites, and massive flowstones dubbed "Frozen Niagara." Visit the park in the summer to enjoy Green River canoe trips and 60 miles (96.6 km) of horseback riding trails.

6 HALEAKALA NATIONAL PARK, HAWAII

Begin your day watching the sunrise from Haleakala National Park's highest point—a 10,023-foot-high (3,055 m) crater carved into the top of the world's largest dormant volcano. Then follow the park's hiking and horseback riding trails to 'Ohe'o's Seven Sacred Pools, ancient lava flows, dense cloud forests, and waterfall camp sites.

7 CABO PUMO NATIONAL MARINE PARK, MEXICO

Sixty miles (96.6 km) north of Los Cabos, the coral reefs of Cabo Pulmo National Marine Park are roughly 20,000 years old. Thanks to 24 years of protection, the reef's UNESCO-recognized ecosystem shimmers with colorful marine flora, 226 fish species, 154 invertebrate species, sea turtles, seabirds, dolphins, and whales.

8 ISLE ROYALE NATIONAL PARK, MICHIGAN

Isle Royale National Park can be reached only by ferry or float plane and is visited by fewer people in one year than Yellowstone sometimes hosts in one day. The park's 43-mile (69 km) Greenstone Ridge Trail extends east to west through forest paths, wild thimbleberry patches, scenic high points, and scrubby wolf habitat.

9 NEW RIVER GORGE NATIONAL RIVER, WEST VIRGINIA

West Virginia's New River Gorge National River is a 70,000-acre (28,328 hectare) playground of white water, waterfalls, and snaking limestone canyons. Activities along the river include Class V white-water rafting, float fishing, rock climbing, rappelling, fat tire biking, zip-lining, and spelunking.

10 JASPER NATIONAL PARK, ALBERTA

One jump off an 80-foot-high (24 m) cliff into Jasper's Horseshoe Lake, and you'll be coming back for more. And there's plenty to be had: Jasper Provincial Park offers more than 600 miles (966 km) of hiking trails, the world's second largest Dark Sky preserve, waterfalls, canyon ice climbing, hot springs, and a glass-bottomed Glacier Skywalk.

OPPOSITE: The 'Ohe'o Gulch—or Seven Sacred Pools—at Haleakala National Park in Maui **ABOVE:** Two caribou graze on a ridge in Denali National Park.

Half Dome is reflected in the Merced
River in Yosemite National Park.

Scale the Dome

You need to secure a permit to attempt the Half Dome Day Hike, a trek so popular it must be protected from overcrowding. But it's not a trip for everyone. The 14-mile (23 km) route includes 4,800 feet (1,463 m) of elevation gain, the last 400 feet (122 m) or so tackled with the aid of fixed cables. Respect the dangers of this hike, particularly the threat of bad weather, and heed rangers' advice. But if your nerve and luck hold, expect a big-time payoff in the kind of rare air often reserved for mountaineers.

See the Trees

The Mariposa Grove of giant sequoias underwent a restoration project to create a more natural, asphalt-free experience among the big trees. In the meantime, visiting sequoias requires some well-rewarded effort. Tuolumne Grove's two dozen mature trees require an approximate two-mile (3.2 km) round-trip hike, while Merced Grove is a three-mile (4.8 km) round-trip. Both hikes descend steeply from their respective trailheads for some 500 vertical feet (152 m).

Catch the Falls

Don't miss the aptly named Bridalveil Fall, 630 feet (189 m) of delicate white water tumbling down a granite face beneath Cathedral Rocks. Continue along the Southside Drive to the Merced River, the spot for swimming, tubing, rafting, and fishing. Cathedral Beach is a great place to soak and stare at El Capitan looming high above the valley.

HIGHLIGHTS

• Museum-hop through San Diego's renowned Balboa Park—the "Smithsonian of the West."

• Get your floral fix at the historic Ganna Walska Lotusland or along the wildflower-covered Hite Cove Trail.

• Zip through the skies on high-flying lines strung just south of Yosemite Valley.

Sinking Into the Cenotes of the Yucatán

By Kate Siber

BENEATH LUSH GREENERY, Mexico's Yucatán Peninsula is like Swiss cheese. The bedrock is pocked with more than 6,000 sinkholes—some large open pools, but many more small, sheltered openings with sheer drops, formed when limestone fully or partially collapses and cool groundwater seeps in.

In centuries past, the Maya relied on cenotes for freshwater and believed they were portals to the gods. Many do hold that quality of sacred space. Now, divers explore the depths and venture into dark underwater networks—but you don't need special certifications to enjoy the pools at the surface.

Down a dirt road fringed by jungle, north of Tulum, on the Caribbean coast, Dos Ojos Cenote is almost ready to close by the time we get there. Divers in wet suits and kids in swimsuits trundle out into the parking lot, faces wet and glowing from the day's excitement. But happily, the attendant lets us in. Down the creaky wooden steps that lead into the pool, we discover we are completely alone.

We sink into 76°F (24°C) water, illuminated in gem-tone shades of blue and green by the late afternoon light, and so clear we can see all the way to the bottom. (The natural filtering of the rainwater by the limestone removes impurities and leaves the water fresh and sparkling.) Our hushed voices echo against the cave ceiling, which sweeps dramatically over our heads like an opera house.

Below, rock formations sink away into a 30-foot-deep (9.1 m) pool, while passages lead deep into the half-submerged cavern. We float and breast-stroke until our fingers are raisin-like and wrinkly, taking in the delicate stillness of this singular window into the Earth.

A couple of days later, we visit Gran Cenote. Just down the main road from Dos Ojos, it's one of the most famous cenotes in Mexico and sports a lively, fiesta-like vibe. Families and couples picnic on a small lawn as we descend stairs to the large sunlit pool, teeming with snorkelers. Through our masks, we watch fish and turtles circle stalactites and stalagmites. About 30 feet (9 m) below, divers' headlamps light up and beam into the craggy depths. We swim back and forth, then warm up aboveground with others who have come to delight in the luminous pleasures and wild wonders of this stone-rimmed pool in the jungle.

• *A frequent contributor* to National Geographic Traveler, *Kate Siber is a freelance journalist and author of* 100 Hikes of a Lifetime. *She is based in Durango, Colorado.*

LEFT: Visitors prepare to descend in Dos Ojos Cenote (Two Eyes Cenote).
OPPOSITE: Divers explore the rocky depths of a cenote lit by the sun.

Snorkelers swim in Dos Ojos, a cenote near Tulum on the Yucatán Peninsula.

CANOEING THE EVERGLADES

Glide through Florida's "river of grass" on a search for crocs and alligators.

Everglades National Park is like no other place on Earth. Established in 1947 to preserve the biological diversity and resources of the Everglades ecosystems, the park protects 1.5 million acres (607,028 hectares) of Florida's southern tip. Famously called a "river of grass" by Florida writer and environmental activist Marjory Stoneman Douglas, the vast subtropical wilderness is a mix of freshwater and coastal prairie; mangroves, marshland, and pine and cypress woods; and the waters and islands of Florida Bay.

Self-guided and ranger-led canoe and kayak trips make it possible to explore the ubiquitous mangrove forests and travel along the Everglades' life source: the freshwater sloughs, or marshy rivers, that channel water through the park every day. Paddling trails crisscross the area, and canoers and kayakers can camp (permit required) in primitive backcountry sites aside or above the water.

Since the Everglades is a massive and complex mosaic of habitats, where you choose to canoe will shape your view of it. If possible, try two different experiences—one launching from or near the Everglades City Visitor Center on the western Gulf Coast side south of Naples and the other starting from or near the Flamingo Visitor Center at the southeastern edge on Florida Bay south of Homestead. Or take one long, challenging paddle along the epic Wilderness Waterway.

Travel Tips

WHEN TO GO: December to April is best for lower temperatures, drier weather, and fewer mosquitoes.

PLANNING: Adverse weather, tides, strong winds, and shallow areas can make paddling difficult. Plan a route using nautical charts and maps, and share your itinerary with others. Back-country camping permits are required for overnight canoe trips.

WEBSITES: nps.gov/ever; flamingo everglades.com; evergladesnationalpark boattours.com; floridapaddlingtrails.com; kayakfloridakeys.com

A roseate spoonbill takes flight.

WHERE **TO GO**

Florida Bay

Rent canoes and kayaks at the Flamingo Marina, close to the Flamingo Visitor Center. For an easy paddle, follow the freshwater Nine Mile Pond canoe trail. The scenic five-mile (8 km) loop packs a full view of the Everglades ecosystem in a half-day trip. Paddle a shallow sawgrass marsh, navigating tight turns around mangrove islands and through narrow tree tunnels. Watch for white-crowned pigeons, found in the United States only in southernmost Florida and mainly in mangroves; alligators and crocodiles, which coexist only in the Everglades; and, of course, the white PVC-pipe trail markers that keep you on course. To learn more about Nine Mile Pond ecology, register in advance for one of the free ranger-guided canoe trips.

Flamingo is also a starting point for the Hell's Bay Canoe Trail, famously described as "hell to get into and hell to get out of" due to its maze of mangroves. The trail is a good choice for a one-night backcountry canoeing trip. Pick up a camping permit (available a day in advance) at the Flamingo Visitor Center to stay in the chickee—a sheltered wooden platform built over the water—at Hell's Bay, your destination for the night. (Heads up: The sides are open on the chickee, so lie down in the center to avoid rolling off into the water.) From the canoe launch site, paddle about 6 miles (9.6 km) to the shelter, passing through mangrove-lined waterways and across wider channels and shallow lakes.

The Gulf Coast

Everglades National Park Boat Tours in

Everglades City rents canoes and kayaks for day use and overnight (camp at backcountry beach, ground, and chickee sites accessible only by water) paddling trips on the Gulf Coast side of the park. If you're short on time, rent a canoe for a couple of hours to paddle around Chokoloskee Bay before low tide. In addition to seeing bottlenose dolphins and the occasional manatee, you'll have a water-level view of roseate spoonbills, white pelicans, black skimmers, brown pelicans, white ibis, ring-billed gulls, and other waterbirds feeding in the shallows and on mud flats and sandbars.

Wilderness Waterway

If you're an experienced backcountry paddler, the 99-mile (159 km) Wilderness Waterway is the ultimate Everglades trip. The Ironman-worthy endurance paddle from Everglades City southeast to Flamingo takes about 10 days to complete, depending on your pace. Canoers up for the challenge

glide along narrow rivers and creeks and around thousands of mangrove islands. Most of the time is spent in total solitude, save for regular sightings of marine creatures from both saltwater and freshwater environments, including alligators and crocodiles.

Making the trip requires serious preparation. Start by studying the park's *Wilderness Waterway Guide,* which, if it doesn't scare you off, offers practical advice and potentially lifesaving safety warnings. There are no services along the route, so you need to carry all of your food and water (a gallon per day per person is the standard recommendation) and get a ranger to approve your itinerary before launching. Backcountry permits and reservations are required to camp on the beaches and chickees along the route.

For a slightly tamer take on the Wilderness Waterway, make a four-day loop beginning and ending in Everglades City. With this version, you'll travel across Chokoloskee Bay and into the Turner River to start the first leg, a roughly nine-mile (14.5 km) paddle down the river and along connector creeks to the Crooked Creek chickee. The next day, go another nine miles or so down to Opossum Key to camp at Darwin's Place, a partially shaded patch of high ground equipped with a portable toilet. From there, it's 8.5 miles (13.7 km) to the Gulf of Mexico and camping under the stars on the beach at Mormon Key. End the trip with a 17-mile (27.4 km) Gulf Coast paddle back to the Everglades City launch site.

HORSEBACK RIDING

1 BANFF NATIONAL PARK, CANADA

Ride through scenery largely unchanged since the pioneers first came to the shores of the Bow and Spray Rivers. A one-hour ride takes you through the stunning scenery of Banff National Park, including the natural sulfur springs. Should saddling up not be your thing, 15-passenger sleigh rides are available in the winter.

2 MONARCH BUTTERFLY BIO-SPHERE RESERVE, MEXICO

Millions of monarch butterflies migrate to the oyamel fir forests just a few hours west of Mexico City. The Monarch Butterfly Biosphere Reserve offers horseback rides to Cerro Pelón sanctuary. Climb from the Sierra Madre valley floor to high-altitude cloud forests where monarchs cluster in the trees to keep warm. Noon on a sunny weekday in January or February is the optimal time to visit.

3 WRANGELL–ST. ELIAS, ALASKA

Alaska's sprawling Wrangell–St. Elias National Park is the size of Yellowstone, Yosemite, and Switzerland combined. Wrangell Outfitters' 12-day summer horse pack trip does its best to scratch the surface, teaching riders how to pack a horse and set up gold rush–style camps as they explore the remote frontier in search of moose, caribou, black bears, grizzly bears, graylings, and dozens of alpine songbirds.

4 SNAKE RIVER, IDAHO

The Snake River flows through Hell's Canyon; Hagerman Fossil Beds National Monument; McGarry Ranch, located on the fringe of Yellowstone National Park; and Idaho's Rocky Mountains. The McGarry family welcomes guests to spend days atop quarter horses to lead herds to pastures across trout-filled mountain stream and aspen grove trails as you keep an eye out for moose, elk, and wild horses.

5 KING'S CANYON NATIONAL PARK, CALIFORNIA

Cedar Grove is the only permitted pack station offering half-day and multiday horseback rides within the boundaries of Sequoia and Kings Canyon National Parks. On the 41.4-mile (67 km) Rae Lakes Loop, riders are carried past lake basins, misty waterfalls, foxtail pines, suspension bridges, sunset-colored canyons, and streamside camp sites.

6 GREEN MOUNTAINS, VERMONT

One of the world's oldest horse breeds, calm and sturdy Icelandics are also the world's only naturally five-gaited horses, perfectly suited to energetic pleasure riding in the mountains. Revel in peak fall foliage season on horseback as you trot inn to inn from the Vermont Icelandic Horse Farm in Vermont's Mad River Valley.

7 BIG BEND, TEXAS

Big Bend National Park protects dinosaur digs, 1,200 plant species, 75 mammal species, 56 reptile species, limestone canyons, the entire Chisos Mountain range, and 118 miles (190 km) of the Rio Grande. Saddle up to take in the salt cedar-lined shores, wildflower-covered cliffs, painted buntings, and summer tanagers.

8 CASCADE LOOP, WASHINGTON

Trace a portion of Washington State's Cascade Loop on horseback to take in its overwhelming range of landscapes: canyons, volcanoes, rainforests, Pacific coastline, desert, moss-drenched forests, apple orchards, vineyards, turquoise lakes, charming towns, jagged alpine peaks, and more waterfalls than you can count.

9 VAÑALES VALLEY, CUBA

Cuba's sleepy Viñales Valley is a lost-in-time landscape of colorful cottages, orchid-filled botanical gardens, tobacco fields, and karst limestone domes beloved by avid rock climbers. It's also one of the best parts of Cuba to travel by horseback. Half-day rides travel the World Heritage site's soft dusty streets, hidden cave pools, and massive outdoor murals.

10 VANCOUVER, BRITISH COLUMBIA

Vancouver's Academie Duello Centre for Swordplay—a school of Western martial arts—offers horseback archery lessons, a one-week immersive mounted combat intensive, and a two-hour riding, horsemanship, and swordplay program for those interested in raising the bar on their horseback riding finesse.

OPPOSITE: A visitor rides along Stoney Creek in Banff. ABOVE: Horses make their way through the mountains of King's Canyon National Park.

HIKING THE OLYMPIC PENINSULA

Experience the wildest corner of Washington State.

Perched in the most northwestern corner of the lower 48, Washington State's Olympic Peninsula seems a world away from civilization. The 3,600-square-mile (9,324 sq km) area is bounded by the Pacific Ocean on the west, the Strait of Fuca on the north, and the Hood Canal on the east. Most of the land is covered by Olympic National Park, nearly one million acres (404,685 hectares) of wilderness featuring three distinct ecosystems: the glacier-capped Olympic mountains; lush, temperate rainforests; and 73 miles (117.5 km) of wilderness coastline, the nation's longest undeveloped coast outside Alaska.

The remarkable diversity, which earned Olympic National Park designation as an international Biosphere Reserve and UNESCO World Heritage site, provides a wide variety of hiking experiences on about 600 miles (965.6 km) of park trails. Over the course of one weekend, you could hike through a fog-shrouded rainforest, walk among some of the largest trees on Earth, navigate narrow switchback trails through an isolated wilderness, and explore a wild stretch of coast sculpted by wind and pounding waves. Park trails also regularly connect to other hiking and recreational paths, expanding the possibilities for adventure.

To help you chart your course, we've curated a collection of six hikes, each highlighting a different aspect of this wild and wildly diverse peninsula.

Travel Tips

WHEN TO GO: Visit June to September when most trails, roads, campgrounds, and facilities are open. Rain is always a possibility, and snow can fall as late as June and as early as September.

PLANNING: Pack rain gear and water-proof hiking boots. Check weather and trail conditions before heading out. From May to September, Olympic Hiking Co. offers guided small-group hiking tours and a trailhead shuttle.

WEBSITES: nps.gov/olym; hikeolympic.com; olympicdiscoverytrail.org; olympic peninsula.org

Lush Quinault Rain Forest in the Olympic National Forest

Take a Low-Tide Hike to Hole-in-the-Wall

The Olympic Peninsula's Pacific coast is a gallery for otherworldly rock art sculpted by nature. Vertical rock sea stacks, huge boulders, and stone arches rise from sand and sea along Olympic National Park beaches like Rialto, north of La Push. When the tide is out, hike north along Rialto Beach about 1.5 miles (2.4 km) to the Hole-in-the-Wall rock arch. Look offshore to see otters, sea lions, and whales. Peer down to examine tide pools teeming with intertidal life like barnacles, crabs, mussels, and multicolored sea stars. Watch your step to avoid the driftwood and exposed boulders on shore.

Beyond Hole-in-the-Wall, the coastal trail quickly turns from a beach walk to a strenuous wilderness backpacking experience. So if you're not equipped to scramble over seaweed-slick boulders and navigate rope-aided headland trails, get someone to capture an Instagram-worthy shot of you standing under the Hole-in-the-Wall arch and then retrace your route to the beach.

Hike to the Most Northwestern Point in the Lower 48

Cape Flattery, the most northwesterly tip of the contiguous United States, is located in the Makah Nation on Neah Bay, ancestral home of the Makah people. Stop at Washburn's General Store on the way to the trailhead to purchase the Makah Recreation Pass (nominal fee) required to explore tribal land. The hike to Cape Flattery point is short (less than a mile/1.6 km), but plan to take a long time savoring the unending Pacific views from four observation decks. Climb down to the lowest deck to see his-

toric Cape Flattery Lighthouse (built in 1857) on offshore Tatoosh Island.

Head Into the Wild on the Olympic Adventure Route

The Olympic Discovery Trail (ODT) makes it possible to hike across the northern Olympic Peninsula from Port Townsend west to the Pacific via 54 miles (87 km) of shared road and 80 miles (129 km) of paved and gravel trail. For a wilder (and much shorter) ODT experience, hike a section of the 25-mile (40.2 km) Olympic Adventure Route (OAR), running from SR 112 west to Lake Crescent. The OAR is a wilderness alternative to the paved ODT segment between the Elwha River and Lake Crescent and is open to hikers, mountain bikers, and horseback riders craving backcountry solitude and scenery. In densely wooded sections of the trail, you'll likely see more moss species than people.

No services are available along the physically challenging and isolated OAR route, which twists and climbs through old growth forests and cougar habitat via a three-foot-wide (0.9 m) trail. Since the trail is open only during daylight hours, take a day hike on one of the four OAR sections. The 5.2-mile (8.3 km) Olympic Skyline segment delivers

views of the Olympic Mountains, Vancouver Island, and Strait of Juan de Fuca.

See Elk and Centuries-Old Cedars on the Way to Five Mile Island

The Hoh River Trail parallels its namesake river for 17.3 miles (27.8 km) of a meandering 50-mile (80.4 km) route from Mount Olympus to the Pacific. The first five (and back) miles (8 km) of the route are mostly flat and a fairly easy walk in the park. Hike through a rainforest blanketed in moss and ferns to see the slate-blue Hoh River and the centuries-old cedar trees of Cougar Grove. The turnaround point, Five Mile Island, is a glacier–ground gravel bar and popular hangout for the park's free-roaming Roosevelt elk, the largest variety of elk in North America.

Take a Peak-to-Lake Trek From Hurricane Ridge

On a clear day, you can see forever—or at least the Strait of Juan de Fuca and the glacier-capped Olympic Mountains—from Hurricane Ridge, named for the hurricane-force wind gusts that can pummel the peak. Despite the moniker, the ridge is one of the most accessible mountain areas in the park

OPPOSITE: A backpacker takes in the sights along a trail in Olympic National Park. ABOVE: Cape Flattery Lighthouse sits on the most northwesterly point of the lower 48 states.

Hurricane Ridge is a year-round destination open to hikers, skiers, and snowboarders in Washington's Olympic National Park.

thanks to a 17-mile (27.3 km) scenic drive leading up to the Hurricane Ridge Visitor Center, elevation 5,242 feet (1,597.7 m).

There are trails up here for varying fitness levels. Arguably the best for views (and lighter foot traffic) is the Klahhane Ridge Trail, a 12.6-mile (20.2 km) round-trip ridge-to-lake hike beginning across from the Visitor Center and ending at Lake Angeles. The route is rated moderate, but it has a steep switchback section, providing a challenging workout. Steer clear of the nonnative and sometimes aggressive mountain goats that regularly travel the same trail. Take rest stops at the numerous overlooks for (clear-day) views of glacier-capped Mount Rainier, Washington State's iconic and highest (elevation 14,410 feet/ 4,392 m) peak.

Take a Walk Among Giants in the Quinault Valley

Known as the Valley of the Rainforest Giants, the Quinault Valley boasts a veritable tall-tree hall of fame. Among the towering Douglas firs, hemlocks, Sitka spruce, and western red cedars are six champion conifers. Four are the largest living specimens of their species on the planet, and two are the largest of their kind in the United States.

The valley's 174-foot-tall (53 m), world's largest western red cedar (with a hollow trunk you can climb into) is the largest living tree in the world outside California. To see the behemoth and a Sitka spruce estimated to be more than 1,000 years old, hike the southern valley trails—beginning with the half-mile (0.8 km) Quinault Rain Forest Nature Loop—near and around Quinault Lake, situated on the border of the Quinault Indian Nation and Olympic National Park.

HIGHLIGHTS

• Walk among some of the largest red cedar trees on Earth in the Valley of the Rainforest Giants.

• Visit Makah Nation and Cape Flattery, the most northwestern point in the continental United States.

• Trek a segment of the rugged and remote Olympic Adventure Route.

BANFF BY HORSEBACK

Saddle up to see the best of Canada's first national park.

Western Canada's horseback-riding heritage lives on in Banff, Canada's first national park and part of UNESCO's Canadian Rocky Mountain World Heritage site. Established in 1883, Banff is a wild, rugged area protecting 2,564 square miles (6,640 sq km) of incomparable snowcapped mountains.

First Peoples and European explorers blazed the original horse trails circling glacier-fed lakes, cutting through high mountain passes, and crossing valleys, meadows, and rivers. In 1892, the enterprising Brewster brothers, founders of the sixth-generation Brewster Mountain Pack Trains outfitter, introduced guided horseback rides to the park. Today, the Brewster family, Timberline Tours, and Banff Trail Riders lead trips out of stables based in the park's two main communities: Banff, Canada's highest elevation town at 4,540 feet (1,383.7 m), and the hamlet of Lake Louise, Canada's highest permanent settlement at 5,052 feet (1,539.8 m).

Whichever lofty starting point you choose, traveling by horse allows you to climb higher, cover more ground, and go deeper into the less visited backcountry than you could on foot. As a bonus, sitting up in the saddle gives you a better view of all that mountain majesty. Choose your ride based on your abilities and appetite for adventure. Options range from a half-day tour to a six-night pack trip.

Travel Tips

WHEN TO GO: May to October for trail rides, June to September for backcountry pack trips

PLANNING: When you're not in the saddle, use car-free options, such as the Parks Canada Shuttle, Roam Public Transit, and the four Banff–Lake Louise gondolas to get around. Space is limited on backcountry horseback riding trips, so book early. Bring riding boots, rain gear, and a hat with a snug fit.

WEBSITES: banfflakelouise.com; pc.gc .ca/en/pn-np/ab/banff; timberlinetours .ca; brewsteradventures.com

American buffalo graze in Banff National Park.

WHAT TO DO

See Snowcapped Peaks and Roaring Cascades in Three Hours

The Sulphur Mountain ride rounds up about a week's worth of Banff National Park sights into one three-hour ramble. From start to finish, you're treated to elevated views of alpine forests and the snowcapped Canadian Rockies. Saddle up in Banff and climb two-thirds of the way up Sulphur Mountain, passing the historic Rimrock Resort Hotel, founded in the 1850s, and ambling underneath the soaring Banff gondola. From there you'll ride into the valley and follow the Spray River Loop Trail, an old fire road tracing the path of the river.

Channel your inner cowboy and steer your steed across the river to continue the ride along the base of Mount Rundle, the much-photographed tilted, pointy peak south of Banff. Make a second Spray River crossing just below Bow Falls, the roaring cascades made famous in Otto Preminger's 1953 film *River of No Return* starring Robert Mitchum and Marilyn Monroe.

Watch for Wildlife on a Half-Day Ride

For a somewhat wilder half day on horseback, choose the Bow Valley ride. The typical route follows the wildlife-rich Bow River (watch for bald eagles and muskrats) north before heading west past the Cave and Basin National Historic Site, considered the birthplace of Canada's national park system. The site protects the Banff thermal springs uncovered by Canadian Pacific Railway workers in 1883 and long considered sacred waters by the indigenous Stoney (Assiniboine) First Nations people.

Continue west along the Bow River to the Sundance Canyon Trail. As you ride through the moss-covered walls of the canyon, look for wildflowers, elk, coyotes, and the occa-

sional black bear. The sheltered canyon gives way to steep and rugged Windy Knoll, a scenic viewpoint that gets its name from the regular gusts (hold onto your hat) blowing over the ridge. Continue climbing up Sulphur Mountain for a final panoramic sweep of the Bow Valley before heading back to town.

See Ten 10,000-Foot (3,048 m) Summits in One Day

From the Brewster Lake Louise Stables, set out on a full-day, high-alpine ride. Not recommended for rookie riders due to some steep and rocky sections, the expedition travels along the east side of Mount Fairview, through alpine forests to turquoise-green Lake Annette, tucked beneath the north face of 11,000-foot (3,352.8 m) Mount Temple. After lunch by the lake, the route climbs through a rock field to the Highline Trail and down past the aptly named Giant Steps (elevation 6,980 feet/2,127.5 m),

cascading waters falling over a rock-ledge staircase. From here, ride above the tree line to savor the monumental mountain majesty of the Valley of the Ten Peaks—a row of 10 summits topping 10,000 feet (3,048 m).

Explore the Backcountry on a Six-Day Pack Trip

You'll meet your cowboy guides, group, and, most important, your horse at Warner Stables, located across the Bow River from downtown Banff. The trip begins with a van ride to crystalline Lake Minnewanka. Flanked by evergreens and craggy peaks, the 13-mile (20.9 km) glacier-fed lake is the largest in Banff National Park. Hidden beneath the surface of the blue lake is an underwater ghost town, the eerie remains of a resort community flooded with the construction of a dam in 1941. Saddle up in the trailhead corral for the eight-mile (12.8 km) ride from the lake into the Banff backcountry.

OPPOSITE: Horseback riders make their way along a trail from Lake Louise. RIGHT: Mount Rundle and Sulphur Mountain pose above the Vermillion Lakes.

The route primarily parallels the Cascade River and Stoney Creek. Overnight in the shadow of the Palliser Mountain Range at historic Stoney Creek Camp, named for the indigenous Stoney (Assiniboine) First Nations people who once lived and hunted here.

The second day's 10-mile (16 km) ride offers wide-open views of the Canadian Rockies and, maybe, members of the wild plains bison herd released into the Banff backcountry in 2018. Seeing free-roaming wild bison is a rare treat, since few populations remain in North America. Ride through fertile river valleys where bison regularly roam, and stop for lunch on the banks of the Cascade River. Settle in at Flint's Park Campsite, one of the park's original warden outposts. The remote backcountry camp is nestled in subalpine meadowlands at the base of Flints Peak.

Flint's Park is home base for two full days, giving you the chance to take a deep dive into the Banff backcountry on horseback. Take day rides surrounded by densely forested slopes and jagged mountain peaks. Climb high above Cuthead Lake for top-of-the-Rockies panoramas. Watch roaring cascades on a rest stop along the trail. Spend nights swapping stories around the campfire.

Pack up your gear and take a different river trail 10 miles (16 km) back to Stoney Creek Camp on day five. The next morning, climb back in the saddle for what's arguably the most scenic ride of the trip. The 13-mile (20.9 km) route leads past small alpine lakes and across grassy ridges on the way up to Elk Lake Summit backcountry campground. The picturesque summit is the ultimate spot for a picnic lunch before making the final ride down to the corral at Mount Norquay ski area.

HIGHLIGHTS

• Explore the backcountry wilderness on a six-day pack trip.

• Ride above the tree line to see 10 summits topping 10,000 feet (3,048 m).

• Cross a river and climb a mountain trail on a half-day ride.

A visitor rests up in a hammock aside Morain Lake and the Valley of the Ten Peaks.

VOLCANOES IN MEXICO'S CENTRAL VALLEY

Take on epic climbs within the "Ring of Fire."

The Trans-Mexican Volcanic Belt cinches Mexico's midsection along a 621-mile-long (1,000 km) arc of more than 20 active and dormant volcanoes—including one of the world's most active volcanoes, Popocatépetl ("Smoking Mountain"). Indeed, the peaks of the central valley hold this land in a state of dynamic equilibrium, with the constant threat of falling apart at the seams if one were to suddenly blow its top.

Far removed from the bustle of Mexico City—in spirit, if not in geography— you can ascend here to heights dizzying enough to take your breath away, to say nothing of the heart-stopping views from the top. There are slopes shrouded in jungle and forest that turn to ice and snow as the altitude climbs, dreamy crater lagoons, and signs of indigenous reverence for these sacred mountains.

In recent decades, cleaner air and improved roads have put these once forgotten peaks on the map for hikers and climbers, resulting in more outfitters and guides to help visitors experience the region safely. Even so, trekking Mexico's volcanoes feels remote and daring, tantalizingly rugged and unpredictable.

This ambitious itinerary outlines a plan to tackle a few of Mexico's superlative summits. Pick and choose the peaks you find most alluring—and be sure to hire local guides and add as many rest days as your body needs.

Travel Tips

WHEN TO GO: The dry season between late October and May provides ideal hiking and climbing conditions. During the winter, snow covers glacial ice at the highest elevations and renders the slopes easier to traverse. Weather on volcanoes can change suddenly and turn dangerous. Monitor conditions carefully.

PLANNING: Stay hydrated and spend sufficient time acclimatizing to the elevation—including warm-up hikes—to avoid the effects of *mal de montaña,* better known as altitude sickness.

WEBSITE: visitmexico.com

A woman enjoys the view from Tepoztlán.

11-DAY **ITINERARY**

Day 1

Base yourself in Mexico City, which stands at more than 7,000 feet (2,134 m) above sea level. Simply walking the bustling streets of this high-altitude capital begins the acclimatization process that will prove essential in the days to come. Venture off the beaten path to check out the Museo Anahuacallí, a striking repository for Diego Rivera's pre-Hispanic objets d'art built from black volcanic rock.

Day 2

Ease into your hiking adventure on a day trip to the Tepozteco Mountain and pyramid. An hour south of Mexico City, the culturally vibrant village of Tepoztlán serves as a welcoming trailhead. Soak up some of the town's purported healing energy as you set off on foot down the cobblestone main street, which becomes a hiking trail as it winds up the jungle-shrouded slopes of the mountain. Scramble up the rocky path, gaining 1,200 feet (366 m) in less than a mile (1.6 km) and fortifying your lungs against exertion in thinner air. At the summit awaits an archaeological oddity: a 30-foot-high (9 m) pyramid dating to the 12th century that is said to have once housed a statue of Tepoztécatl, Aztec god of fertility and the milky fermented *pulque* drink.

Day 3

Set out on another hiking day trip, this time to snowcapped Ajusco, about an hour and a half southwest of downtown Mexico City and technically situated within city limits. This lava-dome volcano rises nearly 13,000 feet (3,962 m) and rewards hikers with sweeping views of the Valley of Mexico, including the sprawling capital. Choose

among three trails—with varying degrees of difficulty—and hike through scrub oak and pine forests on a corkscrew climb to the first of two summits—Eagle's Peak, once a sacred Aztec place of worship. If you'd like, continue on to the highest point, crowned by a white cross. Once you're back off the mountain, enjoy a meal at one of the local *cabañas* along the route.

Day 4

Today's challenge is Mexico's fourth highest peak, the 15,350-foot (4,679 m) extinct volcano Nevado de Toluca. *Nevado* translates to "snowcapped," named for the white dusting that frosts the summit throughout the wet season, but typically ice equipment is not necessary here. Trek up the mountainside to enter the enchanting landscape of its 13,800-foot (4,206 m) caldera, where a pair of turquoise lagoons—Lake of the Sun and Lake of the Moon—sparkles against the dusty rocks. Ambitious hikers can carry on a few more hours to the highest summit of Pico de Fraile. Otherwise, turn around at the crater lakes.

Days 5 and 6

If your body is still adjusting to high-altitude hiking, plan for another acclimatization hike before tackling the country's loftiest volcanoes. Head east from Mexico City to the base of the dormant La Malinche, Mexico's fifth highest mountain and a popular hiking destination. Follow in the footsteps of Mexican Olympic athletes who have used this volcanic peak as training grounds. Hike through a pine forest up the sweeping slopes, setting your sights on reaching the tree line above. Stop to save your breath amid a high-alpine meadow or press on to reach the summit at 14,640 feet (4,462 m). On a clear day, you can look out over the bigger volcanoes in the valley.

Days 7 and 8

From the gateway village of Amecameca, set your sights on the Paso de Cortés. The 12,000-foot-high (3,658 m) pass cuts across the saddle between Mexico's twin volcanoes, Iztaccíhuatl and the highly active (and closed to hikers) Popocatépetl—Izta and Popo, for short. This is where Spanish

SEA-KAYAKING THE SEA OF CORTEZ

Paddle your way through Mexico's Baja California peninsula.

Famously christened "the world's aquarium" by legendary oceanographer and conservationist Jacques Cousteau, the Sea of Cortez off the east coast of Mexico's Baja California peninsula teems with wildly large marine life. Blue whales, manta rays, and whale sharks thrive in the plankton-rich waters flanked by towering cliffs and desert landscapes.

Myriad smaller mammals and fish, seabirds, corals, crustaceans, reptiles, and other marine and desert wildlife make their home in and around the vivid turquoise waters of what's alternately called the Sea of Cortez and the Gulf of California. While the wealth of sea creatures merits the nickname that Cousteau bestowed, the image of an aquarium belies the notoriously rough waters. Kayaking is challenging, to say the least, and yet it is the best way to explore the sea and its rocky islands, move among dolphins and sea lions, and reach remote beaches.

Boat-assisted kayaking and camping expeditions offer opportunities to island-hop without battling massive swells. Motorized skiffs called *pangas* carry small groups and their gear between islands. Nightly beach camps are launchpads for guided kayaking and snorkeling. This five-day trip begins in La Paz, the main gateway to the Sea of Cortez (also known as the Gulf of California), and parallels the rugged coastline 90 miles (145 km) north to Loreto Bay National Marine Park.

Travel Tips

WHEN TO GO: January to April for whale and whale shark sightings and mild temperatures; October to December for whales, warm water and air temperatures, and blooming Baja desert views.

PLANNING: Sign on with an outfitter, such as National Geographic Expeditions, OARS, or Sea Kayak Adventures, for a boat-supported kayaking and camping tour. Pack quick-dry clothing made from synthetic fabrics.

WEBSITES: kayakbaja.com; national geographic.com/expeditions; seakayak adventures.com; oars.com

Giant barrel cactus and cardon cactus on Santa Catalina Island

5-DAY ITINERARY

Day 1

See bottlenose dolphins, pelicans, and up to nine species of whale on a skiff ride from La Paz to Isla Espírito Santo. Dimpled cliff faces rising from blue waters make the island among the trip's most scenic. Get in some sea paddling practice just offshore to prepare for the potentially rough Sea of Cortez waters you'll encounter in the days ahead. Go swimming and snorkeling to spot the kaleidoscope of reef fish under the surface. Stargaze and camp on the sugar-sand beach.

Day 2

Hop back in the skiff for the ride north to Los Islotes, the southernmost rookery of the California sea lion. A few hundred sea lions can regularly be seen barking and basking on the rocky islets and swimming in the swirling water below. For a rare up close encounter (no touching), climb in to swim among the playful mammals.

Cruise north to comma-shaped Isla San Francisco Island. Anchor in the protected cove and hike up the sandstone hills on the west side. At the top, look west toward the Baja coast, where striated gray, pink, and white coastal cliffs rise straight up from the sea. Return to the skiff and ride north to remote Isla San José, one of the largest desert islands in the Sea of Cortez. Set up camp on a golden-sand beach for a two-night stay.

Day 3

Spend the entire day exploring Isla San José by land and sea. Paddle to the south end of the island and pull the kayaks onshore to explore an abandoned salt mine. Walk the red-hued salt flats looking for marine fossils

and the rusted remnants of the saltworks. Continue hiking along the beach to reach the forest of enormous cardon cacti, standing watch on the sandy hillsides. Known as Mexican giant cardon, the spiky green cactus is the world's largest, reaching heights of 60 feet (18.3 m) or more.

Push off again to paddle through the maze of mangrove-lined channels on the south end. Continue kayaking the eastern shore near the raised seabed cliffs. Go ashore to hike up the narrow arroyo (wash) that cuts through the sandstone slopes. Scan the red rocks above for feral goats. Finish the day's excursion on the island's remote northern tip. Kayak through arches and around and along huge rock formations sculpted by wind, water, and weather. Ride the skiff back to camp.

Day 4

Depart Isla San José to cruise the nutrient-rich waters around Isla Monserrate, Isla Danzante, and Isla Santa Catalina in Loreto Bay National Park. Depending on the time of year (most commonly February to early March), you may see blue whales, as well as spotted dolphin pods, sea turtles, and

leaping manta rays. Swim off the skiff at remote Isla Catalina (an oceanic island, not previously part of the mainland) to snorkel in the waters below Elephant Rock. Continue on to camp overnight on Isla Carmen, the national park's largest island. If time allows, hike into the interior to look for bighorn sheep and iguanas.

Day 5

Make your last full day all about the water. Swim and stand-up paddleboard off the beach of Isla Carmen. Kayak along the coast, stopping to snorkel in pebbled coves and marvel at the sheer cliff faces and rust-colored peaks. Head back to the mainland for dinner in Loreto, about three miles (4.8 km) southwest of Isla Carmen.

OPPOSITE: **A kayaker paddles by rock formations off the coast of Espíritu Santo Island. ABOVE: A curious and playful California sea lion swims underwater at Los Islotes.**

KAYAK NORTH VANCOUVER ISLAND

Visit the home of the orcas, and paddle next to them.

Dense colonies of animals thrive in the straits that separate Vancouver Island, the largest island on North America's Pacific coast, from mainland British Columbia. The ebb and flood of the tides through the channels stir up nutrients and oxygenate the temperate water, creating a nutrient-rich cocktail for magnificent marine mammals. Among the assemblage feeding here are sea lions; gray, humpback, and minke whales; and pods of orcas, or killer whales.

One of the best places in the Northern Hemisphere to see orcas in the wild is in the protected waters of Johnstone Strait off Vancouver Island's northeastern, or North Island, coast. Orca- and whale-watching kayaking expeditions typically weave through the strait and around tiny islands and islets in the southern reaches of the Broughton Archipelago Park, British Columbia's largest marine park. Paddlers glide in blissful silence past old growth rainforests, empty stone beaches, and remnants of ancient settlements built by the Kwakwaka'wakw people.

Traveling by kayak provides a water-level vantage point for responsible orca- and whale-watching. Even keeping the required distance away (at least 100 yards/ 91 m), paddlers experience the rare thrill of seeing an orca fin up close and feeling the waves created by an acrobatic humpback.

Travel Tips

WHEN TO GO: Whale- and orca-watching trips off Vancouver Island typically are offered June to mid-September.

PLANNING: Sign on for one of the multiday Johnstone Strait–Broughton Archipelago kayaking and camping expeditions offered by outfitters such as North Island Kayak, ROW Sea Kayak Adventures, and Spirit of the West Adventures. Prepare to kayak five to six hours each day and camp overnight on small islands.

WEBSITES: kayakbc.ca; kayakingtours.com; seakayakadventures.com

A bald eagle swoops in for a fresh catch.

6-DAY ITINERARY

Day 1

Spend your first day on land in Telegraph Cove, your launchpad for North Vancouver Island kayaking expeditions. At the Whale Interpretive Centre (WIC), see the 60-foot-long (18.2 m) fin whale skeleton hanging from the ceiling, and learn about the biology, habitat needs, and threats facing Johnstone Strait's celebrated summer visitor: the northern resident orca. About 300 of the predators—commonly called killer whales, yet actually the largest of the dolphins—return to the area each year to feed in the wildlife-rich waters. Overnight over the water in a rustic cabin or modern dockside suite at the Telegraph Cove Resort.

Day 2

Some kayak trips launch from the boat ramp in Telegraph Cove, while others use water taxis to haul kayaks, gear, and paddlers out to an island launch site in the Broughton Archipelago Provincial Marine Park. Choosing a Telegraph Cove–based trip gets you on the water faster, typically before 9:30 a.m. From there, paddle across Johnstone Strait toward forested Hanson Island, watching for diving humpback whales as you paddle.

The day's winds, tidal currents, and marine traffic dictate your route into Blackfish Sound, located on the northern end of Johnstone Strait. Whether you paddle there via Blackney or Weynton passages, you'll be noiselessly gliding through feeding grounds frequented by an astonishing array of wildlife, including eagles, seabirds, seals, and porpoises. Surge through the strong currents in Blackfish Sound to set up camp on a remote beach. From there, hunters like seeking otters and orcas, Chinook salmon, sea urchins, and other seafood supper

items in the underwater kelp forest close to the shore.

_____

Day 3

After breakfast, paddle up Blackfish Sound, staying close to the shore of Swanson Island in the southern end of the Broughton Archipelago. The high tidal flows here create concentrations of shrimp-like krill, the main food staple for hundreds of different animals, from fish, to birds, to whales. Thanks to the lowly krill, today's kayaking route is likely to produce opportunities to see and photograph foraging marine life—such as humpback whales, orcas, and sea lions—accompanied by a gaggle of diving seabirds.

On some tours, such as North Island Kayak's orca expeditions, kayakers can use a research-grade hydrophone to hear the songs of male humpback whales and how orcas in a pod communicate. The underwater listening device is equipped with an external amplifier, making it possi-

ble to simultaneously record below-surface sounds and above-surface views on your phone. Continue paddling around the top of Swanson Island and into the western edge of the archipelago, ancestral homeland of the Kwakwaka'wakw First Nations people.

_____

Day 4

Wake up early to see the sunrise, and then set out for a day kayaking through several of the narrow channels surrounding the hundreds of small islands in the archipelago. Paddling close to the coast provides some shelter from the winds, making it easier to soak in the breathtaking beauty of the coastal rainforest. Float into secluded inlets and past uninhabited islands shrouded in morning fog. See eagles soaring overhead in the bright blue afternoon skies. As you skim glassy-flat waters, scan the shores of passing islands for all manner of wild things like great blue herons, black-tailed deer, river otters, and sea lions.

OPPOSITE: **Paddling through Johnstone Strait, kayakers take in the views.** RIGHT: **An orca breaches above its pod in the Johnstone Strait.**

Day 5

Today's kayaking route meanders south toward the narrow passages surrounding Hanson Island, home of OrcaLab, a land-based orca research station, established in 1970. From its location at Blackney Pass, researchers and volunteers monitor the movements and behaviors of orcas via sightings, radio signals, and sounds collected by a network of hydrophones, positioned around the orcas' core habitat in the Johnstone Strait and Blackfish Sound.

Look for orcas, humpback whales, and sea lions as you paddle across the still waters, stopping on an island beach for lunch. Push off for the afternoon's paddle near the boundaries of the Robson Bight Ecological Reserve, designated as critical habitat for northern resident orcas. To ensure the area remains a sanctuary for the dolphins to feed, socialize, and use "rubbing beaches" (shallow shores with rocks that the animals scrub against), Robson Bight is closed to the public. Kayak just outside the boundaries for the closest possible views of the pristine marine preserve and its highly intelligent and highly social residents.

Day 6

Spend one final morning paddling among Northern Vancouver Island marine mammals before turning your kayak toward Telegraph Cove or, if you are part of a water taxi tour, the launch site in Broughton Archipelago Provincial Marine Park. The route back to Telegraph Cove hugs the Johnstone Strait shoreline. As you cruise past pebble beaches, you may see black bears turning over rocks in search of crabs, mussels, and other tasty tide pool snacks.

HIGHLIGHTS

• Glide the Johnstone Strait, Blackfish Sound, and the Broughton Archipelago.

• Experience up close encounters with orcas, whales, and other wildlife.

• Paddle among remote forested islands and secluded inlets.

Morning mist surrounds a kayaker gliding in the waters of the Johnstone Strait.

HIKING THE JOHN MUIR TRAIL

Trek the scenic backbone of California's Sierra Nevada.

I n the August 1899 issue of the *Atlantic,* legendary environmentalist and Sierra Club founder John Muir wrote, "Of all the mountain ranges I have climbed, I like the Sierra Nevada the best." Chances are you will too, after hiking part, or all, of the 211-mile (339.5 km) trail named in Muir's honor. Topping many backpacker bucket lists, the John Muir Trail (JMT) runs along the spine of California's Sierra Nevada mountains through some of the most spectacularly scenic and pristine wilderness in the United States. Hikers prepared for high-elevation (almost entirely above 8,000 feet/2,438.4 m) trekking are treated to unparalleled views of gargantuan peaks, waterfalls, cliffs, canyons, and thousands of lakes.

It typically takes about three weeks to through-hike the route, which begins in Yosemite National Park and ends on the summit of Mount Whitney. For most of its length, the JMT overlaps another epic long-distance path, the Pacific Crest Trail. Most hikers travel north to south to slowly acclimatize to the JMT's steadily increasing elevations. The southern half of the trail is the highest and most remote, making resupplying here on a through-hike even more challenging.

If heading into the wild for three weeks isn't possible, you can still experience the high-altitude adventure of the JMT on a section hike. The two outlined here hit several highlights on the northern and southern ends of the postcard-perfect trail.

Travel Tips

WHEN TO GO: Hike July to September to avoid heavy snow and potentially dangerous creek crossings.

PLANNING: Wilderness permits are required to hike any section of the John Muir Trail. Through-hike permits from Yosemite National Park trailheads are limited to 45 per day and are issued via a rolling lottery and on a first-come, first-served basis. Bring or rent a bear canister to store food. There are no shelters, so pack a tent.

WEBSITES: pcta.org; nps.gov/yose; yosemiteconservancy.org

Hikers enjoy a beer along the John Muir Trail.

WHERE **TO GO**

North: Tuolumne Meadows to Devils Postpile National Monument

While this three-day, 31-mile (49.8 km) hike skips the first 20 miles (32.1 km) of the JMT, it's typically easier to get a permit to begin here (via the Lyell Canyon trailhead) than at mile 0 (via the Happy Isle trailhead). The starting point is Yosemite National Park's Tuolumne Meadows, one of the largest high-elevation (8,625 feet/2,628.9 m) meadows in the Sierra Nevada.

On day one, savor views of snow-capped peaks and glacier-carved domes as you head off toward the granite-chunk moonscape of Lyell Canyon and views of Lyell Glacier. Climb above the tree line to Donohue Pass, elevation 11,056 feet (3,369.8 m). The pass connects Yosemite to the Ansel Adams Wilderness in the Inyo National Forest. Descend from the pass to find a flat campsite and enjoy the dark-sky stargazing.

The second day's hike leads you into the volcanic rock landscape made famous by Ansel Adams's classic 1927 photographic print, "Banner Peak–Thousand Island Lake." The scene before you—towering 12,936-foot (3,942.8 m) Banner Peak and its mirror image reflected on the surface of the lake—is among the most awe inspiring on the JMT. Camp along the north shore to take in the view at sunset and sunrise or farther down the trail at Garnet Lake.

Close out the hike in Devils Postpile National Monument, named for its matchstick columns of hexagonal basalt rock towering up to 60 feet (18.2 m) high. Get up close views of the postpile from below

before hiking 2.5 miles (4 km) one way to the scenic overlook above 101-foot-high (30.7 m) Rainbow Falls.

_____

South: Kearsarge Pass to Mount Whitney

This challenging four-day trek covers about 50 miles (80.4 km), climbing along the steep, southernmost section of the JMT to the 14,005-foot (4,268.7 m) summit of Mount Whitney. If you're prepared for high-altitude hiking, the route checks three big JMT boxes: crossing the highest point (13,153-foot/4,009 m Forester Pass) on the Pacific Crest Trail; hiking through Sequoia and Kings Canyon National Parks; and watching the sunrise from the highest peak in the lower 48—Mount Whitney.

Overnight at the Onion Valley campground to get an early start. Take the Kearsarge Pass Trail to connect to the JMT at mile 179.4. The 4.7-mile (7.5 km) trail climbs through the John Muir Wilderness

to the top of Kearsarge Pass, elevation 11,700 feet (3,566.1 m). From the pass, you can see a parade of peaks led by the serrated spires of the Kearsarge Pinnacles in Kings Canyon. Camp in Upper Vidette Meadow.

Pyramid-shaped East Vidette peak dominates the view as you set out the second day on the steady climb up Forester Pass, the natural border between Kings Canyon and Sequoia. As you hike into the wide-open and barren Bighorn Plateau, you'll see the finish line: Mount Whitney. If the wind is calm and the weather is clear, camp on the lunar-like terrain of the plateau for an extraterrestrial overnight.

As you leave the plateau on day three, the trail leads to Crabtree Meadow, a major campsite for JMT through-hikers. Follow the trail across and along creeks, through meadows and rock fields, and watch for fish jumping out of the waters of Timberline Lake. Camp past Guitar Lake at the base of the Eastern Sierra so you can begin the hike up Mount Whitney before dawn.

For your last day, head out by 2:30 a.m., and wear a headlamp to navigate the series of steep, rocky switchbacks on your way up to the summit in the dark. Stand atop Mt. Whitney, the southern terminus of the JMT, and see the sunrise over Death Valley. The JMT ends atop Mt. Whitney, but your hike doesn't: The closest road, Whitney Portal, is 11 miles (17.7 km) away.

HIGHLIGHTS

• Relish the moonscape of Lyell Canyon.

• Watch the sunrise from Mount Whitney's 14,005-foot (4,268.7 m) summit, the highest in the lower 48.

• Backcountry camp beside pristine high-alpine lakes.

OPPOSITE: **The Milky Way provides a stunning backdrop for a hiker along the trail.** ABOVE: **Banner Peak, situated in the Ansel Adams Wilderness, is reflected in Thousand Island Lake.**

WINTER WONDERLAND IN JACKSON HOLE

An action-packed weekend escape to the adventure center of Wyoming

W ith its proximity to stunning national parks (Grand Teton and Yellowstone), a plethora of outfitters, and easy access to massive ski- and snowboard-friendly mountains, Jackson, Wyoming, makes an excellent base camp for a winter adventure—even if that adventure will last only a weekend.

Start your trip off right by accepting one of the complimentary mimosas handed out at Jackson Hole Airport by the local chamber of commerce; then take a 10-minute drive to Jackson's picturesque town square. Once you drop your bags at your lodge, head back outside, where all the real action is, and begin one of the epic experiences you've added to your weekend itinerary.

This is an ultra-athletic town that specializes in the art of "dawn patrol," where people rise before the sun to get in a few backcountry ski laps or miles on the trail before work. Residents also relish quirky athletic competitions like the multisport Pole, Pedal, Paddle spring tradition where teams, typically in costume, combine downhill skiing, Nordic skiing, running, biking, and boating. All of this is to say, this is *the* place to be if you're looking for sport and adventure.

To help get you started on those plans, we've compiled a list of five awe-inspiring adventures in the region that you can tackle in one long weekend.

Travel Tips

WHEN TO GO: For winter adventures, things get started around Thanksgiving, and the snow lasts through early April.

PLANNING: Temperatures can plunge to −20°F (−29°C) and below, so pack lots of layers. Jackson Hole has a bustling art community, so leave room in your suitcase for a souvenir or two.

WEBSITES: jacksonhole.com; fs.usda .gov/btnf; tetonpinesnordiccenter.com; jhsleddog.com; nps.gov/yell; anvilhotel .com; togwoteelodge.com; jhecotour adventures.com; fws.gov/refuge/ national_elk_refuge/

Visitors partake in a horse-drawn sleigh ride.

WHAT TO DO

Skiing and Snowboarding

Spend a morning at Jackson Hole Mountain Resort, the primary winter ski and snowboard destination in Jackson Hole. With more than 2,500 acres (1,011 hectares) in Bridger-Teton National Forest, the resort has the longest continuous vertical rise of a ski area in the United States, and nearly half of its runs are rated for experts. There are also plenty of intermediate runs, and the resort's guides are equipped to teach novices how to perfect turns and explore new terrain. With private lessons, you also get lift-line priority and early tram and gondola access.

For the best of Jackson's cross-country skiing, visit Teton Pines Nordic Center in Wilson, Wyoming, just four miles (6.4 km) south of Jackson Hole Mountain Resort. Accessible for all abilities, trails encompass nearly 10 miles (16.1 km) of track, groomed daily for both skate and classic cross-country skiing.

Dog Sledding

With Jackson Hole Iditarod Sled Dog Tours, you're in good company with eight-time Iditarod veteran Frank Teasley running the show. Drive 30 miles (48.3 km) southeast from Jackson to learn the ins and outs of mushing with the outfit's over 170 Alaskan racing dogs, all professionally trained to compete on sled-dog teams.

On a half- or full-day tour, embark to Bridger-Teton National Forest, part of the Greater Yellowstone Ecosystem that encompasses over 3,000 road and trail miles (4,828 km) and thousands of miles of unspoiled rivers and streams. During a full-day trip, you will cover 20 miles (32.2 km) of this wilderness with sled dogs at the helm. Your destination is Granite Hot Springs, where you can take a soothing dip in piping-hot (105°F/40.6°C) thermal waters.

OPPOSITE: Skiers ride the chairlift ready to conquer Jackson Hole's 116 named runs. ABOVE: A musher is pulled along by Alaskan huskies.

Snowmobiling

Experience the wonder of winter by snowmobile during Anvil Hotel's exclusive Explorer Program to Yellowstone National Park. Before departing Jackson and traveling through Grand Teton National Park to Flagg Ranch, Togwotee Adventures will outfit you in the proper gear, including waterproof gloves and snowshoes. Once you arrive, zip through the snow on one of two 100-mile (160.9 km) round-trip tours. Journey to Old Faithful geyser and Moose Falls, or visit Yellowstone's Grand Canyon, a formation nearly 20 miles (32.2 km) long, 4,000 feet (1,219 m) wide, and 1,200 feet (365.8 m) deep. The most iconic views of the canyon are from the Upper and Lower Yellowstone Falls, which are encased in an icy crust during winter.

Wildlife Spotting

Get a good look at Jackson Hole's abundant wintering wildlife—bison, elk, deer, moose, foxes, coyotes, bald eagles, trumpeter swans, and wolves—on an outing with Jackson Hole Eco Tour Adventures. Embark on a journey to the National Elk Refuge, home to thousands of wintering elk and hundreds of bison, before arriving at Grand Teton National Park to glimpse wildlife during the golden sunset hour. Most of the guides are photographers, so they can help you angle the perfect shot of bighorn sheep resting on stone outcroppings or wolves mating in pastures near a herd of elk.

Sleigh Riding

The 11,000-strong Jackson elk herd migrate to the National Elk Refuge during winter, occupying a 24,700-acre (9,995.7 hectare) natural area bounded by Jackson to the south, Bridger–Teton National Forest to the east, and Grand Teton National Park to the north.

After an action-packed weekend of adrenaline-inducing adventures, relax during a horse-drawn sleigh ride through the snowy refuge. Ride in a wagon through the picturesque grassy meadows and marshes of the area's valley floor to gain intimate access to the grazing elk. The ride lasts about an hour, including the shuttle ride to and from the sleigh ride boarding area, about three miles (4.8 km) north of Jackson.

HIGHLIGHTS

• Ski some of the premier slopes in the continental United States.

• Snowmobile by elk, bison, and geysers through two national parks.

• Race like you are in the Iditarod pulled by professionally trained sled dogs.

A herd gathers in the snowy
fields of National Elk Refuge.

Welcome to Burning Man

By Don George

THE DRESS CODE might best be termed "Come as you wish you were." The styles on display in the stark Nevada desert range from beach to boudoir, Moroccan bazaar to intergalactic bizarre. Think bikinis and big furry boots, medieval robes and Middle Eastern veils, Victoria's Secret meets Star Wars cantina meets Priscilla, Queen of the Desert.

Dressed in Japanese pilgrims' outfits that are tame in comparison, my wife, Kuniko, and I hop on our bicycles to explore the Playa. We're on a stunning tract of 4,400 acres (1,780.6 hectares) of arid alkali flatness, about 110 miles (177 km) north of Reno. For years I've been hearing about Burning Man, a festival that defies categorization. Some of my friends have attended numerous times since Larry Harvey and Jerry James first burned a wooden man in a spontaneous ceremony on San Francisco's Baker Beach in 1986. For me, though, Burning Man has always seemed a bit too cultish—and too primitive. A week enduring blazing days and frigid nights, with freeze-dried camp food, stinky portable toilets, and no showers? No, thanks.

And yet, here we are. On this expanse, where a month ago there was nothing, a C-shaped city grid has taken shape, complete with streets alphabetically arranged from Arno to Lorenzo, and neighborhoods, each filled with tents, trailers, RVs, canopies, campers, and slow-rolling art cars.

A khaki-colored plain stretches to a range of gently

BELOW: A laser-lit dance party draws in some of the 70,000 Burning Man attendees. OPPOSITE: A Burning Man attendee from Seattle, known as Playa Maya, wears goggles to protect her eyes from the dust.

serrated mountains, scattered with gigantic artworks. There is a humpback whale mother and calf made of tiny pieces of stained glass; two wooden gorillas sitting contemplatively in the dust; a bristling metal boar, over whose spiky sides adventurous Burners are clambering. The Playa is studded with more than 200 such installations, each seemingly set at random and each inviting—almost requiring—interaction.

A makeshift road leads from the central plaza to the Man himself, designed in accord with the year's theme—Da Vinci's Workshop—to look like the "Vitruvian Man." The road continues beyond the Man toward the Temple, which will be burned the night after the Man—the contemplative counterpoint to the bacchanalian revel of the Man's burn. Built of wood and embellished by more than a hundred wooden lanterns, the tiered Temple soars to a spire in the Buddhist style.

As the week progresses, we are pummeled by the wind, pounded by the sun, lathered by the dust, and overwhelmed by the scope and spectacle of the scene—and yet we find ourselves surrendering to Burning Man's alchemy.

Since using cash is forbidden except to purchase coffee, tea, lemonade, and ice, a culture of giving permeates the city. Wherever we go, we are invited to stop for chilled wine and ice-cold beer; mojitos, mimosas, and margaritas; s'mores, hot dogs, and grilled cheese sandwiches; bacon, pancakes, and pizza. And it isn't just food and drink. Everything is given away: the all-night dance raves and sunset jazz sets, the yoga sessions and chakra meditations, the talks on mindfulness and space-time physics, even the Introduction to Bondage sessions. Watching a city of 70,000 people function without the use of currency is mind expanding; Black Rock City feels like a socioeconomic Galápagos.

I am shy on my own first foray into gift giving. It just seems odd to stop people I don't know and thrust a gift upon them. But when I see a woman traipsing across the Playa in a lacy black gown and opera gloves, I impulsively pull from my backpack one of the inflatable world globes I'd brought. "Excuse me, but I'd like to give you the world," I say. Her face breaks out into a dazzling smile, "I've got the whole world in my hands!"

I am beginning to understand how this experience can truly be life changing. It coalesces for me in one small but pivotal moment when we drop in on an open-air session, Meditation Through Movement. Eastern music fills a canopied space, and a woman with a dulcet voice is encouraging three dozen people to move however they feel comfortable. At dances, I'm usually the person behind the punch bowl, but in this setting, my balletic baggage is left in the dust. Before long, I am swaying through the space, dipping and twirling, feeling liberated and embraced by all the people dancing around me and throughout Black Rock City.

I'm not quite ready for my naked torso to be covered in shimmery body gel at Glitter Camp or to have a team wash it all off at the Human Carcass Wash.

But maybe next year.

OPPOSITE: A family of Burning Man attendees climb on oversize art.
ABOVE: A man hands out free grilled PB&J sandwiches at the festival.

• *Don George is an editor at large at* National Geographic Traveler.

ROAD TRIP THROUGH UTAH'S NATIONAL PARKS

Discover the road to the Mighty Five: Zion, Bryce Canyon, Capitol Reef, Arches, and Canyonlands.

This multiday adventure on remote byways is a journey through the slickrock heart of the American West, linking Utah's "Mighty Five" national parks—Zion, Bryce Canyon, Capitol Reef, Arches, and Canyonlands. Each park showcases the iconic landscape of the Colorado Plateau, much of it an ancient Sahara now turned to stone. The surreal tableau of arches, alcoves, hoodoos, and epic canyons is so otherworldly that you may wonder what planet you're on.

You may be traveling through Utah, but the trip begins in Las Vegas—the faster way to the first stop, Zion National Park. Along with the parks, there is plenty to see and do along the road. On the way to Zion, stretch car-weary legs on a self-guided walking tour of St. George's Historic District. For a preview of what waits in Bryce, stop for a quick jaunt on the interpretive Pink Ledges Trail in Red Canyon. Stop ahead of Capitol Reef in Boulder to visit the Anasazi State Park Museum and experience life from an earlier culture. Learn about the one-armed wonder who first surveyed the Colorado River at the John Wesley Powell River History Museum on the road to Arches. And on the way to Canyonlands, check out the Moab Giants, a dinosaur tracks museum. Now that you've got the sideshows out of the way, it's on to the main attractions.

Travel Tips

WHEN TO GO: March showers bring April wildflowers, which peak in May and mid- to late June, depending on the park. Visit Capitol Reef in the second week of June and October to harvest orchard fruit. Flash flooding can occur in the Arches between July and August, so be alert.

PLANNING: Layer up: Temperatures can drop or rise 30 degrees Farhrenheit (16.7 degrees Celsius) within hours.

WEBSITES: nps.gov/zion; nps.gov/brca; nps.gov/care; nps.gov/arch; nps.gov/cany

A hiker reaches the top of narrow Angels Landing in Zion.

WHERE TO GO

Zion

A free park shuttle follows the Virgin River, which flows in the shadows of some of the world's tallest sandstone cliffs, creating a walled sanctuary adorned with hanging gardens and emerald pools. Escape the crowds at the park's more remote Kolob Canyons and Kolob Terrace sections (accessible by private vehicle only).

Canyon Overlook is a real rail grabber, with dizzying views of Lower Pine Creek Canyon dropping into Zion Canyon. From the Timber Creek Overlook at Kolob Canyons, views on clear days reach 100 miles (161 km) to Mount Trumbull, marking the North Rim of the Grand Canyon.

Follow the Virgin along the two-mile (3.2 km) Kayenta Trail to Emerald Pools, an oasis of water-filled basins and misting spray. Nerves of steel? Try legging it up the narrow spine of rock to Angels Landing via the West Rim Trail for adrenaline-fueled views of Zion Canyon.

Bryce Canyon

If you think rocks only come in one color, you'll be floored by the polychromatic spectacle of the world's largest display of hoodoos. Be sure to catch a sunrise here. It doesn't matter from where: Sunrise Point, Sunset Point, anyplace in between. Prepare to be transfixed as the rocks unleash their vibrant colors, as if glowing from within. It's arguably the best sunrise on the planet. Of the 14 park overlooks, Paria View is one of the few to catch the last rays of the setting sun; plus, you might glimpse the peregrine falcons that nest here.

For a shifting take on the park's famous hoodoos below (and to lose the crowds thronging the more well known viewpoints), stroll the Rim Trail along the amphitheater's edge, from Sunrise Point to Inspiration

Point. Acrobatic cliff swallows and white-throated swifts entertain hikers along the way.

Capitol Reef National Park

The Reef is the least known and most remote of Utah's five national parks and encompasses the 100-mile-long (161 km) Waterpocket Fold, a wall-like rift of stone in Earth's surface that kept out all but the hardiest of pioneers. Those who persevered found an idyllic oasis pocketed amid the Reef's monumental capitol-like domes, natural bridges, spires, and slot canyons—and you will too.

Hike less than 20 minutes to a solitary bench at the end of the Sunset Point Trail for the park's most elemental panorama: brick-red Moenkopi towers, domes of bone-white Navajo sandstone, and the

distant Henry Mountains. The green swath of trees lining Sulphur Creek as it joins the Fremont River ties it all together.

Don't miss the park's 1908 Gifford Homestead for an authentic taste of Mormon pioneer living. Not for the museum-like displays—okay, for those too—but for the locally baked mini–apple pies available in the gift shop.

Arches National Park

These 120 square miles (310.8 km) contain the highest density of stone arches in the world—2,000 and counting. Some are iconic, such as Delicate Arch (the one printed on Utah's license plates). Others shatter records, including pencil-thin Landscape Arch, one of the world's longest free-standing arches. And some you'll have to search out yourself on trails that lead you

OPPOSITE: **The sun shines behind Mesa Arch in Canyonlands National Park.** ABOVE: **The stunning vistas of Zion National Park**

deep into a sandstone world dating back 300 million years.

To go to Arches and not see Delicate Arch is like going to the Louvre and not seeing the "Mona Lisa." The march to the arch takes close to an hour, most of it uphill, so bring plenty of water.

The safest way to visit Fiery Furnace, a confusing labyrinth of sandstone fins, is on a three-hour tour led by park rangers (offered at least once daily during summer). In the Fiery Furnace, ask the ranger to point out Canyonlands lomatium (also called Arches biscuitroot), which blooms from February to April. It just might be the only time you'll ever see it, as most of the world's supply is only found in the park's Entrada fins.

Canyonlands National Park

This is as wild as it gets. Canyonlands is the largest and most undeveloped of Utah's national parks, so vast it's divided into four sections. The rivers—the Colorado and Green and their tributaries—make up one section. The Maze is rough, remote, and rarely visited. Island in the Sky (I-SKY) floats high above the canyon bottoms, a mesa rimmed with vertiginous vistas. The Needles offers miles of stupendous hiking. If time's an issue, stick to I-SKY. If not, head to the Needles as well.

Drive to I-SKY's Grand View Point overlook for seriously epic views of an endless succession of red rock canyons—with nothing human visible—stretching as far as the eye can see. For maximum effect, settle in for the sunset.

In the Needles, the Cave Springs Trail has it all: an old cowboy camp, a natural spring, ancestral Puebloan paintings, hanging gardens, and wooden ladders to hoist you up on the slickrock for fine views of the Needles' banded spires.

HIGHLIGHTS

• Visit five stunning national parks in one epic road trip.

• Watch the sun rise and set over hoodoos and sandstone arches.

• Hike to peaks overlooking vast expanses of the wild frontier.

The Thor's Hammer hoodoo is a popular site in Bryce Canyon National Park.

EPIC SHOT

A surfer takes on a huge swell in Mavericks break in Half Moon Bay, California. Mavericks has long been considered an ideal spot for surfers looking to ride big waves—50-foot (15 m) swells that challenge even the most experienced riders.

Mavericks, located just offshore from the bluff at Pillar Point Harbor, plays host to an annual surfing competition that is pulled together with just 48 hours' notice when the waves and weather align sometime between November and March. Surfers must be ready to take on the ultimate challenge at a moment's notice.

Winter storms over the Pacific Ocean create a low-pressure front in the north that collides with a high-pressure front in the south, resulting in strong, fast winds that create the big swells at Mavericks. But the waves also gain their size from the unique shape of Half Moon Bay's floor, which rises sharply and drops off steeply, allowing the swells to grow quickly in height.

IMAGE BY **FRANS LANTING**

WHERE TO GO

Destination Arctic Circle

Launch your Arctic adventure in Kangerlussuaq, gateway to the western edge of the
Greenland ice cap (only 12 miles/19.3 km
from the country's largest airport). The Arctic Circle crosses the midpoint of Kangerlussuaq fjord, and the area enjoys clear
weather most of the year, meaning you're
likely to be treated to a spectacular northern light show from October to April. Kangerlussuaq is also the starting point of the
epic 102-mile (164.1 km) Arctic Circle Trail,
a wilderness hiking path following the historic dog-sledding route from Kangerlussuaq
to Sisimiut and the Davis Strait. About half
the trail falls within the boundaries of the
Aasivissuit-Nipisat UNESCO World Heritage
site, and all of it is north of the Arctic Circle,
meaning you'll have around-the-clock daylight for midsummer hiking. If you don't
have a week or more to make the challenging one-way trek, opt for a shorter adventure like camping on the ice cap, hiking and
kayaking on a musk ox safari, or, in winter,
heli-skiing monster peak-to-sea drops (up
to 4,500 feet/1,371.6 m) at the edge of
untouched Eternity fjord.

The Capital Region

Nuuk, Greenland's town-sized capital city—
home to about 16,000 of the country's
56,000 residents—is generating buzz for its
world-class Katuaq (drumstick) Cultural
Center and Nordic-centric food scene (think
glacial-ice vodka and fresh-from-the-fjord
fish). But the capital also sits at the mouth
of massive Nuuk fjord, one of the largest in
the world, making it easy to combine culture and adventure. Explore the fjord system's coves, channels, and islands by
kayak or boat tour. In summer, take the
hour-long boat ride from Nuuk to Qooqqut

fjord, home to one of the world's most isolated restaurants, Qooqqut Nuan, located in
a former sheep breeding station. Catch
your own fish, and they'll cook it with side
dishes, or order off the menu. The restaurant also rents tents and rustic cottages for
overnight stays overlooking the fjord. Hike
around the surrounding valley to see historic Viking ruins and watch for white-tailed
eagles and reindeer.

South Greenland

The southern end of the island accounts for
much of the "green" in Greenland. In summer, emerald meadows, brightly colored
wildflowers, and cobalt lakes dot the landscape. Hike the rolling hills and verdant valleys in and around the Qassiarsuk area to
see Norse ruins, blue icebergs, fjords,
waterfalls, bald eagles, grazing sheep, and,
on occasion, wild ponies. South Greenland
is sheep country, and many families have
converted original farmhouses, most built in
the 1950s and 1960s, into hostels for hikers. Make a sheep farm hostel or guest-
house your base for day hikes and other
adventures, such as a boat ride across

Ikerssuaq Fjord for up close views of the
effects of climate change on Greenland's
ice cap. Hike onshore to touch the ice cap
and see rocks recently exposed by reced-
ing glaciers. On the uninhabited island of
Uunartoq, watch the icebergs float by while
you soak in Greenland's only open-air geothermal pool.

East Greenland

While Greenland's vast and fjord-laced
eastern coast is best explored by sea kayak
or Zodiac, kick off your visit with a hike
from the tiny gateway airport, Kulusuk. Follow the road from the airport across Kulusuk island to Isikajia Mountain. On clear
days, the Isikajia scenic viewpoint offers
sweeping views of fjords, rocky coastline,
and the icebergs floating in the Denmark
Strait. From Kulusuk, hop a boat to Tasiilaq,
East Greenland's largest town and the
region's adventure hub. Rent a kayak or join
a guided tour to paddle through a maze of
steep and rocky fjords. Watch for marine
wildlife, such as harp seals and the rare and
endangered bowhead whale. Listen for the
thunderous roar of calving glaciers as you

OPPOSITE: **Sisimiut village is dotted with brightly
painted houses.** RIGHT: **A pair of walruses poke
their heads above the water to check out their
Arctic surroundings.**

silently glide past icebergs and alongside mountains rising straight out of the water.

————————

Northeast Greenland National Park

Spanning a remote wilderness area more than twice the size of California, 375,000-square-mile (971,246 sq km) Northeast Greenland National Park is the largest park of its kind on the planet. The only way to visit the park, which has no visitor facilities and no permanent residents, is on a guided expedition, employing nimble Zodiacs and kayaks to explore the high Arctic coastline. Make the rugged trek, and you'll be rewarded with brilliant northern light displays; frequent opportunities to spot caribou, musk oxen, polar bears, walruses, and whales; and the privilege of being among the select group to have experienced this untouched corner of the world.

————————

North Greenland

Home to the Ilulissat Icefjord UNESCO World Heritage site, North Greenland is an all-season arctic playground covering the west side of the island from Disko Bay to the far north. Hear the low rumble and crack of Ilulissat's massive icebergs as you hike along the edge of the ice fjord. Sail across Disko Bay to surprisingly verdant Qeqertarsuaq for hiking, whale- and bird-watching, and year-round dog sledding on the Lyngmark Glacier. Head north to explore the Upernavik archipelago's thousands of islands and icebergs on a summer kayaking trip. Or island-hop across the frozen sea ice by sled dog or snowmobile in winter under the glow of the northern lights. Kayak at the top of the world in Greenland's northernmost town, Qaanaaq, an Inuit community located less than 20 miles (32 km) from Canada.

HIGHLIGHTS

• Hike the Arctic Circle Trail wilderness path under the midnight sun.

• Go heli-skiing on summit-to-sea glacial runs at the edge of a stunning fjord.

• Sea-kayak in an Inuit community at the top of the world.

Sea kayaks sit on a beach in the Angmassalik Fjord.

1 SOUTH GEORGIA, ANTARCTICA

Ernest Shackleton's South Georgia hiking route traces black-sand beaches crowded with thousands of king, macaroni, gentoo, and chinstrap penguins. Visit South Georgia from December to mid-February to see downy penguin chicks, fin whales, elephant seals, and fur seals. Or visit late February through March when both chicks and seal pups begin to fledge and wandering albatrosses start to hatch.

2 MACQUARIE ISLAND, TASMANIA, AUSTRALIA

Macquarie Island trembles through an earthquake every year, but that doesn't seem to bother the world's largest colony of royal penguins, which return by the millions every September to breed. The only place where Earth's mantle can be seen above sea level, Macquarie's volcanic shores also welcome elephant and fur seals; albatrosses; Hooker's sea lions; and king, gentoo, and southern rockhopper penguins.

3 WRANGEL ISLAND, RUSSIA

Once home to the world's last family of woolly mammoths, Wrangel's rocky beaches and charcoal mountains now support arctic foxes, musk oxen, reindeer, snow geese, the world's largest population of Pacific walrus, and the world's highest density of polar bear dens.

4 DANGER ISLANDS, ANTARCTICA

Hidden behind enormous ice fragments off the tip of the Antarctic Peninsula, the Danger Islands were not thought to be a crucial penguin habitat—that is, until 2015, when scientists followed guano trail via satellite to a supercolony of more than 1.5 million thriving Adélies. The islands are about as accessible as they sound, reached by only the most experienced captains during the best conditions.

5 SVALBARD, NORWAY

Polar bears, walruses, reindeer, whales, a doomsday seed vault, the northern lights, the northernmost Thai restaurant in the world: all exist in Svalbard. This Arctic Ocean archipelago boasts a polar bear population of 3,500 and growing. Summer is the best time to see polar bears.

6 CHURCHILL, MANITOBA, CANADA

In autumn, Churchill Manitoba hosts the largest concentration of wild polar bears in the world. Tours from Churchill Wild's Nanuk Lodge wander through the Hudson Bay's polar bear territory, also home to wolves, moose, caribou, black bears, and wolverines. Guides have developed safe ways of approaching bears on foot, undoubtedly a thrilling experience.

7 BOUVET ISLAND, NORWEGIAN TERRITORIES

Bouvet's only field station was demolished in an earthquake in 2006 and was not rebuilt until 2014. The inactive volcano at its center is frozen solid. In short, it's a penguin Shangri-La. Thousands of macaroni penguins feast on crustaceans off its chilly shores. Fur seals can also be seen in great numbers. The best way to the island is by ship and then helicopter to shore.

8 ATKA BAY AND THE SOUTH POLE, ANTARCTICA

Skip the islands and head to the South Pole for ice tunnel trekking, rock climbing, abseils, and zip-lining—that is, if you can brave the 13,000-foot-altitude (3,962 m) and below-zero temperatures. White Desert offers all of the activities above, plus day-trips to Atka Bay's 6,000-plus emperor penguin colony and pod-camping between a 200-foot (61 m) ice cliff and a frozen lake.

9 SOUTHERN OCEAN, ANTARCTICA

Why waddle with penguins when you can swim with them? Advanced divers get a new glimpse of Antarctica below the ice where otherworldly icescapes and unreal shades of blue are a spectacular backdrop for penguins, feather stars, Weddell seals, orange sea squirts, and octopus. Less experienced travelers can try penguin-spotting polar snorkeling.

10 NUNAVUT, CANADA

Visit Canada's northernmost Nunavut region between May and July for polar bear viewing under the midnight summer sky. Nunavut's Baffin Island is also home to millions of migratory waterfowl and 4,101-foot-tall (1,250 m) Mount Thor, the world's tallest vertical cliff.

OPPOSITE: A king penguin colony gathers on the beach of the South Sandwich Islands. ABOVE: Guests peer over a ship's edge to catch a glimpse of a strolling polar bear on Baffin Island.

WILD NIGHTS AND NORTHERN LIGHTS

See the dancing sky in the "polar bear capital of the world."

Churchill calls itself the "polar bear capital of the world." A gateway to the Arctic, this tiny Manitoba town 600 miles (965.6 km) north of the provincial capital, Winnipeg, sits on the remote western shore of Canada's Hudson Bay. An adventure and nature destination where tundra, boreal forest, and the waters of Hudson Bay meet, the area has been a traditional hunting zone for First Peoples, whose heritage is honored at Churchill's Itsanitaq Museum (formerly the Eskimo Museum). Today, the region attracts visitors from around the world with its opportunities to watch wildlife and view the aurora borealis.

Manitoba's 110,000 lakes and waterways, abundant wildlife, and diverse arts and cultural experiences entice travelers seeking off-the-beaten-path adventure. From kayaking with belugas to dining on a frozen river, there are plenty of thrills to be had here, especially when it comes to the area's famed bears.

In the 1970s, Churchill resident Len Smith created the Tundra Buggy, allowing visitors to get closer to polar bear habitats than ever before. After a National Geographic crew joined him, their coverage of the region prompted wildlife enthusiasts to make tracks to view bears and belugas.

Whenever it is you decide to make it to this polar paradise, count on catching one of nature's very best shows.

Travel Tips

WHEN TO GO: Summer (for belugas), fall (for polar bears), and winter (for the northern lights) are the best times to visit.

PLANNING: Book your flights early. Churchill is accessible only by plane, and this increasingly popular location can fill up quickly. Be prepared for snow and very cold weather. Pack layers, snow pants and boots, sunglasses, and a balaclava for the wind.

WEBSITES: churchillwild.com; nationalgeographiclodges.com

A beluga whale swims in the Churchill River.

WHAT TO DO

Paddle With Beluga Whales

Nearly 60,000 beluga whales inhabit the western reaches of Hudson Bay. Each summer, thousands head into the mouth of the Churchill River in search of warmer waters to birth, raise calves, and feast on capelin and other fish. Highly sociable and curious cetaceans, belugas are called canaries of the sea for their birdlike calls.

Boat tours bring visitors to waters that belugas often frequent. Many boats have hydrophones so passengers can listen to the whales underwater. Adventurous visitors eager for up close looks can kayak, paddleboard, or snorkel.

Fun fact: Unlike most other whales, belugas don't have fused neck vertebrae, allowing them to turn their heads to look back at you.

Encounter Polar Bears

One of the best ways to spot *Ursus maritimus* (the polar bear) is on a tundra vehicle tour through the Churchill Wildlife Management Area and beyond. The rugged vehicles transport visitors into this realm of the ice bear to watch males spar, cubs play, and mothers snooze.

Helicopter tours provide a bird's-eye view of the sparkling vistas of snow, ice, and water, along with plenty of bear sightings. Normally it's ill advised to walk among the bears, but Churchill Wild offers hiking tours at remote ecolodges to see them safely by foot.

Come fall, bears begin to gather along Hudson Bay, waiting for ice to form so they can hunt seals, a prime time to see these magnificent animals.

Watch the Northern Light Show

Churchill is one of the top places on Earth to witness the aurora borealis, which shimmers into curtains of light here some 300 nights a year. February and March, with their dark and clear evening skies, provide ideal viewing conditions. Green northern lights are most common; red and blue are more elusive.

Temperatures this far north typically are frigid midwinter, but aurora-watchers waiting for the polar spectacle to fan out over the heavens stay warm in tent-size Aurora Domes, a wheeled Aurora Pod, and even an Aurora Lounge. Photography tours offer visitors guidance on capturing the images of this fleeting phenomenon with tips on how to optimize camera settings.

Experience the Clear Lake Life

Clear Lake is the crown jewel of southern Manitoba's Riding Mountain National Park. Located along the Manitoba Escarpment, a tilted rock shelf formed more than 65 million years ago, the pristine park is the traditional territory of the Anishinaabe people. Rent a ride to explore Clear Lake by boat, kayak, or stand-up paddleboard. Walk the leisurely Clear Lake South Shore Trail, part of the more than 250-mile (402.3 km) hiking and mountain-biking trail network crisscrossing the park. Swim and snorkel off the sandy beach in Wasagaming, Clear Lake's friendly resort town. Mid-May to mid-October,

spend the night within walking distance of the lake and the town at Wasagaming Campground. Bring your own tent or, better yet, reserve a yurt, tiny house–like Micro-Cube, or A-frame oTENTik cabin.

Reel in Trophy Fish

Cast a line and catch monster fish in Manitoba, home to 110,000 lakes and waterways and 30 fish species, such as lake trout, northern pike, walleye, and arctic grayling. In remote northern Manitoba, Big Sand Lake Lodge and Gangler's North Seal River Lodge offer fly-in guided fishing trips and outpost expeditions on millions of acres of pristine wilderness waters. Closer to Winnipeg, world-class fishing and a fresh-catch shore lunch await at Aikens Lake Wilderness Lodge in the Atikaki Provincial Wilderness Park.

OPPOSITE: The green aurora borealis performs its nightly dance above Manitoba. ABOVE: A kayaker takes to the waters in Clear Lake.

Lucky tourists enjoy the start of the northern lights show at the Churchill Northern Studies Center.

Deepest Dive Ever Under Antarctica

By Laurent Ballesta

WHEN WE ARRIVE ON FOOT from Dumont d'Urville, the French scientific base on East Antarctica, we have to break up a thin layer of ice that has formed over the hole we drilled the day before. The hole goes right through the 10-foot-thick (30.5 m) ice floe. It's just wide enough for a person, and below it lies the sea. We've never tried to dive through such a small opening. I go first.

Pushing and pulling with hands, knees, heels, and the tips of my swim fins, I shimmy through the hole. As I plunge at last into the icy water, I look back to a sickening sight: The hole has already begun to close behind me. Grabbing the safety rope, I pull myself up inch by inch, but my shoulders get stuck. Suddenly I'm stunned by a sharp blow to the head: One of my dive buddies is trying to dig me out and his shovel has struck my skull. Finally a hand grabs mine and hauls me into the air. Today's dive is over—but it's only one of 32.

This expedition to Antarctica is unlike any other. Here we'll be diving deeper than anyone else has dived before under Antarctic ice—and the conditions will be beyond harsh.

When at last we're ready to topple back into the freezing water, we're wearing and carrying 200 pounds (90.7 kg) each. Moving is a struggle, swimming almost impossible. The cold quickly anesthetizes the few square inches of exposed skin on our cheeks, and as the dive wears on, it intrudes into our suits and gloves, biting harder and harder. It's unbearable, but we must bear it.

What could possibly make this worthwhile? The light, first of all. It's a sight to elate any photographer. At the very beginning of spring, after the long polar night, microscopic plankton have not yet begun to bloom and cloud the water. Under the floe, it's exceptionally clear, because there are so few particles to scatter the light. What little light there is wells down through the cracks or seal holes as if from street lamps, casting a subtle glow over the underwater landscape.

BELOW: Tendrils of ice-covered brine, or brinicles, leak from sea ice near East Antarctica's Dumont d'Urville Station. OPPOSITE: A curious Weddell seal, weeks old, comes in for a close-up look.

And what a landscape! At depths of 30 to 50 feet (9 to 15.2 m), forests of kelp, with blades more than 10 feet (30.5 m) long, create a sober, imposing scene. Farther down, we meet giant sea stars. At 15 inches (38.1 cm) in diameter, they're much bigger than those in warmer seas. Below 165 feet (50.3 m), the light dims and we see no kelp or other plants. Instead, the seafloor is covered with thick carpets of feather hydroids (colonial animals related to corals) and thousands of scallops. The scallops are four inches (10.1 cm) across but may be 40 years old or more—things grow slowly in the Antarctic. At these depths, we also notice feather star crinoids, close relatives of sea stars that snag particles of drifting food with up to 20 undulating arms. Crawling and swimming among them are giant isopods that resemble beetles.

At 230 feet (70 m), the limit of our dives, the diversity is greatest. We see gorgonian sea fans, shellfish, soft corals, sponges, and small fish, their colors and exuberance reminiscent of tropical coral reefs. The fixed invertebrates in particular are enormous. Well adapted to a stable environment, these plantlike animals grow slowly but, it appears, without limit—unless something disturbs them. How will they respond as climate change warms their world?

As we ascend to the surface, the biodiversity diminishes. The shallower waters are a less stable environment. Drifting icebergs and sea ice scour the seafloor, and the seasonal freezing and melting of the sea surface, which removes freshwater from the ocean and then returns it, cause dramatic swings in salinity.

But there is still plenty to occupy the eye. Microalgae cling to the ceiling of ice, turning it into a flamboyant rainbow of orange, yellow, and green. The ceiling is really more like a chaotic labyrinth, with layers of ice at different levels, and we pass through them slowly, cautiously. One day as I'm nearing the hole, I see a mother and baby seal plunge through it. I watch them for a long, envious moment as they move effortlessly through this fairy landscape.

The waters under Antarctic ice are like Mount Everest: magical but so hostile that you have to be sure of your desire before you go. You cannot go halfheartedly; you cannot feign your passion. The demands are too great. But that's what makes the experiences and the images we take so unforgettable.

OPPOSITE: A diver explores what lies beneath Antarctica's ice. ABOVE: A feather star waves its frondlike arms, groping for food particles.

• *Laurent Ballesta is a French biologist and deep-diving photographer.*

EXPLORING GREENLAND AND THE CANADIAN ARCTIC

From soaring icebergs to Baffin Island, historic passageways, rich landscapes, and wildlife

Venture deep into the far reaches of the Arctic, a land where polar bears roam and hardy Inuit communities maintain their traditional way of life. Aboard the *National Geographic Explorer,* trace the rugged fjords of Greenland and navigate the northern end of Canada's legendary Baffin Island. Spot polar bears on the pack ice, get up close to massive glaciers, and hike the islands that dot Canada's shores.

Baffin Island, a 195,928-square-mile (507,451 sq km) landmass in the Arctic Ocean of northern Canada, is extremely remote. But a trip here offers intrepid explorers the chance to see the northern lights, spot a polar bear, ride a dogsled, and kayak between ice floes. Cruising around the island offers spectacular sights on board and escapades on land.

You'll see plenty from aboard the ship as you pass by soaring icebergs at the mouth of Ilulissat Icefjord, a UNESCO World Heritage site. Off the ship on Baffin Island, search for ringed seals, arctic foxes, walruses, and polar bears. Or paddle with beluga and bowhead whales. You'll also encounter Inuit communities and learn about their rich culture. Take in the fjords that Greenland is known for in your own private vessel, kayaking the smooth waterways between stunning scenery and lush landscapes.

Travel Tips

WHEN TO GO: Find different animal encounters in spring, winter, and fall and the mildest temperatures (though they're always frigid at night) in the summer. By mid-July, the midnight sun is beaming and the ocean is ice free. Things begin to freeze up again in October and November, and winter months can be dark.

PLANNING: Add on a few days to either end of the trip to explore more of Reykjavík, Iceland, as well as take a side trip to Oslo, Norway.

WEBSITES: nationalgeographic.com/expeditions

A license plate for Nunavut, Canada

11-DAY ITINERARY

Day 1

The trip begins in Reykjavík, Iceland, where you can soak in the Blue Lagoon or visit a hot spring, geothermal plant, or horse farm. From there, it's a quick plane hop to Greenland, where you'll board the National Geographic Expeditions ship and the real adventure begins.

Dozens of deep fjords carve into Greenland's west coast, many with glaciers fed by the ice cap that covers about 80 percent of the country. Discover this beautiful and rugged coastline in Zodiacs, searching for humpback and minke whales. At Sisimiut, a former whaling port, visit the museum and wander amid a picturesque jumble of historic and modern wooden buildings.

Days 2 through 8

Start by spending a relaxing day at sea where you can watch for whales from the bridge, enjoy a soothing sauna, or learn about the history of polar exploration from on-boat guides or the ship's extensive library. The next stop is the Canadian High Arctic, where you'll have plenty of time for off-boat exploration: You'll spend six days here.

The exploration of the Canadian High Arctic begins with a visit to the small Inuit community of Pond Inlet, Nunavut. Nunavut's 34,000 people live in a land area bigger than Mexico (population 116 million). Formerly part of the Northwest Territories, Nunavut was formalized as a Canadian territory only in 1999. Explore some of the beautiful bays and inlets along Baffin Island's Lancaster Sound, a favorite Inuit hunting and fishing location for hundreds of years. Carved by Ice Age glaciers, Lancaster Sound is also the eastern gateway to the Arctic Archipelago, where European explorers like William Baffin first ventured in

the 17th century to search for the Northwest Passage. Days here will be spent searching for ringed seals, arctic foxes, walruses, and polar bears, as well as beluga and bowhead whales. You may even spot the elusive narwhal, an arctic whale known for its long, spiraled tooth.

Visit Devon Island and take a walk with the ship's archaeologist to learn about the Thule people—ancestors of the modern Inuit—who once inhabited this region. Then venture farther north to the southern reaches of Ellesmere Island. You may take a Zodiac cruise in Makinson Inlet, where tidewater glaciers tumble down to the sea.

Days 9 and 10

Cross Baffin Bay Sail into Disko Bay to explore the UNESCO World Heritage site of Ilulissat Icefjord, a tongue of the Greenland ice cap that extends to the bay. Take an extraordinary cruise among towering ice-

bergs at the mouth of the fjord. Visit the town of Ilulissat and hike in the Sermermiut Valley.

Day 11

The final day will be spent in west Greenland's beautiful fjord lands, exploring the picturesque waterways by Zodiac cruise or kayak. Specialists launch remote-operated vehicles to view marine life inhabiting the floors of the fjords. Watch from their monitors to see what they're discovering.

HIGHLIGHTS

• Observe polar bears, arctic foxes, ringed seals, belugas, and narwhals.

• Explore Lancaster Sound, the gateway to the Northwest Passage.

• Seek out caribou while hiking the landscapes of Baffin Island.

OPPOSITE: Narwhals come up through seal holes and rotten ice to catch a breath. ABOVE: Broad Peak looms large at Sam Ford Fiord and Walker Arm on Baffin Island

Gibbs Fjord's steep cliff faces reflect back on themselves in icy blue Arctic waters.

UNITED STATES

THE GATES OF THE ARCTIC

Channel your inner Iditarod musher, dog-sledding this national park and preserve.

The bush pilot mantra "Where the road ends, the real Alaska begins" captures the essence of Gates of the Arctic National Park and Preserve. All 8.4 million untouched acres (34,287 sq km) lie north of the Arctic Circle, making it the northernmost national park in the United States. No roads or trails lead into or around the vast expanse of arctic tundra, boreal forest, and jagged Brooks Range peaks. The only landmarks on the park's map are six tumbling National Wild and Scenic Rivers.

Being among the fortunate few to experience the solitude and austere grandeur of one of the wildest of the wild places left on Earth isn't easy. Gates of the Arctic perennially ranks among the least visited national parks, with good reason: Most visitors fly in on bush plane (the other option is hiking in from the Dalton Highway or from the village of Anaktuvuk) during the summer. Serious wilderness backcountry skills are required to navigate challenging terrain.

In cold months, however, exploring by dogsled allows you to cover more ground. It's also among the rarest of rare national park adventures. The only outfitter based within the park is Arctic Winter Adventures, operated by veteran Iditarod musher Sven Haltmann. Beginning in March 2020, Haltmann will offer five three-day dog-sledding trips (one person or couple per trip) inside the park.

Travel Tips

WHEN TO GO: The three-day dog-sledding itinerary begins in 2020 and will be offered from late March to mid-April.

PLANNING: Book as early as possible, since only five trips are scheduled each season. Arctic Winter Adventures will provide a packing list and can outfit you with appropriate winter gear. March and April temperatures typically range from below 0°F to 35°F (−17.8° to 1.7°C). There is no cell service in the national park.

WEBSITES: nps.gov/gaar; arcticwinter adventures.com

The Arrigetch Peaks in Brooks Range

3-DAY ITINERARY

Day 1

Arrive inside the park by bush plane, landing on the icy surface of cerulean Takahula Lake. Located at the base of Takahula Mountain, the lake is a regular landing strip for floatplanes. In summer, it is the first stop for the world-class rock climbers who attempt technical ascents in the jagged Arrigetch Peaks, a National Natural Landmark. Unlike the climbers, who face a multi-day hike to the base of the peaks, you have only a short walk from the plane to a lakeside wilderness cabin. The rustic cabin is your base camp for the next three days, and it offers two unexpected luxuries: heat and a hot sauna.

Since Gates of the Arctic has no established campsites or shelters, being able to stay in *any* cabin inside the park is a rare treat. Bunking in this specific one (purchased by Haltmann in 2018) is even more extraordinary since the structure originally belonged to Arctic explorer, pilot, and author Harmon "Bud" Helmericks, who died in 2010. Helmericks, one of Alaska's first and most famous bush pilots, built the cabin after World War II, nearly 35 years before Gates of the Arctic became a national park. After storing your gear, try ice fishing and help—as little or as much as you'd like—with chores, such as feeding the huskies, chopping firewood, and digging water holes in the frozen lake.

Day 2

The day begins with a quick primer on the art and sport of mushing, where the top dogs, Iditarod champions, run nearly 1,000 miles (1,609 km) in only eight days. Afterward, you'll hook up a team of four to six veteran Iditarod canine athletes, all

OPPOSITE: **Pulled by a team of sled dogs, a musher makes his way across the Anaktuvuk Pass in Gates of the Arctic National Park.** ABOVE: **A camper sees the spectacular green northern lights from inside a tent.**

eagerly yipping in anticipation of the adventure ahead. Following Haltmann's lead, you will run your team solo across miles of frozen lakes and rivers. Stand on the runners—the freezing wind whipping at your face—and glide through the vast wilderness, the near-total silence broken only by crunching snow.

After running the team for a few hours, return to base camp to warm up by the fire. At day's end, strap on snowshoes and walk toward the Takahula Mountain lookout point for a full view of the northern lights, which are visible most dark, clear nights in March and April, when this trip is offered.

Day 3

With a full day of mushing experience under your belt, you're ready to push a dogsled team deeper into the wild toward the Arrigetch Peaks. Rising thousands of feet above the surrounding glacial valleys, the Arrigetch (from the Nunamiut name Arigaruitch meaning "fingers of a hand extended") is one of the iconic landmarks of Gates of the Arctic.

As the sheer rock walls and pointy peaks come into clearer view, alternate between

looking up at the mountaintops and scanning ahead and around for caribou. Gates of the Arctic protects much of the natural habitat of the western arctic caribou, a clove-brown member of the deer family known for its superb swimming ability (aided by buoyant hair and wide hooves) and for being the only species in which both sexes grow antlers. The park is also home to other hearty wildlife, including Dall sheep, lynx, moose, red foxes, and wolverines. After an extended lunch break over an open fire, run the team back to the cabin. At night, drive one of Haltmann's "iron dogs" (known as snow machines in Alaska and snowmobiles in the lower 48) around the lake before settling in for a final night under the northern lights. You'll depart the way you arrived, by bush plane.

HIGHLIGHTS

• **Run your own dogsled team above the Arctic Circle.**

• **Stay in a historic wilderness cabin built by a legendary Arctic explorer.**

• **See the northern lights from the northernmost national park.**

EPIC JOURNEYS

Since 1888, the National Geographic Society has funded more than 13,000 research, exploration, and preservation projects around the world. National Geographic Partners distributes a portion of the funds it receives from your purchase to National Geographic Society to support programs including the conservation of animals and their habitats.

National Geographic Partners
1145 17th Street NW
Washington, DC 20036-4688 USA

Get closer to National Geographic explorers and photographers, and connect with our global community. Join us today at nationalgeographic.com/join

For information about special discounts for bulk purchases, please contact National Geographic Books Special Sales: specialsales@natgeo.com

For rights or permissions inquiries, please contact National Geographic Books Subsidiary Rights: bookrights@natgeo.com

ISBN: 978-1-4262-2061-6

Printed in Canada

19/FC/1

The information in this book has been carefully checked and to the best of our knowledge is accurate. However, details are subject to change, and the publisher cannot be responsible for such changes, or for errors or omissions. Assessments of sites, hotels, and restaurants are based on the author's subjective opinions, which do not necessarily reflect the publisher's opinion.

WHAT'S ON YOUR
BUCKET LIST?

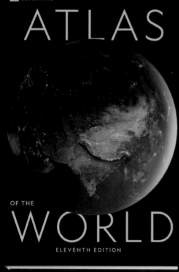

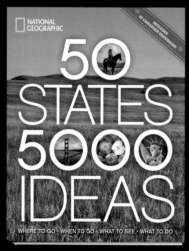

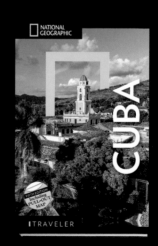